The Complete Book of

BULBS

CORMS, TUBERS, AND RHIZOMES

The Complete Book of

BULBS

CORMS, TUBERS, AND RHIZOMES

A Step-by-Step Guide to
Nature's Easiest and Most Rewarding Plants

BRIAN MATHEW AND PHILIP SWINDELLS

Reader's
Digest

The Reader's Digest Association, Inc.
Pleasantville, New York • Montreal

CONTENTS

The Complete Book of Bulbs, Corms, Tubers, and Rhizomes

A Reader's Digest Book
Edited and designed
by Mitchell Beazley

The acknowledgments that appear on page 240 are hereby
made a part of this copyright page.

Copyright © 1994 Reed International Books Limited

Directories by **Brian Mathew**
Essays by **Philip Swindells**
Editor: **Emily Wright**
Executive Art Editor: **Larraine Lacey**
Assistant Designer: **Barbara Zuniga**
Production Controller: **Sarah Rees**
Commissioned Photography: **Ian McKinnell and Clive Nichols**
Commissioned Artwork: **Fiona Bell-Currie**
Picture Research: **Emily Hedges and Caroline Hensman**
Executive Editor: **Anna Mumford**
Art Director: **Jacqui Small**

Front and back jacket photographs by Ian McKinnell

Library of Congress Cataloging in Publication Data

Mathew, Brian.
        The Complete book of bulbs, corms, tubers, and rhizomes :
a step-by-step guide to Nature's easiest and most rewarding plants /
Brian Mathew and Philip Swindells.
            p.   cm.
    Includes index.
    ISBN 0-89577-546-8
    1. Bulbs.   I. Swindells, Philip.   II. Title.
SB425.M36, 1994
635.9'44—dc20   93-13775

Printed in Hong Kong

FOREWORD

Bulbs are one of the most versatile groups of plants. As self-sufficient storage organs, they adapt well and flourish in a variety of habitats. Once planted, most bulbs maintain themselves for years with minimal care.

This book covers every aspect of gardening with bulbs. First, an important section on getting started provides detailed advice on all practical aspects of growing bulbs, from their purchase to planting and propagation. Accurate step-by-step illustrations clarify specific techniques and practices. The book progresses from season to season, so it is easy to follow. Covering both outdoor and indoor subjects, each seasonal section starts with design and planting ideas, from major naturalization projects to small-scale ideas for containers. The text concentrates on ways of using bulbs, either on their own or with other plants, for the best possible effect. Because bulbs are categorized according to when they bloom—late-winter and early-spring flowering, spring flowering, summer flowering, and fall flowering—each section is followed by a complete plant directory for that season, which is organized alphabetically and contains cultivation details for each bulb.

(above) *The allium bulb (ornamental onion) produces attractive heads known as umbels. These can be dried for winter flower arrangements.*

(right) *In a mixed border alliums hold their own in a dramatic planting, the flower heads echoing the round shape of the formal, clipped box. Alliums are very versatile bulbs and will grow in semishade, as under the laburnum trees seen here* (inset). *The contrast of color and shape makes an unforgettable impression in this lavish garden planting.*

INTRODUCTION

What are bulbs, corms, tubers, and rhizomes?

Throughout this book the term *bulb* is used in a general way to describe any plant with a swollen storage system. This general group of plants consists not only of true bulbs but also corms, tubers, and rhizomes, each categorized according to its shape and makeup.

Bulbs are remarkable plants, distinguishable by their shape, form, color, and adaptability. Understanding the differences between each type of bulbous plant makes it easier to plan and maintain a successful garden.

True bulbs, for example, daffodils, tulips, and lilies, consist of a short basal stem covered with several protective fleshy leaf scales wrapped around the growing point. Some bulbs, such as fritillaries, have a few large scales, while others, like daffodils, have rings of tightly packed scales. The scales are attached to the base of the bulb, known as the basal plate, from which roots grow. Buds develop between the scales and these grow into new bulbs, which then can be separated, cultivated, and grown. In most cases, the whole bulb is enclosed within a tunic of scales, and this forms a tough, dry protective coat.

Corms, which include crocuses, colchicums, and gladioli, look like true bulbs but are usually squatter in shape. Consisting primarily of stem tissue, corms are solid inside, whereas true bulbs have regular layers or scales. The outer surface of the corm is covered by a protective fibrous tunic of modified leaves, which are usually thin and scaly, and roots form at the basal plate of the corm.

Tubers are generally bigger than true bulbs and corms. They have swollen, often irregularly shaped, underground stems that grow with the accumulation of food reserves. Like all stems, tubers have nodes or internodes, and buds or eyes form between the nonfunctioning leaves to produce new shoots and roots. Begonias, anemones, and cyclamens are all popularly grown tubers.

Rhizomes, for example some irises and trilliums, are also bulbous plants. They have creeping stems that act as storage organs and they produce leafy shoots. In the majority of cases, the swollen stems spread horizontally below ground, but occasionally, as in the case of the iris, the stems develop near the surface of the soil.

(left) Amaryllis bulbs can be used for outdoor or indoor cultivation. This bulb is ready to be planted, and the firm, pale green shoots are full of the promise of healthy growth and spectacular flowering to come. All that remains after planting is to supply the bulb with the food and water it needs.

(below) Cross sections (from left to right) of a bulb, a corm, a tuber, and a rhizome. Inside, bulbs contain leaf scales and an embryo flower shoot. Corms are made of modified stem tissue, while tubers consist of thickened stem tissue. Rhizomes are fleshy modified stems, and most grow horizontally.

Life cycles

All bulbous plants have similar life cycles—periods of growth and flowering followed by an annual rest period, known as dormancy. During dormancy, the storage organ sustains the bulb until the growing season begins.

When planted in their dormant states, all bulbous plants quickly initiate roots, and the stems inside begin to grow. As the soil warms up, the plants utilize their food reserves and push up shoots. By the time the plants are flowering, the storage organs are empty of food.

After flowering, the plant foliage continues to grow and, by a process known as photosynthesis, it accumulates new food reserves, which are stored within the bulbous system to sustain the plants through the current and future growing seasons. The presence of the foliage is vital for the continued well-being of the plants; take care never to remove unsightly foliage before it has had time to fuel the plant's energy reservoir. After the foliage dies back, the embryo flowers complete their development within the bulbous system, and the system goes into dormancy, sustained by its internal food reserve, until the next season.

Life cycle of a daffodil

Most true bulbs are perennials, with a life span of three to six years, during which time they self-propagate before dying down. A few bulbs, like some bedding tulips, are exhausted after a single season's growth, and these should be replaced annually by new plants grown from offsets or bulbils. Some bulbs, such as *Lilium lanafolium*, produce bulbils the size of

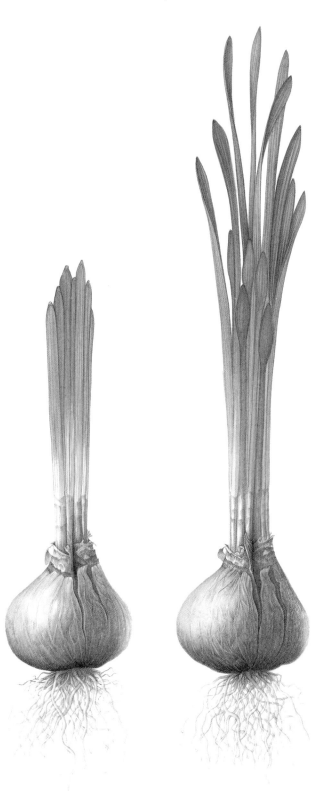

pea seeds in their leaf axils, and these are nothing more than modified stems surrounded by fleshy leaves. When they fall from the parent plant, they sprout to form new plants.

A dormant daffodil bulb consists of an embryo flower, a short stem, and tightly packed leaves. The shoots of the bulb, along with its roots, start to grow during early autumn; the shoots usually remain just beneath the soil or at soil level until the days begin to lengthen during late winter. At the same time, the roots become more active and extensive.

Once the soil has warmed up in the spring sunshine, the leafy shoots quickly extend, although the flower buds are still hidden deep within the foliage. The bulb begins to split into parts and to produce dormant buds at its base. These buds develop into daughter bulbs later on in the cycle.

Flowering lasts for several weeks. Most flowers are insect-pollinated, although many garden varieties have sterile flowers. After pollination the flowers quickly die. Sterile blossoms fade at the same rate as the fertile ones.

When flowering is over, remove the old flower stems to prevent seed formation, which will drain the bulb's resources. The leaves remain green for weeks, building up energy reserves within the bulb. Remove once they are brown and faded. By the time the bulb goes into dormancy, it will have split into two or three parts, each of which, along with the daughter bulbs, will grow as a new bulb the next season.

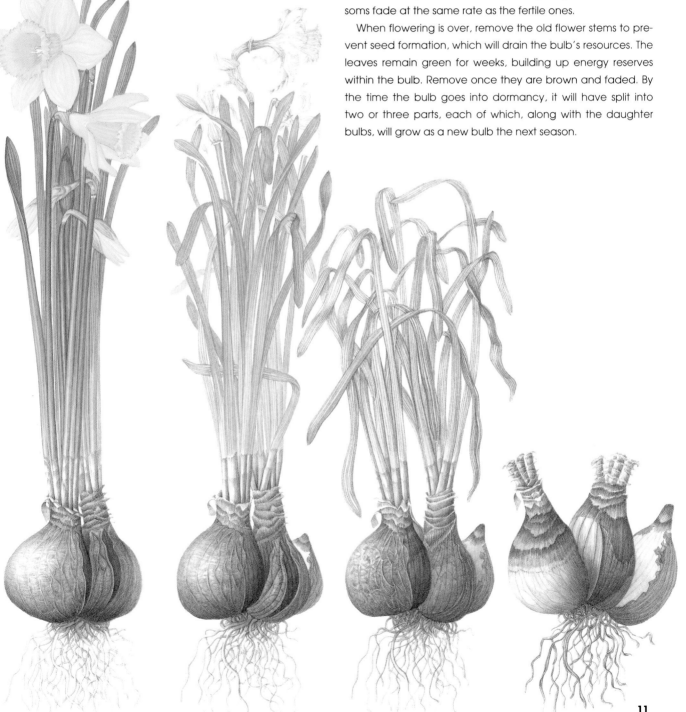

Life cycle of a gladiolus

Corms are very different from true bulbs. They are not permanent but are replaced every year by one or more new corms that grow on top of the depleted corm.

A dormant gladiolus corm is a hard, starchy storage organ. The corm has a protective fibrous tunic and a prominent basal plate from which roots are eventually produced.

Once planted, the corm rapidly produces roots and spearlike shoots. At this stage, there is no sign of a flower spike, although one is beginning to develop in the lower fleshy part of the foliage. As the leaves develop and the root system expands, the central part of the foliage starts to swell as the embryo flower spike pushes upward. The flattened flower head begins to emerge above the foliage. At this stage, the flowers are entirely green.

The leaves reach their full height, and the flower spike continues to grow upward. As it does so, the individual flower buds become separated along the extending stem, and the flower buds at the bottom of the spike begin to show signs of color. The individual flowers open from the bottom of the spike upward over a period of two or three days, each flower blooming for several days before it fades. Once most of the blossoms have faded, remove the flower spike and allow the foliage to remain growing in order to build up a new corm for next season. A new corm will be found on top of its exhausted parent once the leaves have died back completely.

Life cycle of a begonia

A tuber is a swollen stem that, when dormant, consists of a food reserve, a few old roots, and a cluster of tiny dormant buds or eyes. The buds are grouped irregularly on the upper surface of the tuber, although they can occasionally appear at random around the edge.

Tubers are either totally or partially depleted during growth. In the case of popular varieties such as cyclamens and begonias, the tubers wither during flowering but swell in the next growing season and become larger than before.

A newly planted tuber sprouts quite vigorously. Each bud on the crown produces a congested mass of growth, although at this stage the shoots are generally thinned, and the strongest two or three left to grow. If planted, the shoots that have been removed will produce a tuber large enough to flower and survive the winter unaided.

The leaves of a begonia first appear in a cluster at the crown of the tuber, but as the season progresses, it produces succulent stems liberally clothed in handsome serrated leaves. The leaves continue to push up vigorously, and the blossoms grow on short stems from the axils of the upper leaves. Several blooms are usually produced in a congested cluster, the dominant one being a fully double male flower. The smaller single flowers are female and of little decorative merit. If they are removed, the plant will not seed and the main double blossom will attain its full potential.

After flowering, when the foliage has gone into decline and the base of the stems have turned brown, remove all the foliage. The tuber will go into dormancy and can be dug up from the ground and stored until spring.

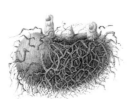

Life cycle of an iris

A rhizome is a continually extending fleshy rootstock that never becomes dormant. It always has some green foliage or a fleshy green shoot, even in the depths of winter.

A newly planted iris begins to sprout in the spring. As the shoots develop, it pushes out an extensive fleshy root system. A healthy young rhizome may have two or three fans of leaves growing from it, each of which may flower, although some of the more recent shoots may produce only leaves during the first season.

The iris grows rapidly in spring and pushes up fleshy flower buds on strong stems. Several buds appear in a congested head, but as the flower stem continues to grow, these become more equally spaced out, although still tight and green in bud.

Once the flower stems have reached above the leaves, the individual blossoms begin to open, first at the top of the spike and then toward the bottom. Most of the flowers are partially sterile, although they produce seed pods occasionally if cross pollination occurs. The seed in the rounded fruits are not worth using for propagation, for they will not breed true. It is much better instead to concentrate on building up the iris for next year by removing the seed heads.

When the flowers have faded, remove the old stalks. Lift and divide, if necessary, cutting the fans of leaves back to within a few inches of the iris.

Hardiness zones

The climatic conditions of an area are of prime importance when deciding what to plant. Even within a particular garden, isolated microclimates need to be considered, as a sheltering wall or a hedge may affect the range of possible plantings. These microclimates can be altered or created by grouping plants and by using mulches. Also, careful siting can modify sun, shade, wind, and humidity.

However, how well a plant grows in an area largely depends on its native climate and how easily it can adapt to its new environment. A plant classified as tender will not endure temperatures below 32°F (0°C). A half-hardy plant can stand a few degrees of frost, but not a cold winter; in contrast, a hardy plant can tolerate considerable cold. Naturally, the degree of hardiness varies from plant to plant.

The maps appearing here have been specially devised to enable you to measure the degree of cold a plant can tolerate. They have been divided into 10 broad climatic areas or zones ranging from –50°F (–45°C) and below in zone 1 to 30°F–40°F (–1°C–4°C) in zone 10. Every plant listed in the Plant Directories cites a hardiness zone, indicating that it will survive and flower at the average minimum winter temperature of that zone. Because weather is variable, hardiness zones, at best, can be considered only relative.

The United States Department of Agriculture issues a Plant Hardiness Zone Map that features an eleventh, almost frost free zone (above 40°F/4°C) on the southern tip of Florida, southern California, most of Hawaii, almost all of the coastline of the Yucatan in Mexico, the southern Baja peninsula, and the Gulf of Mexico. Copies of the USDA map are available from the Government Printing Office in Washington, D.C.

(below and right) *These specially-devised maps are divided into ten broad climatic zones. The key on the right gives the minimum temperature range for each zone.*

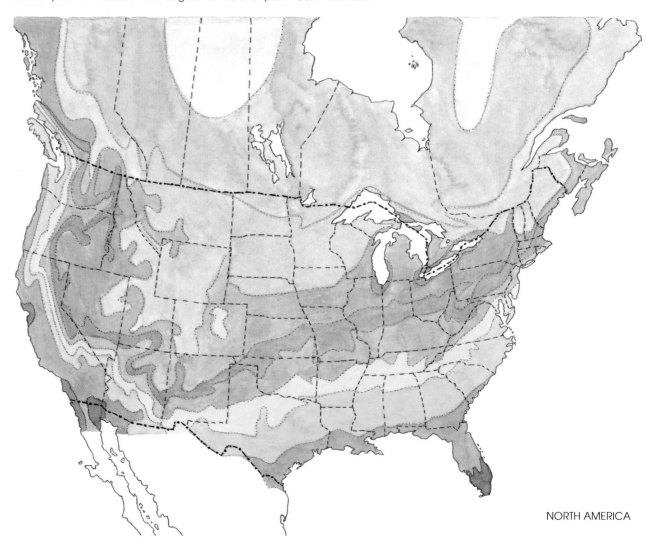

NORTH AMERICA

PLANT HARDINESS ZONE MAPS

Temperature ranges

ZONE 1: Below −50°F (Below −45°C)
ZONE 2: −50 to −35°F (−45 to −37°C)
ZONE 3: −35 to −20°F (−37 to −29°C)
ZONE 4: −20 to −10°F (−29 to −23°C)
ZONE 5: 10 to 5°F (−23 −21°C)
ZONE 6: −5 to 5°F (−21 to −15°C)
ZONE 7: 5 to 10°F (−15 to −12°C)
ZONE 8: 10 to 20°F (−12 to −7°C)
ZONE 9: 20 to 30°F (−7 to −1°C)
ZONE 10: 30 to 40°F (−1 to 4°C)

ZONES OF HARDINESS

GREAT BRITAIN AND WESTERN EUROPE

ZONE 1
ZONE 2
ZONE 3
ZONE 4
ZONE 5
ZONE 6
ZONE 7
ZONE 8
ZONE 9
ZONE 10

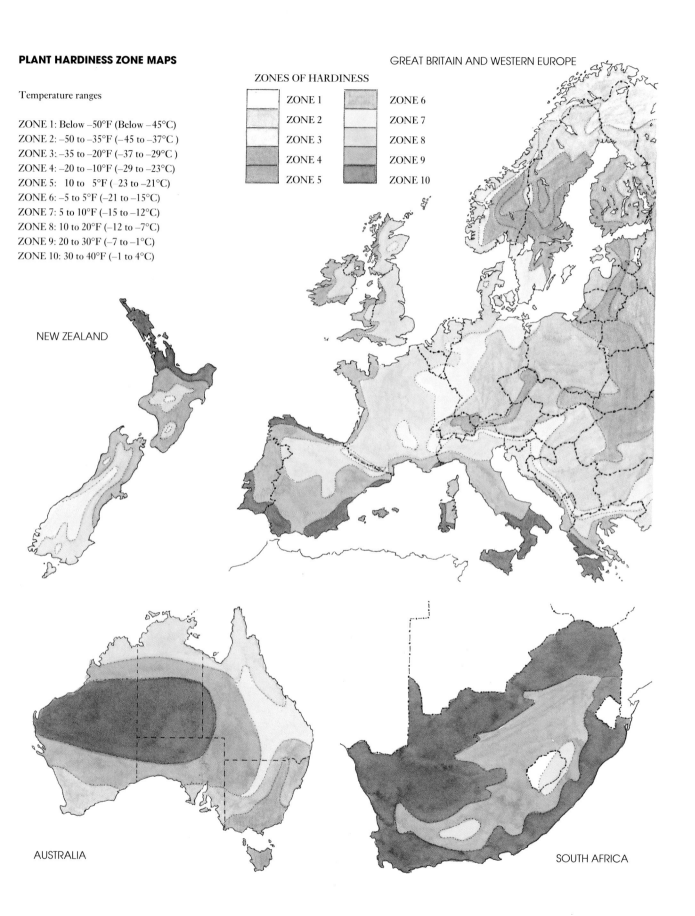

NEW ZEALAND

AUSTRALIA

SOUTH AFRICA

HOW AND WHERE

Bulbs provide spectacular color with little effort. A bulb exists for almost every garden situation, including borders, bedding displays, rock gardens, and raised beds. Many are excellent for naturalizing in grass or soil, while others are suitable for growing in containers and window boxes. In addition, some can be cultivated indoors, either forced into early flowering for the winter season or kept as permanent pot plants. Since they flower only for one season, spending the rest of the year in a dormant state, bulbs are particularly useful for creating short bursts of color. With careful selection, they can supply year-round interest and add variety to more permanent plantings. Although most people think of bulbs flowering in springtime, providing a carpet of daffodils and crocuses, there are many attractive summer-flowering bulbs, as well as ones for fall and winter.

Bulbous plants include a wide selection of different colors and shapes. Some, like daffodils, with their bright primary colors, are good for enlivening dull corners of the garden, while others are more subdued; pastel pink cyclamens are ideal for a soft, subtle planting. For a bold summer display, use one of the tall, imposing bulbs like gladioli or lilies, but a more delicate spring planting might consist of bulbs like crocuses or snake's head fritillaries. A few bulbs, such as hyacinths and lilies, are also grown for their delicious fragrance; they are especially appropriate for container gardens beside a door or under a window.

Most bulbs need well-drained soil to thrive, as well as sun or partial shade, depending on the individual bulb; none will tolerate dense shade. Those that are natives of hot climates benefit from dry, sunbaked conditions, with hot, sunny sites where they ripen, or "bake," in the sun; this enables them to perform better the following year. It is important to note, however, that the majority flourish with summer rainfall. Native woodland bulbs prefer rich organic soil, often dry conditions,

(below) *Finding plants for shady locations can be a problem, but this combination of ferns, hellebores, and trilliums is ideal.*

(right) *Bulbs make an invaluable contribution to the spring garden. Here tulips, grape hyacinths, and daffodils brighten a border.*

and the dappled shade of trees and shrubs. If you are gardening in a dry region, such as California or the Southwest, and are unable to provide such conditions, then it is best not to struggle with these bulbs. Instead, choose those that are native to desert and dry mountainous areas. Many of the botanical tulips thrive under hot, dry summer conditions, and so do South African bulbs such as gladioli, ixias, and babianas. Choose species bulbs rather than the garden cultivars, because hot conditions can sometimes change the behavior of the latter. Some of the large-flowered tulips, for example, will produce incompletely formed embryo flowers if subjected to excessive heat. This causes freakish multiple heads, which can be controlled only by planting the bulbs deeper than usual.

Mixed borders

Bulbs grow happily among other plants that require the same conditions. Early on, when herbaceous plants start to grow, it is possible to grow small spring-flowering bulbs like crocuses and snowdrops. Later on, taller, robust bulbs such as narcissi, tulips, alliums, and lilies are necessary. As permanent members of the border, the bulbs can be lifted and divided as necessary. Most shrubs are less greedy than herbaceous perennials, and a wider range of bulbs can be grown around them.

(left) *Bulbs form an essential part of mixed borders. Here, alliums and Asiatic lilies combine with shrubs and herbaceous plants.*

(below) *These 'Palestrina' tulips add bright color to a spring bedding display of forget-me-nots and honesty.*

(bottom) *Tall hybrid tulips are well-suited to formal borders, particularly with forget-me-nots.*

Bulbs add color and form to a border. They can be grown as highlights in large, prominent clumps or mingled with other plants for a more harmonious, integrated planting. Used as underplanting, they link various taller-growing subjects, and planted in a small patch, they can be used as fillers, providing color and interest to dull parts of a border. In informal settings, allow the bulbs to grow up through other plants, creating a cottage-garden type of border. In formal borders, however, bulbs should be planted in clumps rather than scattered at random; a single well-placed clump will have much more impact than a few spots of color.

Naturalizing

The aim in naturalizing is to create an area that looks as natural as possible. Plant the bulbs at random in lawns or meadows, around trees and shrubs, or on grassy banks; for a more defined feature, plant one or two irregularly shaped areas and mow a path in between. Either use a single type or, to re-create the look of an alpine meadow, grow a mixture of small bulbs. Depending on space, the naturalized area can be as large or small as you wish. Once planted, the bulbs should be left to colonize, or naturalize, at will. Those preferring shady woodland conditions can be naturalized in soil under trees and shrubs.

When selecting a site for naturalizing in grass, remember that the grass cannot be cut for up to 6 weeks after flowering, during which time it may look wild and untidy. This is a problem in formal gardens, where naturalizing is better restricted to small areas. If naturalized in established grass, the bulbs must be carefully selected because not all types can compete with sod. In such cases, it is better to plant the bulbs in well-cultivated soil and sow fine grass over the top.

(below) *The dazzling colors of bright golden daffodils, midnight-blue muscaris, and butter-yellow irises are kept in separate blocks in this generous, formal naturalized waterside planting.*

(right) *The powdery blue of forget-me-nots is ideal for toning down brightly colored tulips. For the opposite effect, however, purple aubrietas can be used to accentuate the yellow of tulips (far right)*

Bedding displays

Beds are formal seasonal displays in which the plants are arranged in colorful patterns. The strong colors of bulbs create an immediate and vivid impact. In fact, some very formal bulbs, like many of the hybrid tulips, only look at home as part of a clearly defined bed. After flowering, the bulbs are removed and stored to make way for the next season's bedding plants or to be replanted. Well-drained fertile soil of a uniform quality is of utmost importance for a good, even display; otherwise some bulbs will grow taller than others.

The best bulbs to use are those, such as hyacinths, that have compact heads of uniform color or simple, bold formal-looking flowers, such as tulips. Plant these in big blocks of color, using one type of bulb for each block, or create a more intricate design focusing on smaller areas. Bulbs can also be used to highlight plants within the plan. Plants such as cannas and galtonias may be scattered among bedding plants to give the display height and interest. A handful of taller bulbs will add height and variety.

Rock gardens

Rock gardens are ideal for displaying some of the smaller, more delicate-looking bulbs. Mixed with alpines, they also provide color and texture.

A wide variety of bulbs can be grown in rock gardens because this type of habitat provides an array of microclimates. Some areas, such as those in the shadow of a rock, are cool and shady; others, such as those facing the sun at the base of a rock, are warm and sheltered. Rock gardens also provide the well-drained conditions that bulbs prefer.

Scale is an important factor when planting rock gardens; make sure the smaller bulbs are not dwarfed by their larger neighbors or their impact will be lost. Dwarf bulbs can be planted on their own in pockets for a highlight display or, if they are tolerant of other plants, they can be integrated with creeping or cushioning plants, which will provide long-term interest after the seasonal display of the bulbs. Where there are established plants, small bulbs can be pushed through the foliage into the soil beneath.

Containers, window boxes, and hanging baskets

Bulbs make excellent subjects for all types of containers, and you can extend the container season into winter and early spring. For year-round color, treat bulbs like annuals and plant a series of seasonal displays, one after the other. After flowering, the bulbs can be lifted and replanted in another part of the garden. Alternatively, for permanent displays, mix the bulbs with other plants that flower at different times.

Bulbs tolerant of warm summer soil temperatures are best suited to container cultivation. All the African species grow well, including tigridias, acidantheras, sparaxis, and ixias. Spring bulbs, such as crocuses and dwarf irises, benefit from quick drainage, and they are good for container growing.

Containers planted with bulbs can be moved around the garden and displayed with other plants. Either plant one species per container and group the pots together, or plant a single pot of mixed bulbs. Use this as a focal point at the bottom of a flight of steps or next to a doorway. When using tall bulbs as the focal point create a balanced display by underplanting them with low-growing bulbs.

Window boxes are less versatile than most containers as their positions are fixed. They must be filled with short-growing bulbs that will not become tall enough to block the view. As most boxes are seasonal, long-term cultivation is of little

concern; a variety of bulbs can be packed together for the greatest impact each season. This is also true of hanging baskets, which are best filled with a profusion of seasonal plants.

Shape is the most important consideration when planting a hanging basket. Remember that it will be viewed from below and sideways rather than from above, and the planting should be as spherical as possible. Since very few bulbs have trailing or hanging stems—the pendulous begonia is the exception—use foliage plants such as ivy as a basic framework. Build up layers of bulbs, poking the small ones like crocuses through the sides of the basket and keeping the taller ones like narcissi for the top of the display.

Cut flowers

Bulbs grown especially to be cut flowers should be planted separately, ideally in an inconspicuous spot like a corner of the vegetable garden. In this way, they can be grown in purely practical rows rather than aesthetic groupings, and the flowers can be cut without ruining the overall display. Grown in neat rows, they are easier to manage.

(above) *A potted cyclamen is combined to excellent effect with cut amaryllis for a vivid display.*

(far right) *The elegance of the amaryllis flowers and foliage can be appreciated in this simple planting.*

(top right) *Densely planted* iris reticulata *look most effective in this traditional basket.*

(bottom right) *Dwarf tulips, ranunculus and trailing ivy are combined here in a wooden container.*

COLOR

Gardening is more than simply growing healthy plants, although that in itself takes patience and a certain amount of knowledge. Successfully combining plants to create living, growing pictures—in other words, designing an eye-catching garden—is an art. First and foremost, think of practical matters, such as soil conditions and aspect. Then, before choosing any plants, decide on the style of your garden and plan a bedding display

A garden usually has many different functions to fulfill, so it must be planned and planted with care. Often it is both public and private. As part of the outside environment, it may be appreciated by someone who passes by. At the same time it is an integral part of the house and should reflect its owner's taste and personality.

How do you begin to create an attractive garden? Planting on the basis of color is a good starting point—after you have taken care of the practical considerations—and, in terms of color, nothing surpasses bulbs. With bulbs, you can have year-round color in your garden, as there are flowering bulbs for each season.

Bulbs come in a wide range of colors, from the palest tints to the brightest hues. For a striking formal effect, plant them in blocks of contrasting colors, either by themselves or mixed with other plants. To create a more relaxed, informal atmosphere, try soft, subtle arrangements using pale, harmonious colors. Although finding the right color for the right place can be difficult, it is worth spending time on this. A well-planned small flowerbed by the front door, for example, can have immediate impact. With a little care and attention, you can establish a number of pleasing color schemes throughout your garden.

(below) *The vibrant combination of orange crocosmias and scarlet dahlias make this border dazzle with color.*

(right) *Plenty of silver-gray foliage helps to tone down the hot pink of the gladioli and the scarlet of the tulips.*

USING COLOR

Although personal taste is the most important guideline when planning and planting a flowerbed or a garden for color, it helps to understand how colors work together and what effects they produce in different styles of plantings. The same color principles can be applied to any garden situation, whether it is an extensive border or a group of containers on a patio.

Color theory

There are many complex theories about color, but one easy point to keep in mind is the division of colors into warm and cool. At the red end of the spectrum, colors seem warm; at the blue end, they appear cool. Greens fall somewhere in between; they are for the most part restful neutral colors, allowing the eye to relax when it perceives them and providing respite from bright hues.

Strong primary colors, such as the red of tulips, the blue of hyacinths, or the yellow of daffodils, can be difficult to place in a garden. They are best used in brightly colored bedding displays. In other spots you may prefer the muted, subtler shades available from a variety of cultivars, as these tones are easier to blend together.

Color and perspective

As well as being decorative, color can be functional, giving a sense of perspective to the garden. Warm colors appear to advance toward the viewer and, as a result, make the garden seem smaller. A sunny herbaceous border, glowing with the vibrant flamelike colors of bulbs like *Crocosmia*, has this effect. In contrast, cool colors and lighter tones recede, creating an impression of space. A springtime bed of pale cream tulips standing over frothy, light blue forget-me-nots will make a garden appear larger than it really is.

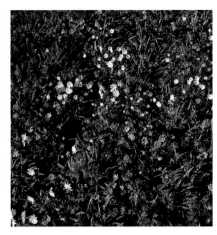

Pale and cool colors, as seen in these naturalized white and blue anemones and blue scillas, make an area of the garden seem relaxed and spacious.

The plentiful green foliage of these erythroniums provides a restful background to the elegant flowers, with their intriguing reflexed petals.

The strongly contrasting hot shades of crocosmias and lilies create a busy, almost cluttered feeling, which can make a border seem small.

Color and mood

Choosing warm or cool colors for a planting creates different moods. Warm colors are generally intense and invigorating, while cool colors are peaceful and harmonious.

When planting for color, think about the function of different areas of the garden and plan accordingly. For example, an informal, meandering path edged with pale cool colors will encourage unhurried lingering, while a straight, formal path lined with glowing warm colors will convey a sense of action. Work on producing specific color effects for specific areas, and plan your garden so that it changes constantly, with the focus moving from one area to another as one seasonal display takes over from the last. The impression will be all the more striking and appealing for being short-lived.

Color and climate

The quality of light has a significant impact on color. Light varies not only with the seasons but also in different latitudes. Where you live will affect your choice of plants, as some colors work better than others in a particular climate, with its distinctive quality of light.

In temperate areas, the soft bluish light can make strong colors look garish and hard, while it lets pastel tints glow, revealing them in all their subtlety. Choose the soft pinks of a plant such as *Nerine* 'Orion,' or the lemony yellows of *Hyacinthus* 'City of Haarlem,' or the very pale blues of *Allium caeruleum*. In hot climates with fierce overhead sun, the light is often hard and white, making pastels look dirty and washed out; only bright colors like reds, oranges, and yellows seem satisfactory. Try the clear red form of *Ranunculus asiaticus*, the strong orange-yellows of *Narcissus* 'Fortissimo,' or for dramatic effect, the deep purple of *Fritillaria persica*.

Color and light

Changes in light during the day, although more subtle, have similar effects on color. Early-morning and late-afternoon light is soft and golden, while midday light is strong and bright. An area intended for sitting outside in the evening can be made truly magical by defining it around the edges with white or blue- and violet-tinted plants. In twilight these colors glow with a light of their own. To enjoy your garden in the evening, avoid dark colors, which disappear into the night as the light fades. Try white and yellow lilies in pots; *Lilium regale*, for example, is superbly fragrant and easy to grow.

Foliage

Almost all gardens start off with plant cover, whether grass, shrubs, or trees. From severe dark green backdrops of yew or holly, to soft, delicate gray-leaved plants, such as helichrysum, santolina, and lavender, there are many varieties of foliage plants. Consider the coloring of these background plants when devising new plant combinations. With a formally clipped hedge of yew, for instance, try a midspring planting of upright creamy white tulips at its base, followed by a mass of white lilies in summer for a simple dramatic effect. Avoid dark-colored tulips and lilies, which would be lost against such a dark background. If you want these plants to show up clearly, you should plant them against a pale silvery green backdrop.

Seasonal variations are important to consider. Foliage colors are usually brightest in spring and summer, when fresh young foliage predominates. In the fall the changes in foliage color are often striking and can radically alter your perception of surrounding plants. Take care to choose a color scheme that complements the bold reds, oranges, and yellows of fall foliage.

These creamy white tulips glow above a bed of purple pansies, particularly in the soft light of dusk, when they stand out even more.

A strong and vibrant display is achieved for springtime by planting bluish-purple hyacinths and gold wallflowers in a formal flowerbed.

This silver-gray foliage calms the bright pink of the alliums and makes them easier to place in a border with other colors.

In winter, when the ground is relatively bare, evergreens provide an elegant backdrop that shows off even very small flowers.

The decorative effect of bulb foliage is often underestimated. Cyclamen leaves, which are frequently marbled and blotched with silver, provide long-lasting ground cover that can act as a foil for other plants. In winter and spring, arum leaves may make a valuable contribution to the garden. They are almost more decorative than the flower spikes. The linear, swordlike leaves of irises are equally decorative and can be used to give both form and texture to a bed of flowers.

Putting colors to work

The choice of color combinations depends on many factors, some of which are beyond your control. The architecture of your house and any garden structures, for example, plays a major role in the overall effect of the garden, as do the framework of the garden and existing background plantings. Any outside features visible from the garden, such as a neighboring tree, also have to be considered in the design. When selecting a color scheme, make sure that your choice blends well with the materials of your house and any other visible structures, such as walls and fences.

Most gardeners admit to learning from their mistakes, so do not be afraid to try new ideas. The following examples should help you start thinking about the different effects that you can produce using different combinations of color. You might combine bulbs with vibrant contrasting colors to create a strong impact, or. you might concentrate on soft neutrals and gentle tints in a subtle harmonious planting. A third idea is to base your garden on a single color for elegance and unity.

CONTRASTING COLORS

For impact planting—to create a bold, colorful display—use contrasting colors. Some of the best color combinations are red and green; yellow, orange, and blue; and pink and purple, but there are countless others to experiment with. Do not forget to take into account the effects of light; bright colors that may clash unpleasantly in full sun will be tempered into a pleasing contrast in shade.

The most successful plantings set up strong focal points using solid, densely planted blocks of color. It is not just a question of throwing the brightest, most forceful colors together, for the effect is lost if the picture becomes confusing, with too many conflicting colors or muddled shapes. The key to success is to keep the planting simple and select only a few colors.

Positioning is important, too. Use strong colors to make a statement and highlight an area. A splash of bright color draws the eye toward it, making the garden seem smaller and deflecting attention from any less attractive areas. It creates a lively atmosphere and brightens up dark spots. Indeed, a garden without areas of contrasting colors can be bland and unexciting.

For a spring display, use a golden yellow daffodil such as the double-flowered 'Tahiti,' which has warm orange inner petals, and underplant it with a simple dark blue muscari, such as *Muscari armeniacum* or the more vigorous *M. neglectum*. A similar effect can be created with *Hyacinthus* 'Delft Blue' and yellow wallflowers. To make a strong statement in a raised bed or rock garden, try muscari with bright pinkish-purple aubrieta.

For a large border in spring, plant red tulips such as 'Toronto' with purple *Lunaria annua* and blue forget-me-nots. For more color, combine the orange-red 'Prinses Irene' tulip and yellow 'Stresa' tulip with forget-me-nots and *Hosta fortunei* 'Albo-Picta.' Summer offers equally good contrasting color combinations for borders, such as *Agapanthus* 'Blue Imp,' the white *Galtonia candicans*, and *Hemerocallis fulva* 'Kwanso Flore Plena,' which has attractive tawny orange flowers. In the pink and purple range, try the dark purple *Iris* 'Wild Echo' and the dark pink *Gladiolus communis byzantinus*.

Planting for impact can be just as successful with naturalized bulbs. In spring, grow a patch of bluebells under a bright yellow or orange azalea. As the seasons progress, fall and winter cyclamens can be naturalized in large areas with contrasting ivy foliage or variegated *Vinca* (periwinkle).

Whatever the season, there are endless plant combinations using contrasting colors. Decide on the colors you wish to use in each area of the garden, and select the bulbs accordingly, paying close attention to the form as well as color of the plants.

(above) *For a bold color statement, plant the hyacinths* 'Queen of the Pinks' *and* 'Blue Peter Stuyvesant' *close together.*

(left) *This glorious bed of tall yellow irises is made all the more memorable by the low border of contrasting purple-blue polyanthus flowers.*

(inset) *These blocks of brightly colored tulips balance each other well, and the forget-me-nots add some variety in texture as well as color.*

HARMONIOUS COLORS

Refined and elegant, spacious and restful—a subtle planting of harmonious colors can be all these things, but it should not be bland. The essence of this style of planting is to avoid strong contrasts of color, form, and texture that would create a single focal point and instead concentrate on painting a uniform picture. The colors used should be restrained and related, so that the eye moves over the plantings without being drawn to any one dominant feature.

Harmonious colors are often used in informal gardens, where a tumbling disorder of flowers and foliage suggests a timeless feeling. A subtle planting makes you want to take your time, so use it to advantage in private areas, where its calming effects can be enjoyed.

Foliage is always important in harmonizing colors. Rely on gray foliage to provide a soft, misty backdrop that tones down adjacent colors and helps link different plants. Do not use very dark foliage, however, particularly if the flower color is very pale. Also avoid large leaves, which tend to look stark; instead, choose small-leaved plants.

Pale and soft colors are preferable to bright colors in this kind of planting. One main color should be combined with only one or two closely related colors.

The icy charm of this white planting is created by the pure white tulips, the boldly variegated hosta leaves, and other silver-colored foliage.

Use subtly different shades to build up a multilayered effect, and draw the varying shades together with some neutral foliage. In spring, for example, try naturalizing the pale blue Spanish bluebell, *Hyacinthoides hispanica*, beneath a spring-flowering shrub such as a pink-tinged azalea. Continue the pink-and-blue theme in another part of the garden with a border of pinkish-purple snake's head fritillaries, *Fritillaria meleagris*, and blue forget-me-nots. Hellebores, with their soft pink, white, and green flowers, are good for subtle effects and can be mixed with cream-colored daffodils and snowdrops.

In a summer border, plant delicate blue irises rising out of the silvery gray foliage of *Dianthus*, continuing toward the back of the bed with purple *Allium christophii* and *Rosa* 'La Ville de Bruxelles.' For fall color, the colchicums are invaluable; the purple *Colchicum agrippinum* harmonizes nicely with any of the silver-leaved herbs, as well as with the pink flowers of *Sedum populifolium*.

As with contrasting colors, the choice of harmonious color combinations is unlimited. However, resist the temptation to select a large number of different types and colors.

ONE-COLOR PLANTING

Whether vibrant or subtle, single-color gardens are always impressive and memorable. The variations in shades of a single color are almost infinite, and they can be used to achieve a remarkable range of contrasts.

Single-color gardens can feature any color, from white through red. When you use one color, the emphasis falls on the texture and form of the plants, as well as their color. Neighboring plants should contrast with each other in one or more of these aspects to avoid a dull and lifeless planting. Foliage plays an important role, serving as a neutral color that supports the color of plants around it; aim at using leaves with a variety of different shapes and densities as well as colors.

When deciding which color to select, look for one that will work well in your climate. In areas with cold winters and late springs, for example, warm colors are very successful. Plant a patch of yellow winter aconites in front of a gold-variegated shrub such as *Elaeagnus pungens* 'Maculata' or one of the smaller mahonias, such as the yellow-flowered *Mahonia aquifolium*. Think bold for spring; red or blue works well, but take care with the shades. In the case of red, avoid mixing bluish

For an atmospheric, nostalgic border planting, select shades of purple-pink and soft, misty white using Gladiolus *'The Bride' and* Allium caeruleum.

This mixed border in warm shades of plum and rose combines Berberis *and lilies, including the reliable* Lilium regale.

This single-colored border is composed of Asiatic lily hybrids and alstroemerias.

crimsons with orange-scarlets. A good choice is to blend red anemones with red tulips. When using blues, do not juxtapose harsh bright blues with purple-blues. Instead, pair plants like indigo-blue hyacinth with dark blue pansies.

Some wonderful white spring displays can be achieved with 'Mount Tacoma' tulips, *Hyacinthoides hispanica,* and the white-edged *Hosta crispula.* But white really comes into its own in summer, when it looks very cool and refined. It is best used in temperate climates, where

the light is softer. Plant a mixture of *Crinum × powellii* 'Album,' calla lilies (*Zantedeschia aethiopica* 'Crowborough'), and any of the white lilies against a dark hedge of yew. In front, try intermingling a cluster of softer *Ornithogalum thyrsoides* with one of the gray-leaved herbs. The yellowish-green lady's mantle (*Alchemilla mollis*) is indispensable in white, yellow, and orange one-color plantings.

In late summer and early fall, before foliage starts to change color, cool pinks work well in a single-color garden. Plant *Colchicum speciosum* in front of

Sedum spectabile, with a few clumps of cherry-red crimson flag (*Schizostylis coccinea* 'Major') behind, and a backdrop of *Fuchsia* 'Mrs. Popple.'

A single-color planting can be effective in a small flowerbed or a large border. In large gardens it is easiest to restrict yourself to planting small areas of one color for a particular season rather than try to coordinate large expanses in a single hue. Whether the planting is small or large, the overall effect will be a sense of harmony and space that a vibrant planting of contrasting colors could never achieve.

GETTING STARTED

Bulbs can be used in many situations and for much of the year. By their very nature, bulbs are intended to grow and flower from year to year. The bulbs, corms, tubers, and rhizomes themselves are storage bodies that contain food made during the growing season. They then use the food to produce growth in subsequent years. So taking a little care fits in perfectly with the bulb's own life cycle and will pay dividends over time.

Choosing, planting, caring for, and propagating are important both for indoor and outdoor plants. But even the most lavish attention cannot make up for a poor-quality bulb or one planted the wrong way. Since the majority of bulbs, corms, tubers, and rhizomes are inexpensive, they can easily be replaced if they do not perform as hoped for after their first year of flowering.

Treat the bulb well as it approaches the dormant season and it will survive in later years. Even the healthiest bulb will start to decline if left in waterlogged conditions winter after winter. Correct storage of lifted bulbs over the dormant season is also critical to their survival.

Indoor bulbs are subject to special demands—root restriction, low light levels, low humidity and high daytime temperatures, and they are often forced to flower out of season. Pests and diseases can be especially troublesome under such conditions. With proper feeding and care, most indoor bulbs can be expected to flower at the normal time in future seasons.

All bulbous plants are vulnerable. During the growing season, whether indoors and outdoors, the foliage and flowers attract unwanted attention from a variety of pests and diseases. In the dormant season bulbs both stored and in the ground are subject to attack from a range of pests, from microscopic viruses to visible insects like aphids. Although defensive action is preferable to dealing with established infestations, prompt corrective action will solve most problems. Unfortunately, sometimes the infected plants must be destroyed to prevent the spread of the disease or to eliminate the pests.

Many gardeners propagate bulbs only by splitting and dividing congested clumps. In fact it is easier to propagate than most people imagine, whether you use a simple seed sowing method or one of the more specialized techniques. And propagation provides plants for virtually no monetary outlay—a definite bonus. For more expensive and unusual bulbs propagation is almost essential, particularly if they are less than totally hardy. With even the simpler techniques a healthy continuity of supply can be ensured for almost all commonly grown bulbs.

(below) *Forced bulbs can be grown in trays, then selected for potting in more attractive containers when ready to flower. This allows you to create displays of well-matched plants, all of similar size and maturity.*

(right) *Growing narcissi in gravel rather than soil gives attractive results. Unfortunately, the bulbs will suffer because of a lack of nutrients and are unlikely to flower the following year.*

FIRST PRINCIPLES

Selecting and purchasing

Bulbs are usually sold in a "dry" or dormant state. It is very important to purchase bulbs at the right time of year according to when they flower. Spring-flowering bulbs should be purchased during late summer and fall, while summer- and fall-flowering bulbs become available in spring and late summer, respectively. While garden centers and plant nurseries offer some that are packaged in nets or plastic bags, others are sold loose in large boxes to be selected individually by hand.

Although bulb storage is highly sophisticated and many bulb varieties can be kept in a satisfactory dormant state all year, they start to deteriorate within about 10 days when stored in areas where the temperature is too high. As a general rule, bulbs should be bought the moment the bulb-selling season gets under way, for the longer they are kept in shops and garden centers, the greater the likelihood that these vulnerable living organisms will be damaged. Without protection, small fritillaries and softer bulbs like snowdrops are the first to spoil; they should never be purchased in pre-packaged

The gladiolus corms on the left are in good condition—plump and firm, with their tunics clean and intact. Those on the right, however, have lost their tunics, and the marked skins show they are bruised.

The iris bulbs in the lower part of this picture are plump and healthy-looking, with clean skins. Those on the upper right are wizened, because they have been stored at too high a temperature.

These begonia tubers are clean, firm, and in good condition. The pink shoots just visible on the upper sides indicate that growth is starting, and the tubers should be planted without delay.

The begonia tuber on the left is plump and firm, and should give an excellent display of flowers. The one on the right, however, is shriveled and unlikely to produce any growth at all.

nets unless bought soon after they arrive on the shelves. Only tough tubers like anemones and winter aconites or bulbs like alliums are likely to survive a protracted period of display. Another problem is that bulbs may begin to produce roots once they come out of storage and will start into premature growth if not planted quickly.

The best variety of bulbs are available from special mail-order companies, plant nurseries, and garden centers. Many mail-order companies offer an extensive range of bulbs, and they carefully package their bulbs before shipping to ensure that they arrive in prime condition. If you buy bulbs from a garden center or nursery, make sure they are stored properly in a cool, dry environment with an average temperature of 45°F (7°C) and a humidity of 75 percent. A quick glance at the display will indicate whether the retailer knows how to store bulbs: lilies, fritillaries, and other soft bulbs vulnerable to rapid drying out should be covered with sawdust, wood shavings, or peat. If, instead, these bulbs are exposed to the drying air, do not buy them.

Once purchased, it is best to plant the bulbs within a few days. If this is not possible, they can be stored for 4-6 weeks. Remove them from the bag and spread them out on a seed tray, covering soft bulbs like lilies and fritillaries with peat or wood shavings. Place the tray in a cool, dry basement, garden shed, or unheated porch with an average temperature of 45°F (7°C).

What to look for

The most important consideration when purchasing bulbs, corms, tubers, and rhizomes is to select those that are firm and healthy looking rather than ones that are soft and shriveled. The entire structure must be solid, especially the area within the ring that forms the roots. To test this, invert the bulb or corm and press your finger or thumb firmly against the center; if it is not solid, do not buy it. Narcissi, in particular, should be tested, as a soft basal plate may indicate an attack of narcissus fly. Cutting open an afflicted bulb will reveal a fat white grub nestling in the center among the badly damaged embryo foliage. Also test the area around the neck for any signs of softness. Tubers and rhizomes should be firm to the touch but not hard. Dried-out ones should be avoided as they are unlikely to grow.

All bulbs must have clean, blemish-free skins, although some hyacinths naturally have dark purple markings on their surfaces. The skins must also be intact, free of cuts or bruises; always closely inspect tulips because the skins tend to split after exposure to dry conditions. Any tulip that has lost most of its outer covering and resembles a small potato should be avoided, because it has no protection against fungal diseases and may become infected.

With the exception of narcissus bulbs, which are often sold by the number of noses they have, most bulbs are sold according to their circumference, as measured around the fattest part of the bulb. This is universally noted in centimeters.

It is important to choose the correct size of bulb, which does not necessarily relate to the size of the fully grown plant. Several large-growing narcissi, for example, are produced from relatively small bulbs. There is a standard bulb size for each variety and charts stating this information are available. When purchasing hyacinths, save any larger than 7 in (18 cm) in circumference for indoor pot cultivation; otherwise the resulting plants will blow over in strong winds because of their tall stems and the extra weight of the flowers. Smaller hyacinth bulbs produce equally good flower spikes that are more weather resistant.

Because all bulbs are prone to storage mold, avoid any showing signs of this. Also, carefully inspect dwarf irises for small black spots or blotches—symptoms of ink-spot disease—which can easily devastate these marvelous plants. Only buy pure, creamy white *I. reticulata* bulbs, and check the brown coats of other types for any dark patches.

If you are in any doubt about the quality of the bulbs you wish to purchase, first buy a trial one. Cut this in half lengthways: if the flower embryo is present the bulb will perform well and several of the same stock can be bought.

Unprepared and prepared stock

Besides choosing bulbs of good size, quality, and health, when purchasing bulbs it is also necessary to distinguish between the identical-looking unprepared and prepared bulbs—this may be indicated by a sign.

Unprepared bulbs form the majority of those sold and are intended for outdoor use. Apart from being graded and cleaned, they are entirely in their natural state, although they may have spent some time in cool storage while awaiting shipment to suppliers.

Prepared bulbs are for forcing into early flowering for indoor displays, hyacinths being a common example. They are more expensive than unprepared bulbs because they have received special treatment prior to selling. To promote premature bud formation, during the dormant period they are lifted and subjected to a higher temperature than they would normally experience. They are available very early in the season and should be planted immediately to take full advantage of their treatment. After flowering, discard or replant them outdoors.

Planting bulbs outdoors

1 *A graduated bulb trowel takes the guesswork out of planting bulbs. Its long, narrow blade has measurements marked on it so that the correct planting depth can be found.*

2 *Before planting a bulb, be sure that it is the right way up, with the growing point upward. This may sound obvious, but with some corms and tubers it can be hard to tell.*

3 *Make sure that the base of the bulb is firmly in contact with the ground before you cover it with soil. If an air pocket is left beneath it, the roots will fail to develop.*

IN THE GARDEN
Preparing the ground

In order to thrive, all bulbs should be grown in fine, crumbly soil. For the best results, thoroughly dig the area a minimum of 7 days before planting; this will give the soil time to dry out and start to weather. Next, break up the soil so it is fine and crumbly using a hoe or a rake; if growing native woodland species such as lilies and trilliums, add a 2-3 in (5-7.5 cm) layer of organic matter such as leaf mold or pulverized bark. To enrich poor soil, dig in some general garden fertilizer, using the recommended amount. For bulbs that do not require very free draining, sunny conditions, manure can be used to enrich the soil prior to planting. A selection of lilies, daffodils, squills and fritillaries benefit from manure-enriched soil. In such cases, only use well-rotted manure that is rich brown, crumbly and odorless. Dig in the manure to below the level at which the bulb will be planted.

Good drainage is essential for all bulbs, and even those requiring moist conditions will not tolerate waterlogged soil. You can improve heavy soil that is too wet and sticky by incorporating sand; depending on how heavy the soil is, incorporate anything from 15-25 percent by volume sand. Conversely, if the soil is too light and free draining, peat can be dug into it to increase its moisture retentiveness. It is also possible to change the acidity of the soil if necessary. Some bulbs, such as lilies, need acid soil. If your soil is too alkaline, incorporate a ready-to-use acidifier in the soil following the manufacturer's instructions. If your soil is too acid, however, dig hydrated lime into the soil at a rate of 2 oz per square yard (50 g per 0.8 square meters).

Planting

After preparing the soil, you are ready to begin planting. A graduated bulb planter is very useful for determining the correct depth; looking like a trowel, it has measurements marked along its length that ensure the right planting depth. When laid horizontally across the surface of the soil, it can also be used to space the bulbs at the right intervals. Alternatively, a garden trowel can be used instead. For areas with heavy clay soil, it will be easier to use a hand-held bulb planter as used for planting naturalizing bulbs (see p. 44) to remove the plugs of soil.

If you are planting individual bulbs, the hole should be twice the depth of the bulb for small bulbs and up to 5 times the bulb depth for large ones. Once a hole of the correct dimensions has been dug, insert the bulb with its pointed end facing up; also insert tubers with any eyes or buds facing up, pressing a little way into the soil. Cover the bulb with soil, firm the surface, then water well and wait for signs of growth.

If you are planting a larger quantity of bulbs, it is both easier and quicker to dig an area to the overall depth required and plant the bulbs together. Once you have dug the area, smooth the soil and, using a garden fork, lightly prick the surface. Space the bulbs as necessary for each individual bulb as detailed in the seasonal Plant Directories. Generally speaking, the bulbs should not be regularly spaced as this will look unnatural, and if a few bulbs fail to grow there will be an obvious gap. Gently scatter the soil over the bulbs, making sure that you do not knock them over in the process. When all the soil is back in place, rake the surface level and water the patch well.

Planting depths

A rule of thumb for planting bulbs is to bury them at least as deep as they are tall, although there are many variations to this rule. Bluebells, for example, should be planted at a depth of at least twice their own height, and tuberous begonias require a shallow planting, just beneath the surface of the ground. For specific requirements, see individual bulb entries in the relevant Plant Directories.

In southern climates, some bulbs—notably daffodils, the majority of large-flowered narcissi, and the larger species tulips and their cultivars—benefit from double-depth planting, which means they are less likely to be damaged by weeding or hoeing. In cold climates, planting at three or four times the height of the bulb is beneficial especially for the large-flowered hybrid tulips, as this protects the bulbs from any severe weather conditions. However, deep planting is not recommended for *Narcissus* 'Sir Winston Churchill,' as the bulb tends to deteriorate over two or three years, or for *Narcissus cyclamineus* cultivars and the more delicate varieties like 'Hawera,' which are too small.

The following seasonal charts, showing a variety of popular bulbs for that season, indicate the planting depths of the given bulbs in relation to their height. Generally speaking, spring-flowering bulbs must be planted in autumn, summer-flowering bulbs in spring, autumn-flowering bulbs in summer, and winter-flowering bulbs in autumn.

Spring-flowering bulbs

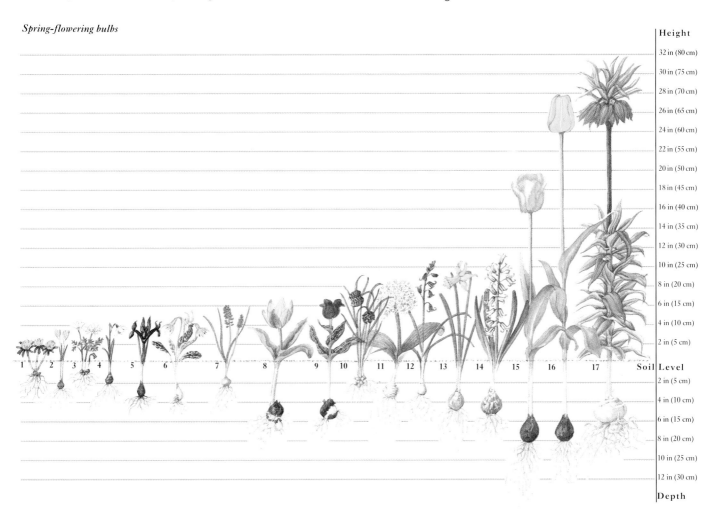

	Height
	32 in (80 cm)
	30 in (75 cm)
	28 in (70 cm)
	26 in (65 cm)
	24 in (60 cm)
	22 in (55 cm)
	20 in (50 cm)
	18 in (45 cm)
	16 in (40 cm)
	14 in (35 cm)
	12 in (30 cm)
	10 in (25 cm)
	8 in (20 cm)
	6 in (15 cm)
	4 in (10 cm)
	2 in (5 cm)

Soil Level

	Depth
	2 in (5 cm)
	4 in (10 cm)
	6 in (15 cm)
	8 in (20 cm)
	10 in (25 cm)
	12 in (30 cm)

Small spring-flowering bulbs like anemones and galanthus need a shallow planting, whereas the taller tulips and fritillaries need a deeper planting to anchor them to the ground.

1 *Eranthis hyemalis*
2 *Crocus chrysanthus*
3 *Anemone blanda*
4 *Galanthus nivalis*
5 *Iris reticulata*
6 *Erythronium dens-canis*

7 *Muscari armeniacum*
8 *Tulipa kaufmanniana*
9 *Tulipa greigii*
10 *Fritillaria meleagris*
11 *Allium karataviense*
12 *Hyacinthoides hispanica*

13 *Narcissus* 'February Gold'
14 *Hyacinthus orientalis*
15 *Tulipa* 'Lady Diana'
16 *Tulipa* 'Golden Harvest'
17 *Fritillaria imperialis*

Summer-flowering bulbs

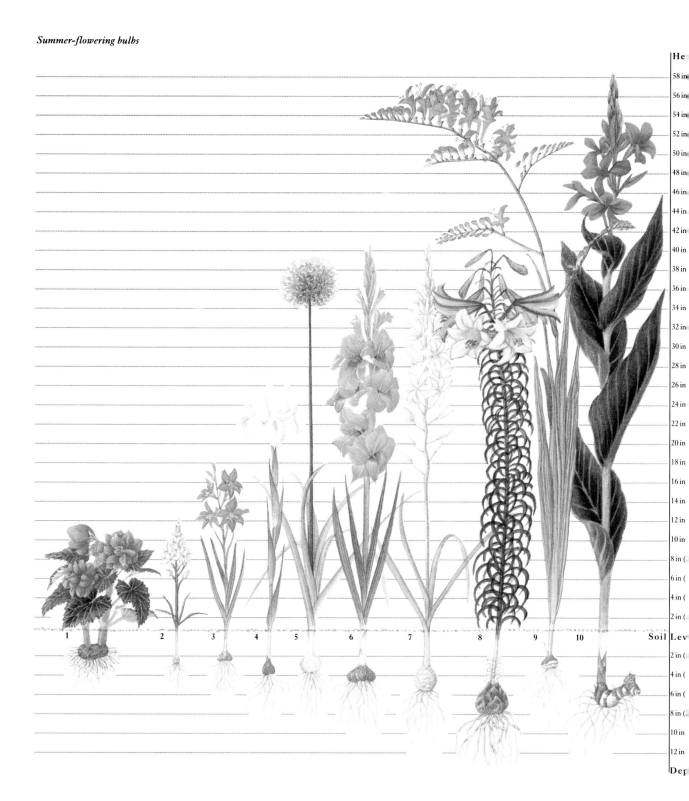

He
58 in
56 in
54 in
52 in
50 in
48 in
46 in
44 in
42 in
40 in
38 in
36 in
34 in
32 in
30 in
28 in
26 in
24 in
22 in
20 in
18 in
16 in
14 in
12 in
10 in
8 in (
6 in (
4 in (
2 in (

Soil Lev

2 in (
4 in (
6 in (
8 in (
10 in
12 in

Dep

Lilies, crocosmias, and cannas grow
into tall vigorous plants. Their bulbs
must be planted deeper than smaller
plants, such as irises and begonias.

1 *Begonia × tuberhybrida*
2 *Ornithogalum thyrsoides*
3 *Gladiolus nanus*
4 *Iris* 'White Excelsior'

5 *Allium aflatuense*
6 *Gladiolus* 'Peter Pears'
7 *Camassia leichtlinii*
8 *Lilium regale*

9 *Crocosmia masoniorum*
10 *Canna × generalis*

Autumn-flowering bulbs

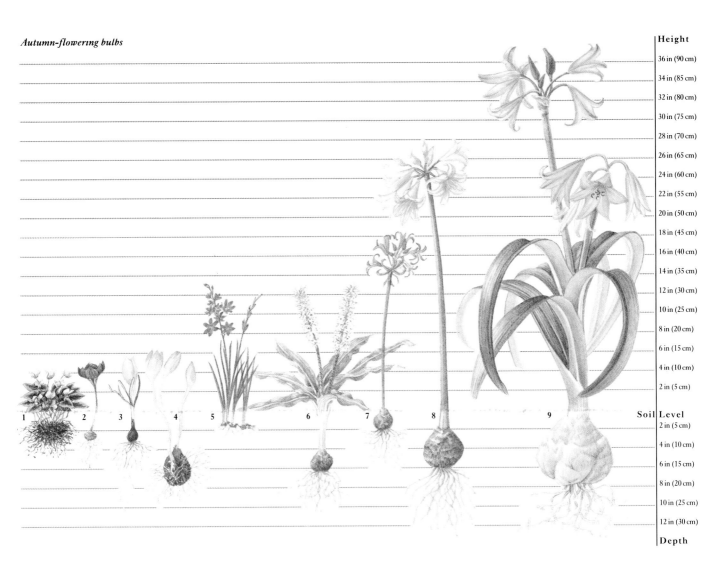

Height
36 in (90 cm)
34 in (85 cm)
32 in (80 cm)
30 in (75 cm)
28 in (70 cm)
26 in (65 cm)
24 in (60 cm)
22 in (55 cm)
20 in (50 cm)
18 in (45 cm)
16 in (40 cm)
14 in (35 cm)
12 in (30 cm)
10 in (25 cm)
8 in (20 cm)
6 in (15 cm)
4 in (10 cm)
2 in (5 cm)

Soil Level

Depth
2 in (5 cm)
4 in (10 cm)
6 in (15 cm)
8 in (20 cm)
10 in (25 cm)
12 in (30 cm)

Colchicums, eucomis, and amaryllis require deep planting, but the large autumn-flowering crinum grows best if planted with its neck just protruding from the soil.

1 *Cyclamen hederifolium*
2 *Crocus speciosus*
3 *Sternbergia lutea*
4 *Colchicum speciosum*
5 *Schizostylis coccinea*

6 *Eucomis comosa*
7 *Nerine bowdenii*
8 *Amaryllis belladonna*
9 *Crinum × powellii*

Winter-flowering bulbs

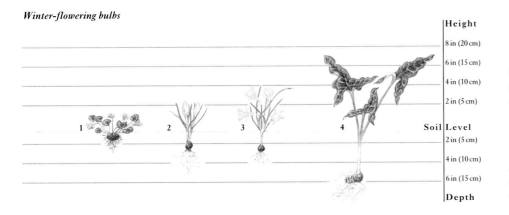

Height
8 in (20 cm)
6 in (15 cm)
4 in (10 cm)
2 in (5 cm)

Soil Level

Depth
2 in (5 cm)
4 in (10 cm)
6 in (15 cm)

With the exception of the arum, which needs a deep planting, the taller the winter-flowering bulb, the deeper it should be planted.

1 *Cyclamen coum*
2 *Crocus laevigatus*
3 *Narcissus bulbocodium romieuxii*
4 *Arum italicum*

Using a bulb planter
A specially designed, hand-held bulb planter provides an easy method of planting bulbs in the garden. It can be used for planting large quantities of bulbs for naturalizing in grass as well as for planting individual bulbs in the soil of flowerbeds. Push the planter into the ground and cut a plug of soil, then lift out the entire plug, leaving a hole. Insert the bulb into the hole, replace the soil plug, and leave the bulbs to grow. A bulb planter is invaluable for planting bulbs around established trees and shrubs.

planting them when they are in leaf rather than planting them as dry tubers or bulbs. Lift and transplant the bulbs immediately, when their flowers have faded but before their leaves start to deteriorate, and water them well.

Cut flowers

If you are growing bulbs specifically for cut flowers, they will require staking. To avoid damaging the root system, insert the stakes or canes as soon as the shoots emerge, but do not tie in the stems until the plant is approximately 6 in (15 cm) tall. Using garden twine, loosely tie the top and bottom of the stem to the stake or cane. Alternatively, use horizontal metal hoops attached to metal stakes.

Naturalizing

Bulbs for naturalizing can be planted in a number of ways. Either scatter them over the designated area and plant them where they fall, or use a special hand-held bulb planter to remove a plug of soil so that the bulb can be inserted and the turf replaced. Although this is a tedious, backbreaking job, it is the only technique that can safely be used around established trees and shrubs. Where you are naturalizing large quantities of bulbs, it is easier to lift the turf in several strips, then plant the bulbs and replace the turf. Alternatively, before seeding a lawn, plant the bulbs in well-cultivated soil and then seed over the top of them.

It is best to transplant some early-spring-flowering bulbs, such as winter aconites and snowdrops, "in the green"—

Seasonal care
Fertilizing

How and when to fertilize bulbs depend on the types and purposes for which they are being grown. If planting an annual bedding display, do not fertilize the bulbs but discard them once flowering is over and replace them with new plants. This also applies to large-flowered gladioli, which may not bloom as well the second year. Most smaller summer bulbs, like sparaxis and tigridia, can be discarded, or they can be lifted from the soil with a hand fork, dried on a wire rack, and stored in a net bag through the winter. Be careful not to over-fertilize them—once every 2 weeks is sufficient—because too much fertilizer can lead to soft growth and a greater vulnerability to diseases, particularly in cool, temperate climates.

Naturalizing bulbs in grass

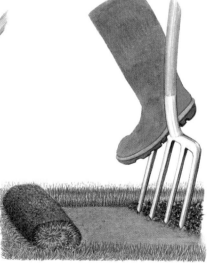

1 *Using a sharp spade, carefully lift a 1–2 in (2.5–5 cm)-thick strip of turf from the area to be planted and place it to one side.*

2 *Once the turf has been removed, loosen the exposed soil with a fork so that the bulbs will be able to root easily.*

3 *Make holes in the soil at random using a graduated bulb trowel. Plant the bulbs and replace the turf.*

Permanent spring-flowering bulbs like daffodils benefit greatly from fertilizing; it builds up their resources during flowering and before leaf loss, enabling the plant to form the next season's flower head. Either apply a single dose of slow-release fertilizer at flowering time, or use an all-purpose fertilizer containing nitrates, phosphates, and potash as soon as the buds emerge. Continue feeding with liquid fertilizer every 2 weeks. The liquid fertilizer supplies more nutrients to the bulbs before they go into dormancy than slow-release fertilizer does. Select a liquid formula with a low nitrogen content—6 parts nitrogen to 12 parts phosphorus and 12 parts potash—to prevent the bulbs from becoming soft and vulnerable to rot, especially when planted in heavy clay. Do not fertilize naturalized bulbs, as the fertilizer tends to feed the surrounding grass as well as the bulbs, making the grass too vigorous and competitive with the bulbs; the grass will quickly swamp any nearby bulbs.

Deadheading

Wherever possible, deadhead all bulbs after flowering to divert the plant's energy into the remaining flowers and, after flowering, into the development of next year's flower spike. It will also improve the look of the plant. Once the flower has faded and started to turn brown, pinch the flower off at the neck. After flowering, perennials should be kept growing by watering until the tips of the foliage turn yellow, after which they can be lifted and stored in a cool, dry place, having been dried first.

Mulching

Bulbs that remain in the ground over winter are usually hardy enough to withstand the conditions, but in very cold areas some will need the protection of a heavy mulch. Once the ground has frozen, cover the earth around the bulbs with straw held in place with evergreen boughs.

Storage

Most of the bulbs, corms, tubers, and rhizomes requiring winter storage are summer-flowering plants, like gladioli, which cannot withstand winter in the open ground and must be lifted and stored in a cool, dry place. Do not lift the bulbs when the foliage is still green because the ends of the leaves may be open to rapid fungal infection. Instead, wait until after the first hard frosts have blackened the foliage and sealed the leaf tissue. In hot climates, most hardy bulbs must be lifted and chilled to produce repeat blooms.

Once the leaves have withered, use a sharp knife to remove any remaining foliage, cutting as close to the top of the bulb as possible. Spread the bulbs out on a wire rack to enable the air to circulate and dry them; corms with a hollow stem must be inverted so that any lingering moisture can drain away. When thoroughly dry, rub off any remaining soil and dust the bulbs with flowers of sulfur as a protection against storage molds.

The bulbs are then ready to be stored in a net bag in a cool, dry place, with an average temperature of 45°F (7°C). Regularly check for signs of softness or disease.

Storing bulbs

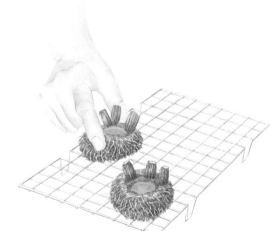

1 *Lift the bulbs from the ground and remove all the frost-blackened foliage to within 1–2 in (2.5–5 cm) of the top of the bulb.*

2 *Spread the bulbs out on a wire rack and, when dry, rub off any soil and dust the bulbs with an insecticide-fungicide powder.*

3 *The bulbs are now ready to store. Place them in a mesh bag and keep them in a cool, dry place until they are ready to plant.*

CONTAINERS, WINDOW BOXES, AND HANGING BASKETS
Growing mediums

Indoor bulbs and bulbs grown in outdoor containers, window boxes, and hanging baskets require a suitable potting medium which has the required humus content and drainage capacity. Despite what some experts say, bulb fiber is not necessarily best for growing bulbs. The various formulas incorporate sphagnum moss or coarse peat moss, or both, with added charcoal and oyster shell. The mixture has virtually no nutrients, and so the bulbs have to depend on their stored energy resources to grow and flower. This usually exhausts them so they do not perform properly or, in extreme circumstances, produce any flowers at all. For the best results, use a good-quality potting medium.

The two main types of potting medium, soilless and soil-based, both have added nutrients—nitrogen, phosphorus, and potassium—although the amount varies according to the manufacturer.

Soilless mixtures consist of peat, pulverized composted bark, or another organic material, and some have additions of sand for extra drainage. Because these mixtures are virtually organic, they are not recommended for long-term planting; they are unstable in structure and will deteriorate after a season. However, they can be used for growing bulbs in pots and planters since these are usually grown for only a single season in the container before being planted outside in the open ground. For raising seed or young plants, a soilless mix or seed starter mix is preferable. To make a soilless mix, use equal parts of perlite, vermiculite, and peat. However, soilless mixtures are commercially available. When using a soilless mix, it is important to fertilize regularly to provide proper nutrients for growing plants.

Use a soil-based potting medium for long-term bulbs such as *Gloriosa*. Additions of up to 25 percent by volume of perlite will act as a moisture reserve, keeping the medium moist but not waterlogged.

Soil-based mediums are generally made of soil or loam, peat, and sand. They are often available in special formulas for differing types of plants. African violet mix and sandy or cactus mix are the most common variations. Depending on the type of bulb being planted, a particular mix may be beneficial. All-purpose potting soil generally consists of equal amounts of soil, peat, and sand. Vermiculite or perlite can be added to boost the soil's ability to retain moisture, as opposed to sand, which enhances the soil's drainage quality. Standard potting soils are suitable for either forced bulbs grown for early indoor flowering or bulbs grown as house plants year-round.

Planting containers

Most bulbs grow well in containers under the right conditions. A good-quality potting medium is the first essential ingredient, but equally important are sufficient root space and good drainage. The success of hanging baskets depends on steady watering as well.

For bulb containers, there is a wide range of possibilities, including imaginative vessels like chimney pots and sinks. Shallow containers less than 6 in (15 cm) high with a large surface area are the least useful because they dry out rapidly; containers measuring 6-24 in (15-60 cm) in height are much better, even if the roots of the bulb are unlikely to penetrate the lower depths, which can be filled with drainage material such as pieces of broken terra-cotta flower pots and small stones about 2 in (5 cm) across. Lilies look best in clay or wooden tubs; large trumpet lilies require a pot at least 9 in (23 cm) in diameter, although the same pot will hold three to five of the smaller Asiatic lilies.

Before adding soil or selecting bulbs, decide where to locate the container. For most bulbous plants, an open, sunny spot is best, but if this is not possible, select shade-tolerant bulbs for shady spots. It is a good idea to position heavy containers before filling them with soil, as they may be difficult to move when full.

Place a $1/2$ in (1 cm) layer of coarse gravel in the bottom of a container with drainage holes and a $1^{1}/_{2}$ in (3.5 cm) layer in one without holes; lilies benefit from a 1-2 in (2.5-5 cm) layer of organic matter such as well-rotted leaves covering the gravel. Fill the container with potting soil for permanent plantings and with a soilless mixture, with up to 25 percent by volume added perlite, for temporary plantings; the few that tolerate damp conditions will require a growing medium mixed with up to 20 percent by volume organic material, such as composted bark. If the bulbs are to accompany an established plant like a miniature conifer, they will have to tolerate the medium already in the container. Plant the bulbs at the correct depths (see pp. 41-43), spacing them as required for each individual type. For stem-rooted lilies, leave a gap of about 2 in (5 cm) between the surface and the rim of the pot so that more soil or well-rotted compost can be added as the stems develop roots above the bulb in summer. If you plant narcissi in a deep container, plant one layer of soil and bulbs and then another immediately above it, making the base of the top layer of bulbs level with the noses of those beneath. This method can also be applied to daffodils grown in pots indoors, but it is not a good method for long-term cultivation.

If you plant in fall, water the bulbs and keep the pot in a cool, frost-free place indoors until spring, preferably plunged in sand. As the shoots develop, bring them into the light and water them so that the medium is always damp but not water-logged. Move the pots outside to a sheltered spot when there is no longer any danger of frost. If you intend to keep the bulb, cut off the stems to the level of the soil once the foliage turns brown and repot the bulbs or top-dress them with new soil. They may require repotting every other year if they increase and become too large and congested for the original pot.

Planting window boxes

As with containers, window boxes must be relatively deep—6-9 in (15-23 cm) is ideal—and have good drainage. Choose window boxes that will not restrict the root development of the bulbs. It is also important to select a lightweight window box that can be fixed to the wall.

Place a 1 in (2.5 cm) layer of coarse gravel in the bottom of the window box and fill it with a soilless mixture. To conserve moisture, you can incorporate up to 25 percent perlite. The soil layer should be a minimum of 4 in (10 cm) deep; a 6 in (15 cm) layer is ideal. Plant the bulbs at the required depths (see pp. 41-43) and water them as necessary. To plan a series of seasonal displays, use several plastic liners. Insert the current season's display in the empty window box and keep the others in a sheltered corner of the garden. As each season comes to an end, remove the liner and replace it with a new one for the next season.

Planting hanging baskets

Hanging baskets can be replanted each season for a continuous show of color. Both plastic and metal baskets are available in a variety of different sizes, and although the plastic ones are less prone to drying out, the wire ones are much more attractive.

Line the basket with a 1½ in (3.5 cm) layer of moist sphagnum moss; this is an ideal medium because it helps to prevent rapid moisture loss but, unlike plastic, does not restrict drainage to the extent of causing waterlogging. Compress it using your fingertips and fill the basket almost to the top with potting medium. Soilless mixtures are best since they are lighter. Using your hand, hollow out planting holes approximately one-and-a-half times the size of the bulbs and insert the bulbs, packing the remaining space with more growing medium. Place the newly planted basket in a container of water and leave it to soak until the potting medium is thoroughly wet, after which you can fix the basket in its permanent position. Subsequent watering can be done with a watering can with a rose attachment.

Seasonal care

Containers and window boxes should be watered regularly—every other day—so that the growing medium is always damp. Keep the window box free of weeds, as well as checking for pests and diseases. When the flower buds begin to show color, start feeding the plants with liquid fertilizer every

Planting containers

1 *Drainage is important for container-grown bulbs. Always put a layer of gravel into the container before adding the soil mix.*

2 *Place the bulbs on the soil so they are correctly spaced and at the right depth. Do not disturb them as you add the remaining soil.*

3 *Water, then top off the soil if necessary. Feed and water regularly, particularly if your containers are made of wood or unglazed pottery.*

2 weeks. Deadhead the flowers as soon as they die to promote good growth.

The success of a hanging basket is almost entirely dependent upon the watering and feeding program. This is because the roots of the plants do not have the space to develop to sustain the plants and, furthermore, the basket loses a lot of moisture because most of its surface is exposed to air. Thoroughly soak the baskets until the water runs out once a day or, in warm or breezy conditions, twice. Every time you water, check for faded foliage and blossoms, removing them immediately. Feed the plants with a liquid fertilizer every 10 days.

Most bulbs planted in containers and window boxes do not survive the winter outside. This is because the soil temperature becomes lower than in a garden bed, and some bulbs may not survive. Either discard these bulbs or store them in net bags indoors, after drying them off on a wire rack. Containers that are planted in early spring, especially with hyacinths, need protection from lingering frosts. Lay a mulch of straw or pine needles over the soil until the weather warms up. In cold climates, use only the hardiest of bulbs in containers and raise them up from the ground on bricks. This will lessen the effect of the cold penetrating the bottom and sides of a container. Pack straw around the container to help insulate it.

IN THE HOUSE

Indoor bulbs thrive in temperatures of 50-60°F (10-16°C) and in light, sunny spots, although some do not like direct sunlight and none will tolerate drafty positions. Growing indoor bulbs is similar to growing bulbs outdoors, with one exception: the majority of indoor bulbs lose their leaves and go into dormancy for part of the year, during which time they should not be watered. Depending on individual varieties, the bulbs remain dormant for 1-3 months. Spring-flowering bulbs go into dormancy in late summer; summer-flowering bulbs become dormant in winter; and fall- and winter-flowering bulbs are dormant in spring.

Some tender bulbs, such as some begonias, are often sold as growing plants, while others, such as amaryllises, can be purchased in their dry state and then need potting. Plant bulbs in a good-quality potting soil, with 25 percent sand added to improve drainage. Achimenes and begonias require a free draining moist soilless mixture. Plant one large bulb or several small ones per pot, allowing a gap of approximately 1 in (2.5 cm) around the edge of the pot. Most bulbs barely need covering, and some prefer to have their tips poking above the surface of the potting medium.

Water the bulbs lightly and then, unless the potting medium dries out completely, do not water them again until the bulbs start to grow, when regular watering should start.

Amaryllises (hippeastrums) are very popular indoor plants. Purchase the bulb in fall or early winter, and pot it in standard potting soil, with approximately half the bulb above the soil surface. The pot should only be ½ in (1 cm) larger than the diameter of the bulb. Once potted, water the bulb well, and place it in a warm, bright spot. A healthy, vigorous amaryllis produces at least four long, bright green straplike leaves and a spike of magnificent colorful trumpetlike flowers. A plant with four healthy leaves throughout the year usually produces good flowers the following season.

Planting indoor bulbs

1 *Amaryllis bulbs are available in autumn and winter, often in kit form with a pot and soil.*

2 *If using your own pot, choose one slightly larger than the bulb and put gravel in the bottom.*

3 *Place the bulb in the pot with about half projecting above the top of the soil and be sure that the soil is well packed. Water thoroughly but carefully around the sides of the bulb.*

Deadheading

Removing spent flower heads not only improves the appearance of your indoor bulbs but lengthens the flowering period, because the plant will not use energy in forming seeds.

Seasonal care

Once flower buds appear, fertilize and water the bulbs with a liquid fertilizer to promote good blossoms and stable growth; this reduces the likelihood of disease during the dormant period. Fertilize every 2 weeks and water the plant so that the potting soil is always damp; this may be as much as every day in hot, dry indoor conditions. Stop fertilizing and watering once the foliage starts to die down, and deadhead the flowers once they start to go limp and fade. With almost perpetually summer-flowering plants like begonias, you must regularly remove the faded blossoms in order to promote the development of new flower buds. With double-flowered tuberous begonias, it is also necessary to remove the single female flowers. These are easy to recognize by the tiny winged seed capsule behind the bud; they do not contribute to the floral display and reduce the strength of the double male flowers. Some bulbs like begonias are also subject to mildew attacks during cool, humid weather and may require spraying with a systemic fungicide.

After flowering, most indoor bulbs go into dormancy but some species may continue to grow. Watch the plant carefully; if it starts to turn yellow and goes into decline, reduce feeding and watering until the bulb goes into dormancy. But if the bulb continues to grow, you should maintain a feeding and watering regime. Indoor bulbs like *Lachenalia* and *Veltheimia* benefit from a dormant period, which you can induce by watering the plant less when the foliage starts to fade and until the potting medium is completely dry. Provided the plant has 4 to 6 strong leaves left several months after flowering, the next season's flower display is guaranteed. If you do not have enough space to store dormant indoor plants in their pots, take the rootstocks out of the pots and place them in an airtight box layered with peat. Begonias should be removed from their pots and the tubers dusted with flowers of sulfur to combat fungal infections and storage molds. Store these plants at a minimum winter temperature of 50°F (10°C), and check periodically for signs of decay; discard any tubers that do not look healthy.

Amaryllises (hippeastrums) can be kept growing through summer, provided their roots are not exposed. They can also be left unwatered over summer and placed in a cool, dark spot until the following winter, when they will start into growth. When winter arrives, scrape away the surface soil until the roots are exposed and fill the container with fresh growing medium. Water the plant and place it in a warm, light spot.

Many indoor bulbs spend the entire year in the same pots, but there are certain exceptions like achimenes and gloriosas, which are better repotted the next season in fresh soil.

FORCING

Specially prepared bulbs can be forced into early flowering for indoor displays. Hyacinths are some of the most widely cultivated prepared bulbs. Among them, 'Pink Pearl,' 'Delft Blue,' and the pure white 'Carnegie' are good choices to provide bowls of color and scent in early winter.

Forcing hyacinth bulbs

1 *Plant specially-prepared hyacinth bulbs for forcing with their shoulders just above the soil level.*

2 *Always place gravel or broken crocks at the bottom of the container to help drainage.*

Planting

For the finest results, the prepared hyacinths should ideally be 9 in (23 cm) in circumference; if you plant only one bowl, restrict the choice to one variety otherwise they may not flower at the same time. As a precaution against skin irritation, wear gardening gloves when handling the bulbs.

Plant the prepared bulbs in late summer or early winter in a multi-purpose soilless mix, with the tips just poking above the top of the soil. Most ornamental bulb bowls have few or no drainage holes; add a 1 in (2.5 cm) layer of gravel in the bottom of the container before planting to help drainage.

After planting the bulbs, water them thoroughly and put the pots in a cool, frost-free place, with a maximum temperature of 45°F (7°C); a garage, shed, or unheated porch is ideal. Leave them there for a minimum of 10 weeks; forced tulips must be left for 12-14 weeks.

After this period, bring the pots into daylight and place them in a cool room. As light is poor during winter and early spring, put the bulbs in the brightest spot in the room, ideally on a window ledge during the day. However, because the air around the window will become colder at night, move the bulbs into the room when darkness falls. if the bulbs become chilled, they will not perform satisfactorily.

Once exposed to the heat and light, the yellow shoots of the bulbs will turn green after a few days. If you wish, top-dress the potting medium with fresh green sphagnum moss to protect the pot against moisture loss. The moss also looks attractive. Water the bulbs so the soil is always moist but not waterlogged; you may need to do this every day in a heated room or once a week in a cool room.

Seasonal care

Forced bulbs flower for 2-3 weeks under average house conditions. If necessary, support tall stems with small, split green stakes and string or specially manufactured wire supports. As the first blossoms fade, cut them off near the base of the bulb. If the dead flower stems are not removed, they drain the bulb's resources so the remaining flowers will not last long. For the best results, start feeding the plants with a liquid fertilizer when the emerging flower buds start to gain color. If you wish to plant the bulbs outdoors once they are over, continue to feed the bulbs after flowering until the tips of the foliage start to turn yellow.

After flowering, either discard the bulbs or plant them outside once danger of frost is over, in which case the foliage must be kept active and green for as long as possible for the bulbs to build up food reserves for the following season's growth and flower display.

PEST AND DISEASE CONTROL

Controlling pests and diseases during the growing period is crucial to maintain a healthy garden. Although major infestations may require using toxic sprays which are harmful to people, pets, and wildlife, most garden problems can be effectively controlled using preventative and non-toxic methods.

The preventative approach is the most environmentally friendly type of pest control. Encourage insect-eating predators, such as birds, toads, fireflies, ladybugs, lacewings, and praying mantises to live in the garden and they will eat the pests. You can also deter aphids, earwigs, and other common pests with commercially prepared insecticidal soap sprays, which are less harmful than chemical sprays. Organic pesticide sprays made from natural pest poisons can be used for more serious problems.

Earwigs

These seemingly harmless insects are, in fact, destructive, causing twisted or distorted, often chewed blossoms. Other signs of earwigs are a stippled chewing of the foliage and tiny irregular holes in the main veins of the leaves. These pests are only active at night, hiding in debris during the day. While an insecticidal dust has some effect if applied around the plants, the best method of control is to capture them. Invert a plant pot filled with dried grass on a garden cane or steel rods, close to the damaged plants, so that the earwigs will hide in the dried grass during the day and can be collected and disposed of each evening.

Snails and slugs

Slugs and snails are also a threat, attacking emergent shoots and leaves of succulent plants like lilies and gladioli, particularly during the spring. In some cases, most notably among lilies, this can have a devastating effect, damaging the growing points and distorting growth. The shoots of summer-flowering *Sparaxis* and *Tigridia* can also be attacked if precautions are not taken, while the flowers of early-flowering *Scilla* and *Puschkinia* are also at risk. You can use slug pellets among the groups of plants most affected; rather than scattering them around the plants, place a handful under a small piece of flat stone that is raised above the soil level. This keeps the pellets dry while preventing birds from picking them up, and slugs and snails will congregate under the stone to devour the pellets.

A more environmentally friendly method of control involves sinking a small plastic carton filled with beer into the ground to soil level. The slugs and snails are attracted to the liquid, and while trying to drink, fall in and drown.

Pests and diseases

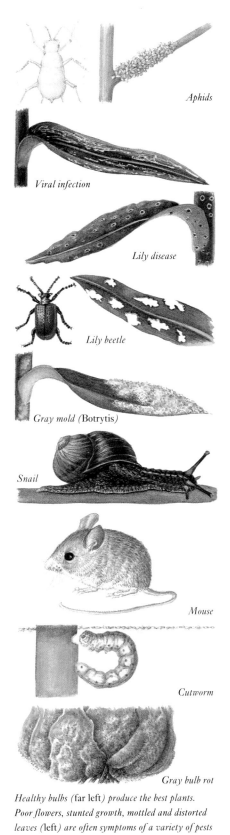

Aphids

Viral infection

Lily disease

Lily beetle

Gray mold (Botrytis)

Snail

Mouse

Cutworm

Gray bulb rot

Healthy bulbs (far left) produce the best plants. Poor flowers, stunted growth, mottled and distorted leaves (left) are often symptoms of a variety of pests and diseases (above).

Alternatively, place the eaten halves of a grapefruit upside down on the soil surface beside vulnerable plants; this will attract the slugs and they will crawl underneath and later can be removed. Replace the grapefruit halves every 3-4 days, once the interiors have dried up.

Aphids

Aphids and other pests can be controlled by the use of a systemic insecticide every 3 weeks. Once the plant has been sprayed, the sap of the foliage absorbs the insecticide, effectively inoculating the plant against sucking insects. However, this is a short-lived measure, and repeat sprayings every 3 weeks are necessary. While a systemic insecticide will not guarantee total protection against virus diseases transmitted by aphids, it is nonetheless a highly effective form of control, particularly benefiting lilies. To avoid using poisons, check your plants regularly and spray with insecticidal soap at the first sign of this pest.

Animals

Animal pests, including mice, moles, deer, squirrels, chipmunks, and gophers, all naturally feed on some part of the bulb plant and can cause extensive damage in the plant world. Many nibble on the foliage and flowers, others dig up and eat the bulbs in their entirety. To deter or trap these pests, use bitter sprays and physical barriers—placed both above and below ground.

Viral infection

Of all the bulbous plants, lilies are the most susceptible to viral infection and, once affected, will die. Typical symptoms include distorted foliage, absence or twisting of blossoms, and when the vigorous young shoots are stopped in their tracks, ugly spreading rosettes of contorted foliage. In such cases, there is no cure and the plants will have to be disposed of. It is best to do this at the first signs of disease so the disease does not spread.

Bulb Diseases

Disease	Symptoms	Plants affected	Control
Basal rot *A fungus living in the soil that enjoys warm conditions*	*Soft, rotting bulbs with a coating of mold around the base; yellow, wilted leaves*	Narcissus	*Remove diseased flowers, buds and leaves and spray plants with a systemic fungicide*
Gray mold (*Botrytis*) *A widespread disease*	*Rotting bulbs and stunted plant growth; gray, fluffy mold on the leaves and flowers, with discoloration and dying patches*	Anemone Lily Snowdrop Tulip	*Dispose of affected plants*
Hyacinth black slime *A disease living in the soil*	*Dry, black decaying bulbs; yellow foliage rotting at the base*	Crocus Fritillary Hyacinth Scilla	*Dispose of affected plants*
Ink spot disease *A disease caused by fungus*	*Black spots on the bulbs; yellow foliage with dark streaks*	Iris	*Dispose of affected plants*
Lily disease	*Reddish-brown spots on withered foliage*	Lily	*Dispose of affected plants*
Powdery mildew *A fungus thriving in drought conditions*	*A white, powdery film on the foliage*	Begonia Cyclamen	*Dispose of affected plants*
Root rot *A disease living in soil*	*Black and decaying roots*	Hyacinth	*Dispose of affected plants*
Tulip fire (*Botrytis*) *A fungus thriving in warm soil conditions*	*Rotting bulbs and stunted plant growth; dark gray fungal blotches on the foliage*	Tulip	*Spray diseased plants with a systemic fungicide*
Tulip gray bulb rot *A persistent fungus living in the soil which infects bulbs shortly after planting or in early spring*	*A dry rot consisting of white, moldy patches; stunted plant growth*	Colchicum Crocus Hyacinth Lily Narcissus Tulip	*Dispose of affected plants*
Viral infection	*Streaked and mottled foliage with pale marks; distorted leaves and wilting*	Gladiolus Lily Tulip	*Dispose of affected plants*

Bulb Pests

Pest	Symptoms	Plants affected	Control
Aphids *Small, green or yellowish insects which suck the sap of the foliage and excrete a sticky deposit*	*A sticky, sooty deposit on the foliage*	Begonia Lily Most other bulbs	*Spray affected plants with a systemic insecticide*
Gladiolus thrips *Brownish-black insects with long bodies*	*A silvery white, black-flecked discoloration on the flowers and foliage*	Gladiolus	*Spray affected areas with insecticide*
Cutworms	*Nibbled roots and chewed soft tissue of bulbs*	Most bulbs	*Dust the soil with soil insecticide prior to bulb planting*
Lily beetles *Bright red insects*	*Chewed leaves and flowers from early spring to mid-autumn*	Fritillary Lily	*Treat affected plants with an insecticidal dust or remove the beetles by hand*
Animals including mice, squirrels, chipmunks, and gophers	*Disturbed often nibbled bulbs*	Crocus Gladiolus Tulip Most other bulbs	*Use bitter sprays and physical barriers*
Narcissus flies *Adult flies similar in appearance to bumblebees*	*Soft bulbs sometimes infested with white maggots; a few grass-like leaves if any*	Hyacinth Narcissus	*Dispose of affected plants*
Snails and slugs	*Chewed foliage, flowers and bulbs*	Gladiolus Lily Most other bulbs	*Use slug pellets and traps*
Stem and bulb eelworms *Microscopic creatures which burrow into the plant tissue*	*Brown and soft bulbs and weak growth; twisted and streaked leaves and undeveloped flowers*	Hyacinth Iris Narcissus Snowdrop Tulip	*Dispose of affected plants*

By diagnosing and controlling pests and diseases in their early stages, you can save a great deal of trouble and expense. Swift and appropriate action may involve digging up and destroying the affected plants. This may seem drastic, but it will prevent the problem from spreading.

Fungal diseases

Fungal diseases like mildew are easier to treat, the majority being dealt with by a systemic fungicide. The more stubborn diseases can be tackled with a copper-based fungicide applied every 3 weeks, but in extreme cases it is easier to buy healthy new bulbs and discard the badly infected ones. The sooner this is done the better, to stop the fungus spreading to other plants. Mildew and leaf spot diseases of various kinds can also be tackled with a systemic fungicide applied every 3 weeks, provided spraying commences early in the growing season, as soon as fresh young foliage appears. The combination of a compatible systemic fungicide and insecticide will considerably reduce the number of sprayings needed.

INCREASING YOUR STOCK

There are numerous ways to increase your bulb stock, some of which are specific to individual genera. For details, see individual plant entries.

Division

During the growing season, many bulbs, such as narcissi, increase by forming offsets from the main plant. If the plants are lifted when dormant, the offsets can be detached and planted as new plants, a process known as division.

Ideally, you should lift and divide the bulbs during the dormant period, but this is often impractical as most gardeners have little idea of the number and position of the bulbs once they have died back. Bulbs can also be divided just as they begin to peep through the soil in spring, provided they are handled carefully, since at this time they will split more easily than when dormant. Snowdrops are slightly different in that they should be divided when in leaf.

To divide the bulbs, use a garden fork to lift the clump carefully, and gently shake off the soil. Separate the offsets from the parent plant with your hands, grading them into flowering and nonflowering sizes; the flowering bulbs will be bigger than the nonflowering ones. Do not force the offsets apart; resistance is a sure indication that the bulbs are not ready to part. Pot the offsets or replant them in their permanent positions.

Narcissi regularly produce "daughter" bulbs as part of the main structure, and these growing points—known as "noses"—slowly separate from the main bulb. Provided the nose is attached to a tiny portion of the base plate, it will grow into a new plant. Never force the daughter bulbs apart, for you may damage the base plate; wait for them to divide naturally before collecting and replanting them.

Some tubers—for example, begonias—can be propagated by dividing the main storage organ. Take a sharp knife and cut through the tuber, making sure that each piece has a dormant bud attached to it. Do not make the portions too small; a few large slices are ideal. A mature begonia usually provides three or four sections. After you divide the tubers, dress all the cut surfaces with flowers of sulfur to reduce the possibility of infection. Pot each individual portion and allow it to grow before planting outdoors.

Division

1 *Bulbs that spread by self-seeding or offsets will eventually form overcrowded clumps. When this happens, the clumps should be lifted carefully with a garden fork.*

2 *Gently tease the congested clumps apart with your hands, taking care not to break the root fibers. Select the largest, healthiest bulbs from the clump and discard the rest.*

3 *Replant the bulbs you have selected, either singly or in small groups. Improve the soil by adding compost or digging in some fertilizer, and water the bulbs thoroughly.*

Propagating bulbils

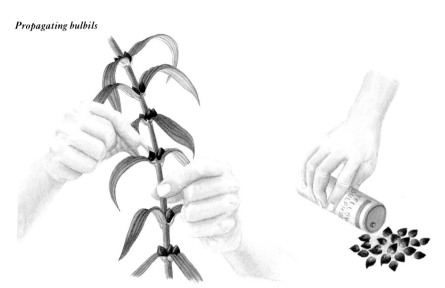

1 *Some lilies form bulbils in their leaf axils, and these can be easily detached when ripe, usually when the foliage starts to die back.*

2 *Dust the bulbils with flowers of sulfur to prevent the spread of fungal diseases, to which some lilies are particularly prone.*

3 *Seal bulbils in a polythene bag with damp moss, and store in a cool place. They will soon grow, ready for planting the following spring.*

Bulbils

Some bulbs, notably lilies, produce bulbils, or small bulbs, which can be used for propagation purposes, although they take a whole summer season to develop into plants. Flowering depends on the variety, but most should perform in their third or fourth year.

Do not pick the bulbils until they are ripe, because they damage easily and will not root properly. Ideally, the foliage of the adult plant should be starting to turn yellow before you gather the bulbils. Detach the bulbils, dust them with flowers of sulfur, and place them in a plastic bag, with a little damp green sphagnum moss. Store the bag in a cool place—such as the vegetable bin in the bottom of the fridge—and, the following spring, plant them, just covered, in seed trays filled with a soilless mixture. You can leave them there, feeding them regularly from early summer until the following spring, when they can be planted outdoors.

Alternatively, remove a section of the stem with the bulbils and take off any leaves. Place the stem horizontally in a tray of soilless mixture, with the mixture just covering the stem, and put the tray in a cold frame. In most cases, the bulbils will root and start to grow.

Once the bulbils have sprouted and are growing strongly, carefully remove them from the old stem. Plant them in a seed tray of soilless planting medium and leave them to grow. During the growing season feed them regularly and transplant them into small pots as they grow bigger. The following spring they can be taken out of the cold frame and planted outdoors.

Cormels

Many corms, such as gladioli, crocuses, and crocosmias, produce masses of tiny cormels around their bases at the onset of the dormant period. These can be grown for propagation purposes.

Gather the cormels and plant them in a tray of all-purpose potting soil, and place the tray in a cold frame. If the winter temperature drops below 20°F (−6°C), the tray will need protecting. Keep the cormels moist through the winter, and start watering in early spring to encourage growth. Once large enough to handle, the plants can be placed in rows outside. It will take approximately 3 years for the cormels to grow into flowering-size plants.

Propagating cormels

(above) *The tiny cormels formed around the base of gladioli and other cormous plants will gradually form congested clumps of foliage. They can be detached and planted in soil to produce flowering-size corms in as little as 3 years.*

Seed

This method of increasing bulbs produces a large stock, but may take from 3 to 5 years to produce flowering-size plants. As a general rule, small-flowered varieties that have small bulbs and seed freely are the best to increase this way. These include the *Scilla* and *Chionodoxa* species as well as mixed *Anemone blanda*. It is pointless to use this method with named cultivars, as the seed gathered from these is often the result of a cross with another plant, which—even if it is of the same type—will not necessarily produce identical progeny.

You can either buy the seed or collect it from the plants. However, freshly gathered seed always germinates much more freely, especially if sown immediately after gathering. This applies particularly to bulbs like narcissi and snowdrops, which belong to the Amaryllidaceae family, whose members tend to yield seed of short viability. The Liliaceae family, which includes lilies and fritillaries, and the Iridaceae family, which includes crocuses and irises, produce seed that, while better sown directly after harvesting, will tolerate being stored in a paper bag for up to 6 months.

For lime-tolerant seed, use all-purpose potting mixture with up to 25 percent sand by volume for improved drainage; for lime haters like some lilies, use an acid formula potting medium with up to 25 percent added sand. Fill a seed tray with the potting medium; smooth the surface and press the surface down firmly before sowing the seed. Barely cover the seed with soil, and gently water the tray using a watering can with a fine rose attachment. Place trays of tender seed in a frost-free greenhouse or on a sunny window ledge. For those that take a long time to germinate, a liberal top-dressing of fine sand can be applied to help prevent an invasion of moss. Trays of hardy seed should be placed in a cold frame. Stubborn seed can sometimes be stimulated into growth by freezing; place the tray in the deep freeze for 3 weeks or so, before moving it to a warm, light place.

Once the seeds start to germinate, scatter a handful of slug pellets around the seed tray so the seedlings are not attacked by snails and slugs. Aphids can also be a problem: spray the seeds with a systemic insecticide every 2 weeks.

When the seedlings are large enough to be handled—usually within 2-3 weeks of first appearing—pot them together in an all-purpose potting medium and water. Once they are well established, you can either pot the seedlings individually or plant them outside in the garden.

Fine seed, like that of double-flowered begonias, requires a rich, organic soilless mixture containing a combination of peat or bark and sand, as this is warmer than soil-based composts. Fill a seed tray with the potting mixture, smooth the surface, and press it down firmly. Drop a pinch of dry sand in the open packet of seed and shake it so that the sand and seed mix together. This will make it easier to distribute evenly. If sown in this way, it will not require covering with soilless mix.

Sowing seed

1 *Although it takes longer than other methods, growing bulbs from seed is an easy and inexpensive way of producing large numbers of bulbs. Use a well-drained soil, and sow the seed thinly.*

2 *The seed should be covered with a scattering of soil. After sowing, water carefully, using a fine spray to avoid disturbing the seed or washing it all to one side of the pot.*

3 *Prick the seedlings out as soon as they are large enough to handle easily. They should be planted about 1-2 in (2.5-5 cm) apart so that they have enough room to develop their root systems.*

Place the tray in a warm place. Begonias need a minimum temperature of 60°F (16°C). Close, humid conditions can lead to damping-off disease, which affects a wide range of seedlings, causing the stems to blacken at soil level; the plant then collapses and dies. The best precautionary measure is to apply a fungicide such as thiram or zineb; a systemic fungicide is of little use since it must be absorbed by green foliage, whereas seedlings are often affected before their leaves have fully developed. Gently water with the compound immediately after sowing and reapply every 10 days, until the plants develop their second set of leaves.

Transplant the seedlings into a tray of soilless medium. If they have germinated in small clumps, gently tease out individual seedlings, taking care not to damage the roots. Leave them to grow for 2 or 3 years, repotting them into individual pots as necessary. If they are to be planted outside, however, they must first be hardened off. If you have a cold frame, put the plants in the frame and close it. After 4 or 5 days, raise the lid a little more every few days until the plants are weaned from the warmth of the indoor or greenhouse environment in which they were raised. Alternatively, if you do not have a cold frame, move the seedlings outside for a day at a time, bringing them indoors for the night. After approximately 10 days, they should be able to tolerate night conditions and can be left outside to grow.

With some bulbs—for example, bluebells—growing plants from seed by hand is unpredictable. Bluebells will self-propagate into naturalized patches if left alone, but you can encourage them and increase your stock. Either let the seed fall naturally to the ground or gently shake the seed heads to dislodge the ripe seed and leave it to grow. In the case of naturalized crocuses and scillas, cut back the old growth when the seed has ripened and the plant will self-seed.

Stem cuttings

Stem cuttings are a way of increasing a variety of tubers, including begonias. It is a good way of quickly producing a large number of plants that will flower the same season without impairing the quality of the blossoms, and it is especially suitable for providing a large quantity of bedding plants.

Space out the tubers in boxes of soilless potting medium, scarcely covering them. Lay brown paper over the top to protect any emerging roots from bright sunlight, and water them regularly. When tiny green shoots appear, immediately remove the paper. When the shoots reach a height of approximately 2 in (5 cm), carefully remove them just below a leaf joint. Allow one shoot to remain on each tuber so that the tuber can be left to grow. Remove the lowest leaf and base of each, and dip the cuttings into a softwood hormone rooting powder or liquid. Plant them in a tray filled with a 50:50 mixture of peat and perlite, or peat and sand, and stand the tray in a warm but lightly shaded place. Within 2 weeks, the shoots will root.

As soon as rooting takes place, pot the cuttings individually in a soilless mixture and provide them with plenty of light and a steady temperature, a minimum of 60°F (16°C). The parent tubers can also be potted and grown alongside the rooted cuttings; they usually make slightly larger plants more quickly, but by the time they are ready for planting outside, all the plants will be of similar size.

If you wish to produce more cuttings than you have shoots for, do not remove the shoots from the tubers until they are 4-5 in (10-12.5 cm) long. Then, remove the shoots and cut them into short lengths approximately 1½ in (3.5 cm) long.

Remove any large leaves and dust the cut surfaces with flowers of sulfur. Dip the ends of each section in rooting powder or liquid and plant them as for single stem cuttings.

Stem propagation

1 *Begonias can be forced into growth for stem propagation. All they need is a little warmth, moist soil, and protection from light until the first shoots show through.*

2 *Cut off all but one shoot from each tuber when the shoots are about 2 in (5 cm) long. Make sure the knife you use is sharp and clean to avoid damaging the shoots or introducing infection.*

3 *Hormone rooting compound will help the cuttings establish quickly. Plant the cuttings and tamp them in. Protect them from drafts and full sun until they are established.*

Scooping

Scooping is a propagation technique used to produce large numbers of hyacinth bulbs. Use a sharp, clean knife or a spoon to avoid bruising the flesh of the bulb or spreading diseases, and scoop out the middle of the bulb.

Scouring

Alternatively, make a V-shaped cut about ¼ in (0.5cm) deep, using a sharp, clean knife, in the basal plate of a hyacinth bulb. Place the bulb, cut side up, in moist sand or soilless mix. The spawn will form around the cut areas.

Scooping and scouring

Hyacinths can be increased by processes known as scooping and scouring. For the first method use a sharp knife to scoop out about a quarter of the central fleshy stem of the hyacinth while it is dormant and discard this, leaving the circular hard ring and basal plate intact. Plant the scooped bulb in a large pot of soilless mix, with the cut end facing up, and it let grow, watering and feeding as usual.

Once the flowers have died back and the foliage has faded, lift the bulb; a mass of young bulbs will be growing around the damaged area. Remove the bulbils and plant outdoors. In 2-3 years, they will reach flowering size.

Scouring is a less adventurous method which involves making two incisions in the shape of a cross through the basal plate of the bulb, removing a sliver of flesh each time. Replant the scoured bulb, with the basal plate facing down, and it will produce approximately a dozen new young bulbs around the cuts. These can be treated in exactly the same manner as those that have been scooped.

Scaling

Unlike most other bulbs, a lily bulb consists of clusters of scales, most of which can be detached for propagation purposes. Increased this way, the scales will take between 3 and 7 years to produce flowering-size bulbs.

Take a deep tray and fill it with all-purpose potting soil, with an extra 25 percent by volume of sand to improve drainage. If the species is a lime hater, like *Lilium canadense*, select acid formula potting soil. Carefully remove the scales from the bulb, each with a piece of basal plate, and insert them into a tray of soil, with the vestige of the basal plate facing down, so that they are completely covered.

Start the scales off in a cold frame, watering them so that the potting medium does not dry out. Depending on the species or cultivar involved, within a couple of months tiny leaves will appear, at the base of which is a small bulb. Keep the bulbs in the tray through the first winter, but protect them from temperatures below 15°F (−9°C). Transplant them outdoors early the following spring.

1 *Lily stocks can be increased by removing scales from a sound, healthy bulb. Any damaged or withered scales should be discarded, and plump ones from underneath snapped off with a little of the basal plate attached. This technique is useful for propagating hybrid lilies that would not come true from seed, and for the types that do not produce bulbils in the leaf axils.*

2 *Handle the scales carefully by the tips, to avoid damaging the base, from which new growth will emerge. Insert them into a pot or tray of compost, base downward, and water in with a solution of fungicide to help prevent disease. Most types of lily will survive quite well in a cold frame or unheated greenhouse, but the tender varieties will need more protection.*

Scaling

1

2

SPRING

Garden highlights

A display of spring-flowering bulbs is an excellent way to bring color into the darkest areas of the spring garden and to create striking focal points. The diversity of bulbs available guarantees something for every situation, from a formal bedding display to an informal mixed border.

Daffodils, with their yellow, orange, and white heads nodding in the wind, are popular spring-flowering bulbs. Although often used for naturalizing, they are also good border plants because they are so bright. Give careful thought, however, to their positioning so that, after flowering, their dying foliage will be hidden by other plants.

The daffodil season lasts from early to late spring, and with careful selection, it is possible to have a continuous display of flowers. For the early spring, *Narcissus cyclamineus* cultivars, such as 'Peeping Tom,' 'February Gold,' and 'Tête-à-Tête,' are particularly useful for borders, either planted on their own in clumps to provide colorful highlights or grown as underplanting beneath shrubs. Although small and delicate-looking, 'February Gold' will tolerate lingering winter weather. With its backswept, golden yellow petals and slightly darker, slender trumpets, it is a handsome daffodil, deserving much attention. Equally attractive is the later-flowering 'Dove Wings,' with its creamy white petals and yellow trumpets. The ivory-colored 'Jenny' makes a lovely focal point planted in a corner with evergreens. For a more unique display, it can be grown under the purple-leaved sand-cherry, *Prunus cistera*.

(previous page) *Similar in general appearance to the bluebell,* Scilla bithynica *spread by self-seeding and offsets to form extensive ground cover.*

(left) *Mixed daffodils look their best when naturalized in clumps. If the leaves are left to die back naturally, the display will improve each year.*

(below) *This mixture of yellow winter aconites, pinkish-purple chionodoxas, snowdrops, and daffodils provide an eye-catching spring display.*

For fragrance, choose a jonquil such as 'Sweetness,' a plain yellow, 'Suzy,' a yellow-orange charmer, or 'Stratosphere,' which bears rich golden flowers with darker gold cups. For a bolder look, use the pretty double-flowered narcissi, which burst into bloom later in spring, sometimes continuing into early summer. They come in a variety of colors, including white and orange ('Bridal Crown'), yellow and orange ('Tahiti'), and white and creamy yellow ('Irene Copeland'), and are excellent for informal mixed borders, grown among a few pale pink hellebores (Lenten rose), interspersed with primroses and bright green fern fronds. Blue can be introduced in the form of hyacinths, grape hyacinths, or bluebells.

Muscari (grape hyacinth) is an invaluable plant for spring border color. Used on its own, it is good for edging paths and for uniform ground cover. Its intense blue can be softened with other plants, including daffodils and primroses and, later in the season, small tulips. It also combines well with hellebores, particularly the green- or purple-flowered *Helleborus purpurascens* or *H. foetidus*. A long-lasting display can be achieved by planting *Muscari armeniacum* 'Blue Spike' with the low-growing *Stachys olympica* 'Silver Carpet' (lamb's tongue). Muscaris will also tolerate semi-shaded spots and are useful for planting under trees and shrubs. First-rate combinations include *Forsythia* 'Ottawa' and *Muscari neglectum*, and the midblue *M. tubergenianum* and early-flowering pale pink viburnums or darker pink camellias.

(above) *The golden yellow of the daffodils is here complemented by the blue* Scilla bithynica.

(below) *This classic spring planting consists of* Narcissus 'February Gold' *and acid-green hellebores.*

A simple but successful grouping for early in the year pairs grape hyacinths with early-flowering heathers (heaths). 'Springwood' varieties and 'Pink Spangles' can be used to provide bold, startling groups of color. *Muscari armeniacum* 'Blue Spike' mixes particularly well with both *Erica carnea* 'Springwood White' and 'Springwood Pink.'

Small irises and delicate-looking scillas are excellent choices for underplanting shrubs. For a spectacular highlight, plant a large cluster of the chunky blue-flowered *Iris histrioides* 'Major' against an evergreen background of *Olearia* × *haastii* (daisy bush), *Mahonia aquifolia*, (Oregon grape) or *Taxus media*. A sprinkling of the porcelain-blue *Scilla tubergeniana* and the common snowdrop looks especially good growing under colorful shrubs like the scarlet-stemmed *Cornus alba* 'Siberica,' the red-stemmed Dogwood, or the orange-stemmed willow *Salix alba* 'Chermesina.' The intense yellow stems of *Cornus stolonifera* 'Flaviramea' seem even more vivid when underplanted with dark blue *Scilla siberica* 'Spring Beauty.' This lovely scilla brings life to a planting of conifers, such as *Chamaecyparis lawsoniana* 'Stardust' or 'Winston Churchill,' both of which have bright golden yellow foliage.

Shrubs such as Mollis and Pontica azaleas look sensational with an underplanting of *Chionodoxa luciliae* (glory-of-the-snow). This wonderful spring bulb, with its starry blue and white blossoms, creates a dense carpet around the leafless shrubs. The intense blue *Scilla sibirica* forms a similar display.

(above) *A raised bed is ideal for this vibrant planting of* Muscari armeniacum *and* aubrieta.

(below) Narcissus *'Suzy' grow with* Muscari armeniacum; *the tulips will flower later on.*

(left) *A formal spring bedding display, with* Fritillaria imperialis *'Lutea' towering above the daffodils and densely planted* Anemone blanda.

(above left) *This vibrant layered effect is made using a foreground planting of muscari backed with* Tulipa greigii *'Toronto.'*

(above) *The dazzling color of* Tulipa *'Orange Wonder' stands out well against the stiff variegated foliage of the iris.*

Fritillaria imperialis (crown imperial) is an eye-catching plant for a spring border. When planted in a group with herbaceous plants, it bursts into color long before its neighbors start performing. A dramatic and beautiful bulb, its stately character demands a prominent position. For the greatest impact, plant a group among a sea of ground cover. A striking display of colors can be achieved using the clear orange *Fritillaria* 'Aurora' and deep blue grape hyacinth.

In addition to the orange and red varieties, look for *Fritillaria imperialis* 'Lutea.' Its brilliant yellow bells stand out best against a dark background planting of evergreen shrubs, in particular, the shorter kinds, such as the fragrant yellow *Mahonia* × *media* 'Charity.' It also becomes a fine architectural feature growing in front of the broad-leaved evergreen *Viburnum tinus.* A gentler use of color involves 'Lutea' and the soft silvery green of rosemary.

Fritillaria persica 'Adiyaman' (Persian fritillary) is much less vibrant than its relative. An elegant plant, it has spires of rich, dark, plum-colored blossoms and handsome blue-green foliage. Enjoying damp conditions, it is ideal for planting near water, where its image may be reflected. In such situations, it can be planted among the ground-hugging foliage of *Ajuga reptans* 'Atropurpurea,' 'Multicolor,' or 'Burgundy Glow,' all of which have colorful leaves. *F. p.* 'Adiyaman' is also useful for informal borders, grown among silver-leaved plants like *Stachys lanata* (lamb's ears) and *Artemisia schmidtiana.*

Allium oriophilum is another good partner, with the dark purple fritillary bells silhouetted against the deep rose pink umbels of the allium. The flowers are best appreciated, however, when mixed with yellow. To create this effect, plant a few of the bulbs behind a cloud of primrose-yellow *Cytisus* × *kewensis* (broom).

There is nothing more lovely than leucojums, or summer snowflakes, as they are commonly known, to brighten up a border. *Leucojum aestivum* is one of the best varieties to use, with its slender stems and nodding white, green-tipped bells. Like *Fritillaria persica* 'Adiyaman,' it looks spectacular when gracefully overhanging the edge of a pond. The two can be mixed together, with a patch of *F. meleagris* (snake's head fritillary). In borders with rich soil, the various species of *Erythronium* (dog's-tooth violet) will thrive. The creamy 'Pagoda' and icy 'White Beauty' are particularly good choices. 'White Beauty' has splendid dark green, marked foliage that mixes well with *Polygonatum multiflorum* (Solomon's seal).

Tulips are also good for spring color, either in a border or in bedding displays and containers (see pp. 74 and 78). The Early singles and doubles make good edging plants in formal borders, and given their elegance, they look excellent in front of low-growing, spreading plants, adding height and form. For an informal planting, Rembrandt tulips are very colorful, along with the red or pink smaller-growing types, such as *Tulipa linifolia* and *T. greigii* 'Toronto.'

Naturalizing

There is nothing finer than a grassy slope covered with daffodils and crocuses or a shady woodland site carpeted with snowdrops and winter aconites.

Although it is possible to naturalize bulbs in any existing landscape, they are much better planted in specially prepared areas that have been sown with fine grass. Choose the area carefully: an informal part of the garden is ideal. This is because the bulbs must be allowed to die back naturally every year before the surrounding overgrown grass can be cut, and this can look untidy.

Crocuses are one of the first bulbs to provide spring color, and the great advantage of naturalized crocuses is that their foliage can be mowed about 6 weeks after flowering. Single colors can be used, but a more exciting display results from mixing yellow, purple, and white with striped blooms. *Crocus vernus* is one of the best and is often sold in mixed colors; grown with the large, deep golden yellow *C. flavus* hybrid 'Dutch Yellow' (also known as 'Yellow Giant' and 'Yellow Mammoth'), it creates a vibrant picture. Also good for grassy areas, *C. tommasinianus* naturalizes well, particularly the deep purple 'Ruby Giant' and the purple and white 'Pictus,' both of which can be mixed with snowdrops and hellebores.

One of the most graceful of all bulbs is *Anemone blanda*. If left undisturbed it will naturalize into extensive patches, and being partially shade-tolerant, is useful for planting under trees and shrubs. It is low growing, with delicate dissected leaves, and the daisylike flowers open wide in the sun to display yellow centers. There are various colors to choose from, including dark blue, pink, magenta, and white; the paler forms are good for planting under brightly colored bulbs such as daffodils. Alternatively, plant a mixed selection to create a multi-colored sheet of flowers.

Galanthus nivalis (the common snowdrop) is a good snowdrop for naturalizing. Although slower growing, the double

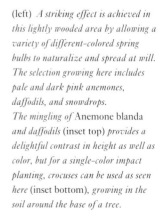

(left) *A striking effect is achieved in this lightly wooded area by allowing a variety of different-colored spring bulbs to naturalize and spread at will. The selection growing here includes pale and dark pink anemones, daffodils, and snowdrops.*
The mingling of Anemone blanda *and daffodils* (inset top) *provides a delightful contrast in height as well as color, but for a single-color impact planting, crocuses can be used as seen here* (inset bottom), *growing in the soil around the base of a tree.*

67

form 'Flore Pleno,' with its frilly head of icy green and white petals, looks attractive. The larger-flowered *G. elwesii* (giant snowdrop) is also suitable for naturalizing. Left to grow undisturbed, it will form a dense ivory-white carpet, but it also mixes well with most other spring bulbs. In the light shade of a tree canopy, snowdrops and winter aconites (*Eranthis*) thrive, and a few small-leaved ivies creeping in between adds to the woodland effect. Bluebells (wood hyacinth) enjoy similar wooded situations. They also thrive in deep shade, which is useful for bringing interest to otherwise dark areas. Often sold as a scilla, the bluebell *Hyacinthoides non-scripta* is the best

for naturalizing in large areas because it is so invasive. In comparison, the smaller Spanish bluebell (*H. hispanica*) does not spread so much, is suitable for localized areas beneath shrubs, and is hardier.

Daffodils are another favorite for naturalizing, either on their own or with a selection of other bulbs in an orchard or meadow. Besides naturalizing in grass, they colonize well in the soil around the base of specimen trees, such as the chalky white-stemmed birch, *Betula jacquemontii*, and the polished, mahoganylike *Prunus serrula*. Their bright colors also make them suitable for growing with rhododendrons and other evergreens like leyland cypress and yew.

There is an overwhelming selection of daffodils to choose from, and in many respects, it is easiest to buy a mixture. For a

(below) *Snowdrops spread rapidly to form first clumps, as here, and later extensive patches.*

(below bottom) *Double daffodils contrast well with the simpler flowers of* Scilla siberica.

mixed display, choose both early- and late-flowering varieties to provide long periods of bloom. However, if you prefer a single type of flower, *Narcissus poeticus* (poet's narcissus, or pheasant's eye) is always good for naturalizing. Large-flowered cultivars should be used only sparingly as they tend to look bold and clumsy; the yellow-green 'Spellbinder' is lovely, and the golden yellow 'Carlton' and 'Golden Harvest' are also popular, as is the yellow and white 'February Silver.' The Cyclamineus narcissi cultivars, with their narrow, pointed, reflexed petals, are excellent for small areas of grass and are weather resistant. 'March Sunshine,' 'Peeping Tom,' and 'Charity May' are top-of-the-line, and 'Satellite,' with its bright orange trumpets, has a strong impact. All flower at much the same time and increase year by year, provided their foliage

is allowed to die back naturally. Many mail-order catalogs now offer mixtures of bulbs especially selected for naturalizing in the average garden. In fairly damp ground, hoop-petti-coat daffodils, snowflakes, and snake's head fritillaries can be planted together for a tapestry of color.

Although a less familiar sight, scillas will successfully natural-ize in grass, *Scilla bithynica, S. siberica* and its white form 'Alba' being the most reliable. Resembling dwarf bluebells, but flowering much earlier in the season, they produce a delicate carpet of blue or white. If planted in soil with fine-leaved grass sown over the top, scillas are likely to seed

(left) *In this natural-looking planting, snowdrops grow among ivy and hellebore foliage.*

(below) *This pink rhododendron makes a vivid companion for the Spanish bluebells beneath.*

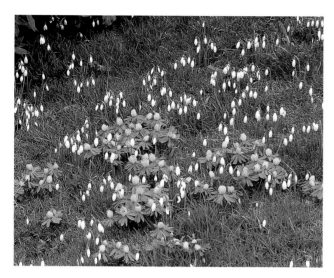

freely, although the pale porcelain-blue *S. tubergeniana* prefers to colonize open soil.

Tulips are not usually associated with naturalized bulbs, but the early-flowering *Tulipa kaufmanniana* and its cultivars colonize grass in much the same way as narcissi. The only disadvantage is that their broad, fleshy leaves destroy the grass beneath if the bulbs are planted too close together.

One of the most attractive ways to landscape with naturalized bulbs is in a meadow. Even though a meadow does not naturally occur in a garden, it is easy to create the right conditions. To start the meadow off from scratch, cultivate but do not fertilize an area of soil, plant the bulbs, and sow a variety of fine-leaved grass seeds over the top. Since typical alpine meadows are fairly damp in spring, incorporate some moisture-retaining organic matter into dry soil before planting the bulbs. The spring-flowering meadow will be a star feature for about 6 weeks, followed by 2 months or so of unruly vegetation, then grass for the rest of the year.

(above left) *A characteristic yellow and white spring planting of snowdrops and winter aconites.*

(above right) Crocus tommasinianus *is a robust bulb, despite its delicate appearance.*

(below) *These sparsely planted tulips lend both color and form to a wild, grassy area.*

(right) *The blue-flowered* Scilla bithynica *is used as ground cover in this woodland glade.*

Plant a generous amount of *Narcissus bulbocodium conspicuus* (hoop-petticoat daffodil) to form large clusters and clumps of bright color. *Fritillaria meleagris*, with its purple or white pendent, checkered flowers, is much more subtle and delicate-looking than the daffodils. It also enjoys meadow conditions, especially wet ones; plant a large quantity for the best effect, mixing them in with the hoop-petticoat daffodils. Species crocuses and their cultivars enhance such areas in early spring. Look for the cultivars of the bunch-flowering *Crocus chrysanthus*, such as 'Cream Beauty,' which is a rich cream with orange stigmas, 'Blue Pearl,' which is a delicate blue shading to darker blue at the base, and 'Zwanenburg Bronze,' a yellow form with a bronze exterior. *C. ancyrensis* 'Golden Bunch' is another possibility. It spreads rapidly to form a dazzling golden carpet during early spring, attracting the first of the spring bees and other pollinating insects.

Another type of naturalized landscape is a woodland garden. *Leucojum aestivum* is a wild plant that enjoys garden conditions, along with *Fritillaria meleagris* and the small-flowered *Allium neapolitanum*. Because many wild species will not adapt to "foreign" climates, choose varieties of bulbs that respond well to garden conditions but look like their wild relatives; for example, plant the wood anemone, *Anemone blanda* 'White Splendor,' instead of its native cousin, *A. nemorosa*, and *Hyancinthoides hispanica* rather than *H. non-scripta*.

(left) Anemone blanda *comes in a variety of flower colors, from white to deep blue.*

(above) *The snake's head fritillary flowers in a range of colors, from white to purple.*

(below left) *A mixture of wild primroses and* Cyclamen repandum *for a grassy patch.*

(below right) Narcissus cyclamineus *is quite at home growing with crocuses.*

Bedding displays

Bulbs are excellent for spring flowerbeds, either massed together on their own or used with other spring-flowering plants. With careful selection, colors, heights, and flowering times can all be coordinated for a stunning display.

Hyacinths are among the most useful spring bedding bulbs because of their short, stiff stems. Available in dozens of colors, the flowers have one of the richest perfumes in the garden and their scent lingers in the air. Arrange the bedding hyacinths in square or rectangular blocks of color, or use them as dot plants among other bedding plants like primroses. The choice of bedding cultivars is wide, but the pure white 'Carnegie,' the blue 'King of the Blues,' the rose-pink 'Lady Derby,' and the lilac-violet 'Amethyst' are all reliable and tend to flower simultaneously; 'Carnegie' is especially lovely grown beside the primrose-yellow 'City of Haarlem,' particularly when surrounded by an edging of low box hedge.

One of the most striking formal arrangements involves creating a small checkerboard using the pure white 'L'Innocence' and 'Violet Pearl.' Both are of similar height and flower together, as do the later-flowering 'Carnegie' and 'Queen of the Violets.' For a variation on the theme of bedding, plant them 8-10 in (20-25 cm) apart rather than close together, so each individual flower stem can be seen.

Tulips make equally successful bedding plants, and there is a type of tulip available for every color scheme. The strong pure red and crimson types can be difficult to place; their intensity is better accentuated with bright bedding plants rather than toned down. *Tulipa kaufmanniana* and its hybrids bloom early in spring. The lovely red and yellow 'Stresa,' the yellow 'Gluck,' and the scarlet 'Brilliant Star' can all be grown with the red and yellow 'Edwin Fischer,' and 'Stresa' makes a dazzling display with rich red primroses. Just as colorful is a combination of 'Brilliant' and golden-flowered primroses. Plant a single-color batch of primroses first, and interplant these with a contrasting variety of tulip. 'Heart's Delight' has deep red flowers edged with pale pink. It looks stunning interplanted with white primroses or pink and white English daisies. In warmer climates, winter-flowering pansies go well with early tulips. A bold blue edging of pansies with a solid center of white tulips is a sensational sight. Taller, later-blooming tulips, such as Triumph or Lily-flowered types, have

(left) *For a traditional bedding display, tulips are planted among forget-me-nots.*

(top right) *Any color of tulip looks good with forget-me-nots. Here, 'Prinses Irene' is used.*

(middle right) *The pink 'Chestnut Flower' and blue 'Dreadnought' hyacinths offer a fragrant display.*

(bottom right) *Primulas can be planted with hyacinths for a formal and colorful effect.*

beautifully sculptured flowers and, like the Darwin hybrids, are best planted among other low-growing spring-flowering annuals or perennials.

The hybrids of *Tulipa greigii* and *T. fosteriana* are extremely useful for narrow beds, where taller-growing cultivars are inappropriate. Their shortness also makes them ideal for exposed sites, but because they have large leaves, the plants' should be well spaced, about 8 in (20 cm) apart. When mingled with a boisterous cluster of hybrid primroses, they form a tough, resilient display that can withstand everything from hailstones to gale-force winds. The purple and brown splashed and striped leaves of the cultivars derived from *T. greigii* are an added attraction, providing a strong foil for white- or blue-flowered pansies before the tulips bloom.

Myosotis (forget-me-not) has traditionally been used as a base for bedding displays, creating a misty azure haze through which white, pink, and yellow sentrylike tulips can be grown. In a formal corner, try *M.* 'Royal Blue' and the 'White Triumphator' tulip or *M.* 'Blue Ball' and the 'West Point' tulip. Double-petaled *Bellis perennis* (English daisy) is an equally good companion plant. If you are designing a small,

informal mixed bed or a border with loose, informal plantings, miniature-flowered English daisies make an excellent chorus for the crumpled and ruffled blossoms of the Parrot tulips, especially 'Blue Parrot' or 'Apricot Parrot.' Fringed tulips—namely, the violet-colored 'Blue Heron,' the wine-red 'Burgundy Lace,' and the pink 'Bellflower'—also work well in displays with English daisies,

The majority of daffodils are unsuitable for bedding displays, but the versatile shorter-growing *Narcissus cyclamineus* cultivars can be used to provide splashes of bright color, and once the display is over, the bulbs can be moved to a grassy spot and allowed to naturalize. 'March Sunshine,' 'February Gold,' and the ivory-white 'Jenny' can be bedded out with grape hyacinth. *N. c.* 'Foundling,' a white dwarf daffodil with deep rose-pink cups, makes an excellent dot plant in a bed of forget-me-nots. The multiheaded 'Tête-à-Tête' is a marvelous plant to pair with *Muscari armeniacum* 'Blue Spike' for a yellow and blue display.

(below) *To create a light and airy feeling, tulips are planted among a selection of pale pansies.*

(right) *Tulips, daffodils, and Fritillaria imperialis enhance and enliven this rock garden.*

Rock gardens

Plenty of dwarf spring-flowering bulbs enjoy the well-drained conditions of a rock garden. They can be used to fill pockets with startling color for highlights, or a collection can be grown together, with summer- and fall-flowering alpines used to fill gaps and hide the dying foliage of the bulbs after flowering.

Narcissi make lovely rock garden plants, and the sheltered conditions provided by the rocks offer an ideal opportunity to grow some smaller species that cannot be grown elsewhere.

Narcissus asturiensis, one of the tiniest of the Trumpet daffodils, is worth growing in a large clump as a focal point in the garden. The multiflowered dwarf *N. canaliculatus*, with its pure white petals, bright yellow trumpets, and pleasing fragrance, reproduces freely and soon fills a pocket in the rock garden. It should be planted in an isolated spot because it will not tolerate any companion plant other than a dwarf shrub or conifer, like *Chamaecyparis lawsoniana* 'Minima Glauca,' *C. l.* 'Ellwoodii,' or *Cryptomeria japonica* 'Vilmoriniana.'

Narcissus cyclamineus is always popular; it is easy to grow and attractive, with narrow, grassy foliage and charming backswept, bright yellow petals and projecting trumpets. Rarely attaining more than 6 in (15 cm) in height, it is perfect for planting next to close-growing carpeting plants like pink-flowered thyme, which bursts into bloom just as the narcissi leaves disappear. Also worth considering are the downy-leaved *Thymus lanuginosus* and the tiny *T.* 'Minimus.' The

daffodils also grow well with the low-growing golden *Arenaria caespitosa* 'Aurea' and green *A. caespitosa*.

Although the natural habitat of snowdrops and winter aconites is an open woodland glade, they tolerate a sunny spot in the rock garden if plenty of organic matter is mixed into the soil. Plant a few dwarf azaleas or small rhododendrons first, then insert several bulbs each of snowdrops and winter aconites into the soil at the base of the plants. The effect of pristine white snowdrops or glowing yellow aconites peeping in between the branches is delightful.

Crocuses provide a long-lasting colorful display in the rock garden, especially the *Crocus chrysanthus* cultivars, and dwarf irises look very attractive among the rocky outcrops. The two combine well; plant a group of the cobalt-blue *Iris reticulata* 'Cantab' or *I. r.* 'Joyce' next to a patch of *Crocus chrysanthus* 'Cream Beauty.' However, for a touch of stark simplicity, try 'Cantab' or the plum-colored 'J.S. Dijt' in a cluster on its own. The blue *Iris histrioides* 'Major' makes a colorful contribution; flowering before its foliage develops, it often makes a surprise appearance while snow is still on the ground. When the foliage does appear, it tends to swamp any nearby carpeting plants, so the bulbs should ideally be planted at the edge of the rock garden. Also for the lower areas around and leading up to the rock garden, a bold clump of *Ipheion uniflorum* (starflower), with its soft blue flowers, grows well in well-drained, sunny conditions.

Containers, window boxes, and hanging baskets

Many excellent opportunities exist for growing spring-flowering bulbs in window boxes and containers. Concentrate on daffodils, tulips, and crocuses, which bloom reliably. Avoid snowdrops and winter aconites, as these may take 2 or 3 years to establish themselves before blooming. For an instant display, purchase hyacinths or other prepotted bulbs that are on the verge of blooming. In cold regions, they can be repotted outdoors when the temperature has warmed up.

For the widest range of interest, there is nothing to surpass the tulip. The taller kinds are best avoided as they may blow over, but all the other types will thrive in the well-drained conditions of containers and window boxes.

The most useful is the early-flowering *Tulipa kaufmanniana* (waterlily tulip), a

(above) *In a simple wooden container, vivid blue muscaris supply additional interest at the base of the* orange Fritillaria imperialis.

(above) *Single container plantings can be very effective. Here, pots of muscaris and hyacinths are displayed with a bowl of pansies.*

stocky plant that is able to cope with spring gale-force winds and even scatterings of snow. The ordinary species is compact, rarely more than 8 in (20 cm) tall, with pointed cream or pale yellow blossoms, flushed red, opening out into a dazzling display. The leaves are stiff and formal, giving the plant an architectural appearance. For a mixed window box, plant these tulips through the ivy *Hedera* 'Anne Marie' with a patch of *Crocus ancyrensis*. There are a number of hybrids between *T. kaufmanniana* and *T. greigii* that make an even more dramatic statement; the multiflowered 'Toronto' is pinkish-red, 'Shakespeare' carmine-orange and yellow, 'Berlioz' yellow, 'Stresa' red and yellow, and the ever-popular 'Red Riding Hood' a solid red. *T. greigii* and its many cultivars have distinctive purple-striped foliage, but since they differ slightly in height and flowering period, it is unwise to mix them if you want a uniform formal display.

Tulipa clusiana is another exciting choice, with pink-flushed blossoms carried in profusion among crowds of gray-green rushlike foliage. Like most tulips, it looks best alone, although it can be mixed effectively with pastel shades of *Aubrieta* tumbling over the edge of the box. The curious-looking *T. acuminata*, with its long, thin, vertical yellow and

red petals, is another first-rate choice, especially for gardens with an old-fashioned atmosphere. For a less flamboyant look, select a paler tulip, such as the soft yellow *T. batalinii*. The attractive apricot-colored 'Bronze Charm,' if planted in full sun, will produce a reliable show of flowers. It mixes well with mound-forming plants, such as *Armeria maritima* (pink thrift).

Most other tulips give only a short display, but they still present a marvelous, if temporary, spectacle. The Lily-flowered

cultivars, with their beautifully sculpted blossoms and long, straight stems, are the aristocrats of the tulip family. In a large, round wooden tub, a bold central planting of just one variety, surrounded by single-color primroses, creates a splendid picture. If grown in window boxes, however, the tulips are best planted alone, as they need the room to grow.

Hyacinths are among the best bulbs to plant in a container; it is the one place where they excel above all

other bulbs. They are available in an enormous range of colors and are wonderfully fragrant. In addition to large-flowered cultivars, the multiflora kinds are worth considering; try a mixed planting of the blue hyacinth 'Bismarck' and blue or yellow pansies, or the pink

(right) *Tulips and hyacinths are planted in plain flower pots, and these are placed in attractive glazed containers so they do not show.*

(below) *The glowing colors of these narcissi, tulips, pansies, and hyacinths are set off beautifully by the terra-cotta containers.*

hyacinth 'Lady Derby' and white pansies. Primroses can also be added, along with a few clumps of daffodils for a multicolored display.

Narcissus cyclamineus hybrids such as 'Jenny' and 'Peeping Tom' are ideal for container planting as they can cope with any lingering bad weather, an important consideration for window boxes in exposed sites. For a bright display of contrasting colors, plant the daffodils among clusters of red primroses. Sweetly scented single jonquils or jonquil hybrids, such as the red and yellow 'Suzy' or the ivory-white and pink-cupped 'Waterperry,' make a fragrant show, especially when massed together. The *N. triandrus* hybrids, such as 'Ice Wings' and 'Thalia,' are equally lovely, enjoying the well-drained conditions provided by large containers. 'Thalia' is a very good white narcissus cultivar; planted alone in solid blocks or interspersed with the velvety blue or golden early-flowering pansies, it is spectacular. Another delight is the lemon-flowered *N. triandrus* 'Liberty Bells.'

(above) *The bright scarlet-orange of* Tulipa *'Aladdin' looks quite flamboyant in these two plain, clay pots.*

All the daffodils look at home planted with variegated ivy because the foliage complements the simple flower heads of the daffodils. However, more substantial companion plants include small evergreen shrubs or conifers, such as *Rhododendron* 'Blue Diamond' and *Sarcococca confusa*. These can be treated as permanent plants, whereas the daffodils will have to be replaced after flowering.

To provide early-spring interest before the main spring display begins, insert several crocuses; simply push the corms into the soil among daffodils, primroses, pansies, or English daisies and let them grow. By distributing them evenly among the companion plants, the problem of their unattractive fading foliage can be minimized.

Of all the many spring-flowering bulbs, few surpass the fritillaries. The common snake's head fritillary, *Fritillaria meleagris*, is one of the most attractive. It has nodding flowers, held on upright leafy stems, and is available in white and various shades of pink and purple, checked a darker color on the outside of the petals. Requiring well-drained soil and full sun or partial shade, the snake's head fritillary is a good window-box subject because its beauty can be enjoyed at eye level or below.

(above) *The white spring-flowering* Ranunculus *and multiflora hyacinths are especially appropriate for container plantings.*

While relatively few bulbs can be used successfully in hanging baskets, both *Scilla siberica* and its cultivar 'Spring Beauty' prosper and look especially fine when contrasted with a blue or white strain of Universal pansy. The smaller narcissi are also amenable to hanging-basket cultivation. The sweet-smelling *Narcissus canaliculatus* and *N. cyclamineus* look lovely tucked in a basket planted with shorter-growing winter heathers or creeping variegated ivy, and *N*. 'Tête-à-Tête' makes a strong showing grown as a centerpiece in a basket full of plain green ivy, such as *Hedera helix* 'Parsley Crested,'

(left) *The red ranunculus provides a splash of color in this cool-looking display of the* Hyacinthus *'Ostara,' muscari, and ivy.*

(above) *This planting consists of narcissi and trailing ivy in a simple wire basket, which has been covered with moss.*

Indoors

Provided they are kept as cool as possible, many popular outdoor bulbs can be grown indoors. For a very early spring indoor display, plant the multiflora *Hyacinthus* 'Borah.' Available in white, blue, and pink, it resembles a dwarf bluebell and is lovely. Good container companions include *Selaginella martensii* and *S. helvetica*, soft green fernlike plants, with foliage of a delicate mossy texture. The larger hyacinth cultivars such as 'Delft Blue' and the primrose-yellow 'City of Haarlem' can be grown in bowls, grouped around a tiny pteris fern and top-dressed with green sphagnum moss. The double-flowered hyacinths, which look stiff and unyielding in the garden, unless used in a

(below) *Inspired use of wood makes a spectacular centerpiece with narcissi, lilies of the valley, and* Tulipa *'White Dream.'*

(above) *Hyacinths will grow well in a glass container filled with water, provided it is deep enough to allow the roots to develop.*

formal bed, are most rewarding when grown indoors.

A good reason for having a container of tiny jonquil daffodils inside is their sweet perfume, which will soon fill the room. Both 'Trevithian' and 'Sweetness' are delightful, producing scented yellow blossoms. For a small container, try the lemon-and-white 'Pipet,' top-dressed with green sphagnum moss. Tazetta narcissi are also excellent for indoor displays. 'Cheerfulness,' with its highly fragrant creamy white flowers, blossoms during the early part of the season. The equally fragrant yellow form 'Yellow Cheerfulness' and the orange-cupped cultivar 'Soleil d'Or' are also highly recommended.

Tulips can also be grown indoors, and what they lack in fragrance, they make up for in color, an important consideration on dull early-spring days. *Tulipa kaufmanniana*, *T. greigii*, and *T. fosteriana* are all suitable; for the greatest impact, restrict each container to a single color. A reliable display is easy to achieve using *T. praestans* 'Fusilier.' These stately multiflowered tulips have green leaves and upright heads of bright red blossoms, three or four per stem. Unless the temperature is hot, they will last for several days inside.

There are many miscellaneous dwarf plants that adapt well to indoor cultivation. Do not mix the bulbs but grow a single cultivar per container; mixed displays of several different bulbs look messy and unruly.

The dwarf scillas grow well inside, especially the bright blue *Scilla siberica* 'Spring Beauty.' For the best results, keep the scillas as cool as possible until the flowers start to show color, then bring them into the warmth. Once inside, they should be kept in a cool room to prolong their flowering period.

(above) *If you use a wicker basket, like this one filled with muscaris, be sure to line it with plastic before you plant in it.*

(right) *This metal bucket is an unusual but attractive container for a planting of blue hyacinths. The randomly placed decorative twigs are another striking touch.*

(below) *This informal-looking arrangement consists of fragrant narcissi and ivy in a simple moss-lined metal basket, with catkin twigs used as an extra ornamental touch.*

Cut flowers

Provided they have a long-enough stem, most spring-flowering bulbs will last up to a week in water. However, before cutting the flowers are sometimes damaged by strong winds and rain. So growing some in the greenhouse is a good idea.

Daffodils yield first-rate cut flowers. The sticky sap that drips out of their stems, however, can kill other flowers in the same vase. To minimize this problem, stand the daffodils in water for 24 hours, wash the stems, and place them in fresh water that has a drop of bleach in it.

(above) *Here* Tulipa *'Snowflake,' ranunculus,* Hyacinthus *'Carnegie,' and lily-of-the-valley are combined with mixed fruit.*

The Split corona or Orchid-flowered daffodils are easy to grow and some of the best for cutting. The Small-cupped daffodils also provide good-quality blossoms. 'Barrett Browning,' with its distinctive orange-red cups, is pleasing both indoors and growing outside, but it must have a little protection; otherwise its pristine white flowers will turn brown in wet weather. This also applies to the yellow-and-orange 'Birma,' as well as Large-cupped cultivars such as the pink 'Mrs. R.O. Backhouse' and the pure white 'Ice Follies.' Some of the best Large-cupped cultivars for cut flowers are the bright yellow 'Carlton,' 'Golden

(above) *This informal arrangement of vivid ranunculus is enhanced by the bold color and design of a striking vase.*

(left) *Narcissi are tightly bunched together, tied with garden string, and placed in a modern glass vase in this unusual display.*

Harvest,' 'Dutch Master,' 'Spellbinder,' and 'Mount Hood.' 'Cassata' is a widely grown white kind with a yellow split corona, and 'Baccarat' is yellow with an orange-red segmented corona. However, their stems may bend under the weight of their flower heads, and the flower heads may drop into the dirt during bad weather, such as heavy spring rains.

It is well worth growing a range of tulips for cutting as they are so versatile in flower arrangements. Either they can be used to add color and form in a mixed display of spring blooms, or a few

A little later on in the season, Lily-flowered tulips are ready for cutting. 'Aladdin' is scarlet, edged with yellow, and 'White Triumphator' is snowy white. For something truly unusual, the Viridi-flora types are a delight for flower arrangers. They have strange, often feathered blossoms with green stripes or bands; 'Greenland' is pink with prominent green markings, 'Spring Green' is greenish cream, and 'Esperanto' is more of an oddity, with pink- and green-shaded flowers with white-edged leaves. All look splendid in a single-color vase on their own.

Florist's anemones are useful in the spring, particularly the St. Brigid and De Caen strains. A bunch of reds, purples, and blues makes a magnificent display. For a smaller arrangement, place a few snowdrops and hardy cyclamens in a glass or vase with some primroses and ivy leaves. Grape hyacinths can be added, although they will only last a few days in water.

Among the many snowdrop varieties are two large-flowered types: *Galanthus elwesii* and *G.* 'Samuel Arnott.' Both these are particularly useful for cutting, and 'Samuel Arnott' continues to flower late in the snowdrop season. Similar in general appearance to the snowdrops, but with larger flowers consisting of six petals, leucojums (snowflakes) are also good for indoor flower arrangements. Snowdrops and snowflakes look best in plain or colored glass vases.

For fragrance, hyacinths can be used for indoor displays. If growing the bulbs outdoors for cutting, plant large clumps so that the cut flower spikes will not ruin the display. It is also possible to cut the flower spikes of forced hyacinth bulbs when the flowers are nearing their end; they will last longer in water than in soil.

stems can be placed in a vase on their own, in which case the erect stems will start gently curving, creating a natural, informal look.

Any of the Single late tulips are ideal; 'Golden Harvest' and the silky salmon-pink 'Clara Butt' are good choices, but for something extra-special, try 'Queen of Night,' with its velvety midnight-blue flowers. The blooms look spectacular on their own in a simple vase, but the purple-black cups also stand out well when mixed with cream or white flowers. 'Sorbet' is one of the best pink-flushed cultivars, and for a bold display, the red 'Halcro,' with its distinctive orange-red edges, is hard to beat. Among the Darwin hybrids, the yellow 'Gludoshnik' and the carmine 'Holland's Glorie' both last well in water, and these brightly colored tulips can be enhanced by adding a few sprigs of dark-colored foliage.

(above) *Here, flowering narcissus bulbs are mixed with violets, twigs, candles, and an old bird's nest.*

(below) *A warm opulence is created by this floral display of white ranunculus, scarlet-orange tulips, and mixed narcissi.*

ALLIUM
Ornamental onion

There are dozens of attractive, unusual alliums that bloom in spring, beside the better-known edible species—onions, garlic, chives, shallots, and leeks. Although some of the early flowering members of this genus die off over the summer and require a dry place during their dormant period, most are easy to cultivate and care for and are hardy bulbs.

Alliums are a distinctive group of bulbs because they produce small star- or bell-shaped flowers in spherical or hemispherical heads, known as umbels. Most give off an unmistakable onion smell when cut or bruised. The species below bloom in late spring and are fairly short, less than 1 ft (30 cm) high when flowering; they are therefore suitable for the front of a border or rock garden, where they can be left undisturbed to form clumps. Since the many species and varieties flower at different times of the year, others are listed in the summer and fall directories on pp. 150 and 203. Propagation is by offsets, which in some species are produced quite freely, or by seed, which may take up to 3 years to produce flowering bulbs. Hardiness zones: 3-8.

A. karataviense (*below*)

This striking plant has broad gray-purple leaves at ground level that spread 8-10 in (20-25 cm). It needs a sunny position and good drainage. In late spring, stout 6 in (15 cm) stems carry large umbels with many small, pale pink flowers.

A. karataviense

A. neapolitanum

In midspring, the wiry 8-12 in (20-30 cm) tall stems of this species bear loosely flowering umbels of small white flowers.

A. oreophilum 'Zwanenburg'

This dwarf species adapts well to rock gardens. It requires sun and good drainage. It has narrow gray leaves and 2-6 in (5-15 cm) high stems carrying large carmine flowers in umbels $1\frac{1}{2}$-$2\frac{1}{4}$ in (4-6 cm) wide.

A. triquetrum

A. triquetrum (*above*)

Best used for naturalizing, this species can be left to seed and increase at will. This attractive plant stands about 4-8 in (10-20 cm) high, with channeled pale green leaves and umbels that bear only a few pendent, bell-shaped white flowers in midspring; each petal flaunts a distinctive green stripe.

A. unifolium

A. unifolium (*above*)

Usually sold under the name '*A. murrayanum*,' this American species produces large, flat pink flowers in midspring. The loose umbels grow on about 6-12 in (15-30 cm) tall stems.

ANEMONE
Windflower

Among the most colorful plants of spring, most windflowers come in white and shades of pink, red, blue, and purple.

Although unrelated to most other bulbous plants, they do have tuberous rootstocks and are usually obtainable wherever bulbs are sold. The showy, often lushly petaled flowers of the St. Brigid types are well known for their cut flowers, while the hardier *A. blanda* and *A. apennina* make effective ground covers and handsome rock garden plants. Propagation is by division in autumn. Hardiness zones: 4-8.

A. apennina

An excellent plant for semishaded areas. The fernlike dissected leaves are topped by 1-$1\frac{1}{2}$ in (2.5-4 cm) diameter blue flowers that exhibit up to 20 petals. This anemone grows to about 6 in (15 cm) high and may spread into clumps up to 1 ft (30 cm) or more across. The pure white form is known as 'Alba.'

A. blanda 'Atrocaerulea'

A. blanda (*above*)

This anemone grows well in partial shade but also flourishes in full sun. A rock garden or border is an excellent location for planting this species. Its daisylike blue flowers are produced in early spring on 2-4 in (5-10 cm) long stems above fernlike divided leaves. The deep blue flowers of 'Atrocaerulea', the stark white of 'White Splendour,' the attractive soft pink blooms of 'Charmer,' and the vibrant magenta flowers of 'Radar' are often used for single-color collections, but mixed collections are also available. Plantings of one-color clusters, however, tend to look better than mixed plantings.

A. coronaria

This is the species from which the St. Brigid and de Caen florists' types have been raised. The hard, knobby tubers can be planted at any time of the year and—except in moist climates—may perform better if first soaked in tepid water overnight. Those planted in autumn flower by midspring, but require a sheltered, sunny position and benefit from being protected with a transparent cover in cold weather. Subsequent plantings will flower in late spring or summer. They grow about 6-10 in (15-25 cm) high with parsleylike leaves and large, flat flowers. St. Brigid have semidouble layered flowers, while de Caen's are single.

A. pavonina

A. pavonina (*above*)
This anemone is very similar to *A. coronaria* but has less finely divided leaves; the cultivation requirements are much the same. Best known are the large-flowered selections called the St. Bavo strain. The varieties come in a wide color range.

ARISARUM
This strange tuberous-rooted plant is grown for curiosity, although the carpet of arrow-shaped leaves has some value as ground cover. Propagation is by division in early fall. Hardiness zone: 7.

A. proboscideum

A. proboscideum (*above*)
Mouse plant
In midspring, small chocolate-colored

spathes, with 6 in (15 cm) long, tail-like appendages, appear amid the leaves, giving the appearance of a mouse diving for cover. *A. proboscideum* is only 2-4 in (5-10 cm) high but can spread by tuber division into patches over 1 ft (30 cm) across. It grows best in a semishaded spot in humus-rich soil.

ARUM
Lords and ladies or cuckoo pint
Characteristic of this large and interesting group of tuberous-rooted plants are their many tiny flowers clustered together and enclosed within a hooded or sail-like spathe on a pencil-shaped spadix; the leaves are often arrow-shaped. The Arum lily *Zantedeschia* is probably the best-known to gardeners, but there are several other hardy species well worth planting for an unusual touch.

A few of these plants are worth considering for the spring garden, and in some cases the foliage is a noteworthy ornamental feature. Those mentioned below die down over summer, although some have spikes of berries that ripen to a bright red in autumn. Propagation is by removal of offsets in fall. Hardiness zones: 6-8.

A. creticum

A. creticum (*above*)
This unusual species has a bottle-shaped yellow spathe; the upper part is twisted and reflexed, leaving a projecting yellow spadix. It appears in midspring, accompanied by deep green arrow-shaped leaves. *A. creticum* reaches 1-1⅓ ft (30-40 cm) in height and slowly increases into a compact clump about 1 ft (30 cm) in diameter.

A. dioscoridis (*next column*)
Mediterranean in origin, this dramatic plant needs a warm, sunny position in order to reach its characteristic 1-1⅓ ft (30-40 cm) in

height. It has the usual arrowlike leaves, but the spathes are either deep velvety purple or pale green, strikingly blotched with blackish purple. Unfortunately, this plant has an unpleasant smell.

A. dioscoridis

A. italicum (*below*)
This hardy species has highly ornamental autumn foliage, which is retained throughout the winter into spring. The leaves are arrow-shaped and shiny green, with a marbling of silvery white veins; they are good for flower arrangements. This species grows well in semishade but is less likely to flower than in the sun. In a warm position it may produce pale green spathes in spring, followed by showy red berries in fall. A variety with particularly fine foliage is 'Pictum', sometimes known as 'Marmoratum.'

A. italicum 'Pictum'

BULBOCODIUM
This small, seldom-seen bulb is related to *Colchicum* (see p. 203, Fall) but flowers in spring. It is best grown in a terrarium on account of its height of under 1½ in (4 cm), but it will grow outside in a sunny raised bed. Propagation is by division in early fall. Hardiness zone: 4.

B. vernum

One small corm may produce two or three pinkish-purple funnel-shaped flowers about 1-1½ in (2.5-4 cm) in diameter. These are almost stemless and are accompanied by short, narrow leaves, which later elongate. These plants are native to the Pyrenees and Alps.

CHIONODOXA; × CHIONOSCILLA
Glory-of-the-snow

This close relative of the scillas, or squills, owes its name to the melting snow patches around which it grows in the mountains. The various species are very hardy and do well in a semishaded or sunny location, provided the spot does not become too hot and dry in summer. When growing well they seed freely, giving a welcome early-spring display. Chionodoxas have flat, star-shaped flowers held in short racemes, less than 6 in (15 cm) high, produced between a pair of narrow leaves, which die down fairly soon after flowering and seeding. Propagation is by division in early fall or by seed in fall. Hardiness zone: 4.

C. luciliae

C. luciliae (*above*)

(Note that *C. siehei* is often sold under this name.) The most common species has large, upward-facing, pale lilac-blue flowers—only 1-2 per stem. The white *C.l.* 'Alba' bears 2-3 flowers per stem.

C. sardensis

This species has up to 12 rich, deep blue flowers in a raceme, facing outward. Each one has an indistinct white eye.

C. siehei (*next column*)

(Note that this is sometimes sold as *C. luciliae* or *C. forbesii*.) Probably the best garden plant of all, this species is excellent for

naturalizing. It has one-sided racemes of up to 12 lavender-blue flowers, each with a large white eye in the center. 'Pink Giant' is a vigorous form with pink, white-eyed flowers.

C. siehei

× Chionoscilla allenii (*below*)

A hybrid between *C. luciliae* and *Scilla bifolia*, this bulb flowers very early in spring, with a raceme of deep blue starry flowers about 4-6 in (10-15 cm) high. Like its parents, it grows well in dappled shade and is suitable for planting beneath deciduous shrubs or in a cool spot in a rock garden. In a border, it looks well with hellebores, pulmonarias, and other shade-loving plants.

× Chionoscilla allenii

CORYDALIS

Although a few of the tuberous-rooted corydalis have been known for centuries, new introductions and selections provide some exciting and unusual choices for the spring garden. These early-spring-blooming tubers are low-growing—no more than 4-6 in (10-15 cm) high when in flower—and produce spikes of white, purple, pink, or red long-spurred flowers over attractively divided foliage. Cultivation is easy: provide reasonably well-drained soil in partial

shade where the dormant tubers will not become too hot and dry over summer. They should be planted at a depth of approximately 1-2 in (2.5-5 cm) in the fall. They are ideal for naturalizing, together with snowdrops, crocuses, winter aconites, and anemone blandas. Individual plants may form clumps up to 6-10 in (15-25 cm) across. Propagation is by division in early fall or by seed as soon as it is ripe. Hardiness zones: 4-6.

C. bulbosa (syn. C. cava)

This common species, originally from Europe, usually produces masses of 2-lipped purple flowers and long spurs. 'Alba' is an attractive white version, and 'Cedric Morris' is a selected form with white flowers and dark purple bracts. Unlike *C. solida*, the tubers do not often divide, but seedlings are produced.

C. solida

C. solida (*above*)

The most commonly seen form of this excellent little spring plant has dull purple long-spurred flowers, but beautiful pinks and reds are now available from nurseries specializing in bulbs. 'George Baker' has rich, glowing red flowers, while 'Beth Evans' comes in clear pale pink. The small yellowish tubers increase quite rapidly, usually doubling in number each year, and the established clumps can be lifted and divided in early fall. Seedlings may appear but often have different-colored flowers.

CROCUS

No other bulb group epitomizes the early spring like the crocus, which produces wineglass-shaped flowers in a great array of sizes and colors from late winter onward. Crocuses are mostly easy to grow and increase readily when given suitable conditions. All require well-drained soil that dries out to some extent in summer, but they are not fussy about the pH, if anything slightly preferring alkaline soils. Most like open ground, but they can do equally well in the light shade of deciduous trees and shrubs. The dormant corms are sold in late summer or early autumn and should be planted about 2 in (5 cm) deep. A few of the species may seed and spread widely, but most crocuses produce compact clumps, no more than 2-4 in (5-10 cm) in diameter; they barely reach 4 in (10 cm) in height. Propagation is by division in late summer or by seed; seed takes 3-4 years to produce flowering plants. Hardiness zones: 4-6.

C. ancyrensis

C. ancyrensis (*above*)
The Ankara crocus sends up small, bright orange flowers in early spring, several per corm produced in succession. One commercial variety is called 'Golden Bunch' because of its free-flowering nature.

C. angustifolius (syn. *C. susianus*) (*below*)
Cloth-of-gold
This small crocus with a bronze stain on the outside of the petals opens up in the sun to display a shiny orange-yellow interior.

C. angustifolius

C. biflorus

C. biflorus (*above*)
Scotch crocus
This variable spring crocus comes in a wide range of shades from white to blue, sometimes marked with stripes or stains on the outside. All forms make good rock garden plants, or they can be grown at the front of sunny borders. *C. b. alexandri* has bicolored blooms, white inside and purple-stained outside. *C. b. weldenii* is white-flowering, but the cultivar 'Fairy' has a pale, soft lilac-blue tint, while *C. b.* 'Argenteus' is white with brownish-purple stripes.

C. chrysanthus '**Cream Beauty**'

C. chrysanthus (*above*)
An early-spring-flowering species, the wild version of this crocus has yellow flowers, although the name is now attached to a range of cultivars with lovely medium-sized, goblet-shaped fragrant flowers in a wide color range. Some are hybrids (*C. biflorus* × *C. chrysanthus*). They succeed in rock gardens, sunny borders, and grass, but may also be grown in pots for blooming indoors. When forced for early flowering, move them into the warmth only when the buds are showing color; otherwise they may fail to bloom. Most *C. chrysanthus* varieties increase well by offsets, and the resulting clumps can be lifted

and divided in early autumn. The following are all recommended: 'Blue Pearl' has soft blue flowers with yellow throats; 'Cream Beauty' is one of the most vigorous, with large, cream-white flowers and yellow throats; 'E. A. Bowles' has deep yellow flowers striped bronze at the base; 'Zwanenburg Bronze' is yellow, shaded bronze over the outer surface; the striking 'Ladykiller' is purple outside and white within; and 'Snow Bunting' is a good clean white.

C. corsicus

C. corsicus (*above*)
This species flowers in mid- to late spring, with small lilac flowers that are heavily striped and feathered purple on the outside. It requires a sandy, quick-draining soil.

C. dalmaticus
This midseason crocus produces pale lilac flowers with yellow centers; the outside is pale yellow-brown, with a few purple stripes.

C. etruscus '**Zwanenburg**'

C. etruscus (*above*)
Very similar in color to *C. dalmaticus*, often flecked and veined on the exterior, this is a robust species. 'Zwanenburg' is a selected form with lilac-colored flowers.

C. *flavus* 'Dutch Yellow'

C. *flavus* (*above*)

This original wild species has small, deep yellow flowers and is not readily obtainable, but 'Dutch Yellow'—also called 'Yellow Giant' and 'Yellow Mammoth'—can be found in most bulb catalogs. It is a large, robust hybrid of vigorous growth and does well in grass. The flowers boast a large gobletlike shape and deep golden yellow colors with dark veining at the base.

C. *gargaricus*

C. *gargaricus* (*above*)

This rare species is sometimes available through rare-bulb catalogs. The small, bright orange-yellow blooms appear in midspring. It flourishes in a moisture-retentive, humus-rich sandy soil—but avoid waterlogging. The corms produce stolons and are capable of forming clumps.

C. *imperati*

This late-blooming crocus has a striking appearance, with large, slender, elongated flowers that are buff-colored on the outside and bright purple within. The vigorous selection 'Jager' increases well by offsets. It does well in open ground but can also be grown in a greenhouse.

C. *korolkowii* (*below*)
Celandine crocus

A central Asiatic species flowering in mid- to late spring, the celandine crocus has yellow flowers that open wide in the sun to reveal shiny inner petals.

C. *korolkowii*

C. *minimus* (*below*)

This small late-spring crocus has rich violet long-tubed flowers, shaded even darker black-violet on the outside. It can be grown outdoors in a well-drained, sunny spot, but it also grows well in planters.

C. *minimus*

C. *olivieri*

Requiring a hot, sunny location, this Greek species blossoms in midspring with fragrant orange-yellow flowers.

C. *sieberi* (*next column*)

Also from Greece, this is one of the best early-spring crocuses. The most commonly seen form, which is lilac-blue with a yellow throat, makes an excellent choice for a rock garden, for planting in short grass, or for the front of a border; when properly cultivated it may grow in clumps. Equally reliable variations include 'Violet Queen,' a robust grower

with rich deep violet-blue flowers; 'Bowles' White,' one of the best of the white crocuses with large, white, yellow-centered flowers; 'Hubert Edelsten,' with white flowers overlaid with bands of purple; and 'Tricolor,' the most colorful, with rich purple, yellow and white flowers.

C. *sieberi* 'Tricolor'

C. *tommasinianus* (*below*)

The 'tommies' are usually the earliest spring crocuses to appear. The flowers are small and slender, graceful, despite any wind and rain, opening wide the moment the sun appears. C. *tommasinianus* is very accommodating and grows in partial shade or full sun, in light or heavy soil, and often seeds profusely across gravel paths and in cracks between nearby paving. It is at its most delightful when seen in numbers and it dies down rapidly after flowering. The common form is pale lavender with a gray-white exterior, but there are several selections available, all equally valuable, including 'Albus,' the white-flowering version; 'Whitewell Purple,' a deep purple-blue; 'Ruby Giant,' a somewhat larger and more robust version, with rich deep purple flowers; and 'Pictus,' with purple and white marks on the tips of its lavender-colored blooms.

C. *tommasinianus* 'Whitewell Purple'

C. vernus

C. vernus (*above*)

The common spring crocus of the Alps is seldom cultivated in its true wild form. Dutch expertise in selection has produced the fine range of large cultivars that are now available, suitable for forcing gently in pots and bowls or for naturalizing in grass or borders. These cultivars have larger flowers than most of the species crocus and are very robust, increasing rapidly to form clumps, which may be divided in early fall or when the leaves turn yellow, from late spring to early summer. They are available in single colors, white, purple or striped, but mixed colors are also available. 'Jeanne d'Arc' is an extremely good white; 'Pickwick' has striking purple stripes; 'Queen of the Blues' is an excellent rich violet-blue; 'Vanguard' is a soft, silvery lilac-blue; and 'Remembrance' is one of the best of the deep purples with attractive shiny petals.

C. versicolor

This species is now seldom seen except for the cultivar 'Picturatus.' It has white flowers with purple veins on all 6 petals, but the wild forms can vary from lilac-blue to white, usually marked with purple veins or stripes. It does well in extremely well-drained soil, enjoying full sun.

CYCLAMEN

The highly popular florists' cyclamens sold in winter and spring are tender plants selected from the wild *C. persicum* (see Winter Directory, p. 226). Although native to the islands and shores of the Mediterranean, several species are frost hardy to varying degrees, and all differ subtly in flower shape and color, as well as in the attractive mottled patterns on the foliage. All are dwarf plants, only 2¼-4 in (6-10 cm) high when in flower, with a spread of some 4-6 in (10-15 cm). The following are

ideal for growing in the dappled shade of a rock garden. They are best planted in light soil with added leaf mold and sand to give good drainage. Propagation is by seed sown in autumn or winter; it takes about 2-3 years to produce flowering-sized tubers. Hardiness zones: 7-8.

C. balearicum

C. balearicum (*above*)

A native of Majorca, this is one of the smaller species. It produces silvery heart-shaped leaves and boasts fragrant white flowers.

C. creticum

This cyclamen is very similar to *C. balearicum*, but it usually has darker green leaves.

C. libanoticum

This Lebanese plant is one of the most beautiful cyclamens, with larger flowers than most species. It is soft pink, marked with a jagged carmine zone near the mouth.

C. pseudibericum

C. pseudibericum (*above*)

This Turkish plant has striking bright carmine, fragrant flowers, with white and dark purple areas around the mouth. The leaves are patterned with light and dark silvery green.

C. repandum peloponnesiacum

C. repandum (*above*)

This native of Italy, Greece, and Yugoslavia performs later than other species, producing its deep pink-red, deliciously fragrant flowers in mid- to late spring above ivy-shaped, deep green leaves. 'Album' is the white form. The subspecies *C. r. rhodense* from Rhodes is similar but has bicolored flowers that are white with pink mouths, and the leaves are splashed with silver. *C. r. peloponnesiacum* is like the *C. r. rhodense*, but has pale pink flowers with dark pink mouths.

C. trochopteranthum

The curious name of this Turkish species refers to the flower shape, each petal being twisted like a ship's propeller. Its flowers are variable, from near-white to pale pink or carmine with a darker stain at the mouth, and they have a musty fragrance. The leaves exhibit light and dark silvery patterns.

ENDYMION (see HYACINTHOIDES)

ERANTHIS
Winter aconite

Winter aconites display honey-scented, yellow to golden cup-shaped flowers in late winter. They are ideal for dappled shade in a leaf-mold-rich soil. The knobby tubers may be obtained soon after spring flowering while still in growth, in which case they should be planted at once. They can also be purchased in the dried state during autumn. In the latter case they are best soaked overnight or placed in damp peat for several days before planting at a depth of about 1-2 in (2.5-5 cm). All winter aconites are low-growing, reaching only 2-4 in (5-10 cm) in height, with the flowers carried on short stems and surrounded by a ruff of deeply toothed leaves. They grow well in acid soils but are particularly good in alkaline conditions.

When thriving, they self-seed to form extensive patches. Propagation is by seed when ripe or by division of clumps after flowering while the plant is in leaf. Hardiness zones: 4-5.

E. hyemalis

E. hyemalis (*above*)
The European winter aconite has green-yellow flowers surrounded by a frill of pale green, coarsely toothed leaves. These tubers are fairly inexpensive and look best naturalized in large quantities.

E. × tubergenii (*below*)
This hybrid between *E. hyemalis* and the related Turkish *E. cilicica* has bronzy, heavily divided leaves. It produces larger flowers than either parent in a rich gold, and the young leaves are slightly bronze-green. The deep yellow-bronze 'Guinea Gold' is a vigorous-growing variety with large flowers.

E. × tubergenii

ERYTHRONIUM
Dog's-tooth violet

Among the most graceful of all spring bulbs, these outstanding plants are instantly recognizable by their pendent bell-shaped flowers. With its 6 petals above a pair of spreading leaves, the flower bears a striking resemblance to the cyclamen. These hardy plants are suitable for growing in dappled shade beneath or between deciduous trees and shrubs, or in a cool spot in a rock garden. Most of the better-known species have bold, beautifully marbled foliage with light and dark patterns. They are all compact plants, the most vigorous being no more than 1 ft (30 cm) high when in flower. Propagation succeeds both by seed and by division of established clumps. The plant's curious common name refers to the long, pointed bulbs that resemble canine teeth. Hardiness zones: 3-6.

E. americanum
A dwarf eastern North American species, *E. americanum* has brown-mottled leaves and solitary yellow flowers, shaded bronze on the outside. When growing happily, the stolons spread to form sizable patches.

E. californicum
One of the easiest erythroniums to cultivate, this North American species adapts well to gardens. Its creamy white, yellow-centered flowers display a ring of brown angular marks around the throat. The ornamental leaves are marbled with silver-green patterns. The 'White Beauty' variety thrives especially well.

E. dens-canis

E. dens-canis (*above*)
The European dog's-tooth violet is a popular species and one of the easiest to grow and earliest to flower in spring. It is a dwarf plant, only $3\frac{1}{4}$–$4\frac{3}{4}$ in (8-12 cm) high when flowering. The dainty, elliptical, brown- and green-mottled leaves make a good foil to the rose-purple or white flowers with dark center zones. Attesting to its ease in cultivating, this plant grows well in short grass.

E. hendersonii

E. hendersonii (*above*)
This species has several lilac, dark purple-centered flowers and mottled leaves.

E. oregonum

E. oregonum (*above*)
White-flowering and very similar to *E. californicum*, this version has conspicuous yellow stamens protruding from the bells. It is a native of western North America.

E. revolutum (*below*)
This western North American species has elegant pink, yellow-centered flowers held over brownish-purple mottled foliage. It seeds liberally. A rich pink form is 'Johnsonii.'

E. revolutum

E. tuolumnense (*below*)
This California plant has plain, bright green leaves topped by 10-12 in (25-30 cm) long stems, bearing several rich yellow flowers. It is vigorous and increases by bulb division.

E. tuolumnense

E. 'Pagoda' (*below*)
This vigorous hybrid reaches 1 ft (30 cm) in height with large, bright green, faintly brown-mottled leaves spreading 6-8 in (15-20 cm). It has several pale yellow flowers per stem, each with a central brown zone.

E. 'Pagoda'

FRITILLARIA
Fritillary
This stately relative of the lily makes a stunning accent in the spring garden. The pendent bell-shaped flowers borne near the top of leafy stems give fritillaries a distinctive appearance, making them recognizable, regardless of color. The height varies from a few inches to over 3½ ft (1 m) in the case of the crown imperial.

Most fritillaries prefer well-drained, sunny locations that dry out to some extent in summer. The bulbs should be planted with about 1½-4 in (4-10 cm) of soil above the top of the bulb; the larger the bulb the

deeper the planting. The smaller species are best grown in a small outdoor terrarium or cold frame. The more robust ones are suitable for undisturbed, sunny borders or for naturalizing in grass and between shrubs. Because the flower emits a skunky odor, it is often planted near shrubs, where its scent is reputed to deter squirrels. Propagation is by seed sown in autumn or winter, or by bulblets, which may be removed from the parent and potted or planted individually. Hardiness zones: 3-8; most are hardy in zones 4-6.

F. acmopetala

F. acmopetala (*above*)
This species exhibits slender stems 6-14 in (15-35 cm) high. It carries alternating narrow gray-green leaves and 1-2 wide green bells that are 1-1½ in (3-4 cm) long. These bells are stained brown on the outside.

F. affinis

F. affinis (syn. *F. lanceolata*) (*above*)
This North American species may reach 3½ ft (1 m) in height. The leaves are carried in whorls up the stem; the ¾-1½ in (2-4 cm) long bells vary in color, from purple to green-purple with a checkered pattern and sometimes several in a spike.

F. armena
This small species grows only 2-4 in (5-10 cm) high, with a few scattered gray-green leaves and 1-2 small, conical, deep blackish-purple bells, often greenish-yellow on the inside.

F. bucharica

F. bucharica (*above*)
This attractive species from central Asia is 4-14 in (10-35 cm) high, with scattered gray leaves and several shallow, cup-shaped, green-tinged, white flowers, about ½-¾ in (1.5-2 cm) long. It grows best in well-drained soil.

F. camtschatcensis.
Black sarana
An unusual shade-loving plant from eastern Asia, this fritillary produces up to 8 black flowers carried on ½-2 ft (15-60 cm) long stems, which bear whorls of glossy green leaves. It prefers cool conditions in humus-rich, well-drained soil.

F. crassifolia (*below*)
This stocky, 4-8 in (10-20 cm) high plant has scattered gray leaves and up to 3 green bells about 1 in (2.5 cm) long, usually checkered with brown. It is suitable for growing in an outside terrarium.

F. crassifolia

F. graeca

This fritillary varies from 2–8 in (5–20 cm) in height, with alternate gray leaves and up to 4 wide, bell-shaped flowers $\frac{1}{2}$–1 in (1.5–2.5 cm) long. These are usually green checkered with brown, with a bold green stripe along the middle of each petal.

F. imperialis

F. imperialis (*above*)
Crown imperial

This is one of the largest fritillaries, with stout stems up to 5 ft (1.5 m) tall and glossy green leaves held in whorls. The several large reddish–orange bells, about 2 in (5 cm) long, are carried in a dense cluster and topped by a crown of small leaflike bracts. The plant has a skunklike odor. It is a striking border plant for rich, well-drained soil and is good in alkaline conditions. 'Lutea' is a showy variety with large yellow bells; 'Aurora' is rich orange-red; and 'Argentea Variegata' and 'Aureo-marginata' have variegated leaves.

F. latifolia

F. latifolia (*above*)

This European species, up to 14 in (35 cm) high, grows well in open, sunny spots. It has scattered gray-green leaves and 2 in (5 cm) long, brown–purple, vividly checkered bells.

F. lusitanica (syn. *F. hispanica*)

This easily cultivated species varies in height, but rarely exceeds 20 in (50 cm). It has narrow, alternate leaves and up to 3 wide bells $\frac{3}{4}$–1$\frac{1}{2}$ in (2–4 cm) long, in shades of brown and green.

F. meleagris

F. meleagris (*above*)
Snake's head

This widely grown fritillary has a tall, slender stem and scattered narrow, gray-green leaves topped by drooping bell-shaped 1–1$\frac{3}{4}$ in (3–4.5 cm) flowers. These are pink tinged purple and often conspicuously checkered. Other forms include pure white ('Aphrodite'), purple ('Charon'), and strong red-tinged violet ('Saturnus'). This is the best species of fritillary for naturalizing in grass so long as it is not too dry and does not bake in summer; it is also suitable for planting in semishaded areas between shrubs where the bulbs will not become desiccated when dormant.

F. michailovskyi

F. michailovskyi (*above*)

This species is small, about 4–8 in (10–20 cm) high, with a few gray leaves and up to 4 striking bicolored, bell-shaped flowers,

$\frac{3}{4}$–1 in (2–2.5 cm) long. The lower two-thirds of each flower is purple-brown and the upper third bright yellow. This fritillary grows well in well-drained soil that does not dry out excessively in summer.

F. pallidiflora (*below*)

This central Asiatic species ranges from $\frac{1}{2}$–2$\frac{1}{4}$ ft (15–68.5 cm) high. It has bold, glaucous leaves and up to 5 large, pale yellow and faintly brown checked, bell-shaped flowers that reach a maximum length of 1$\frac{3}{4}$ in (4.5 cm). The inside of the bells is speckled red. It requires well-drained but cool conditions and is hardy.

F. pallidiflora

F. persica (*below*)

This is one of the taller fritillaries with large, unpleasant-smelling bulbs. The stems, which may reach up to 5 ft (1.5 m) in height, are densely clothed with narrow gray-green leaves. It has 10–20 small, conical flowers, each only $\frac{1}{2}$–$\frac{3}{4}$ in (1.5–2 cm) long. Among the wild versions color varies from pale straw-yellow to dirty brown and deep plum-purple. The most commonly available good form is 'Adiyaman'. *F. persica* comes from the Middle East and requires a hot, sunny, sheltered spot, but will withstand winter cold.

F. persica 'Adiyaman'

F. pontica

F. pontica (*above*)

One of the easier species to grow, *F. pontica* requires a semishaded spot where the soil does not become too hot and dry. The $\frac{1}{2}$-$1\frac{1}{2}$ ft (15–45 cm) long stems carry pairs of gray-green leaves, a whorl of 3 topping the solitary, wide bells. Green flowers tinted with brown range $\frac{3}{4}$-$1\frac{3}{4}$ in (2–4.5 cm) in length.

F. pudica

This very small but charming North American species is only 2–6 in (5–15 cm) high, with a few scattered gray leaves on its stem and 1–2 deep yellow, conical bells 1 in (2.5 cm) long. It grows best in a small outside terrarium or cold frame, in sandy soil that is in an open, sunny location.

F. pyrenaica

F. pyrenaica (*above*)
Pyrenean fritillary

After *F. meleagris* and *F. imperialis*, this is probably the most successful fritillary in the garden, doing well in a range of ordinary soils and sometimes forming dense clumps. The $\frac{1}{2}$-1 ft (15–30 cm) tall stems carry scattered gray leaves and 1–2 checkered, broad, black-tinged, purple bells, flaring out at the tips to show a green interior. The bells are about 1 in (2.5 cm) long.

F. sewerzowii (*below*)
(Sometimes known as *Korolkowia sewerzowii*)

This central Asiatic species is a fairly stout plant with thick, 6–10 in (15–25 cm) tall stems bearing broad, almost succulent leaves and a spike with up to 10 green or purple bell-shaped flowers. They flare out at the mouth and are 1–1$\frac{1}{4}$ in (2.5–3.5 cm) long. It needs a sheltered spot to avoid early-spring frosts and may do best in a terrarium.

F. sewerzowii

F. tubiformis (**syn.** *F. delphinensis*) (*below*)
Slender stems 6–14 in (15–35 cm) high carry scattered narrow, gray-green leaves. The solitary 1$\frac{1}{4}$–2 in (3.5–5 cm) long bells display a soft shade of purple-tinged pink, overlaid with gray on the outside, and are checkered.

F. tubiformis

F. uva-vulpis
(Also incorrectly called *F. assyriaca*)
Perhaps best appreciated in a small outdoor terrarium or frame, this fritillary also enjoys a well-drained spot outside. Growing 4–10 in (10–25 cm) high, it has scattered shiny green leaves and 1–2 narrow bells $\frac{1}{2}$–1 in (1.5–2.5 cm) long. These are a metallic shade of deep purple with yellow tips on the petals.

F. verticillata

F. verticillata (*above*)

The cultivated variety of this hardy species, *F. v. thunbergii*, adapts easily to deep, rich soil in an open site or partial shade; it should not be left to bake in the hot summer sun. If it thrives, it will form large clumps. The slender stems grow 1$\frac{1}{3}$–2 ft (40–60 cm) high, bearing whorls of very narrow leaves that coil at their tips like tendrils. There may be up to 6 wide, conical, creamy-colored, 1–1$\frac{1}{4}$ in (2.5–3.5 cm) long, green-checkered bells.

GALANTHUS
Snowdrop

Probably the best loved of all spring bulbs, snowdrops appear through the bleak, late winter into spring. There is even an autumnal one, *G. reginae-olgae* (see p. 208, Fall), for those who seek the unusual. Despite many variations, the several species and many named selections and hybrids are all unmistakably snowdrops in flower shape and color. Each translucent blossom is composed of 3 long, white petals on the outside and 3 short, green-tipped petals on the inside; slender leaves wither away in late spring.

Snowdrops prefer cool growing conditions in partial shade where the bulbs will not bake in the summer; a spot between and beneath deciduous trees and shrubs is ideal. Although not especially fussy about soil type, they do particularly well in heavy, neutral to alkaline soils. They flower at about the same time and enjoy the same conditions as hellebores.

Snowdrops may be obtained as dried bulbs in the fall or occasionally as growing plants in spring, while still in leaf. In both cases, plant immediately since they suffer if allowed to dry out. If established clumps in the garden become crowded, lift and divide into smaller groups, even down to single bulbs if necessary, and replant at

once. This can be done in early autumn or spring, either during or soon after flowering. Snowdrops often seed themselves, but with named clones the offspring will not necessarily be the same as the parents.

The following snowdrops all grow from 2-6 in (5-15 cm) high, the vigorous growers sometimes reaching 10 in (25 cm). Hardiness zones: 4-6.

G. caucasicus

G. caucasicus (*above*)
This species with gray-green leaves and large, rounded flowers produces blossoms in late winter, where conditions allow.

G. elwesii

G. elwesii (*above*)
Giant snowdrop
This Turkish species is very similar to *G. caucasicus*, with broad gray leaves and large flowers, but it can be distinguished by the 2 green blotches on each of the inner petals, one at the apex and one at the base.

G. gracilis (**syn. G. graecus**)
This species, like the giant snowdrop, has 2 green spots on each of the inner petals, but the flowers are smaller and the leaves are much narrower and twisted lengthwise.

G. ikariae

G. ikariae (**syn. G. latifolius**) (*above*)
This distinctive snowdrop with broad, glossy green leaves often blooms slightly later than *G. elwesii* and *G. caucasicus*.

G. nivalis

G. nivalis (*above*)
Common snowdrop
Compared with *G. elwesii*, this snowdrop is quite small, with narrow gray-green leaves. It often flowers a little later and is excellent for naturalizing in quantity. The bulbs normally increase well so that clumps can be divided every 3-4 years. There are many named selections including 'Flore Pleno,' which has tight double flowers with many extra petals.

G. plicatus
This robust species increases well by offsets. It usually flowers a little later in the snowdrop season than other types and has distinctive leaves with down-turned edges. The variation *G. p. byzantinus* is similar, but its flowers have 2 green marks on each of the inner petals.

Named cultivars
Some of the best snowdrops include 'Atkinsii,' a particularly graceful snowdrop with stems up to 10 in (25 cm) high, bearing elegant long flowers; 'Magnet,' a distinctive

variety with the flowers held away from the stem on long, threadlike stalks; 'Sam Arnott,' with large, beautifully formed flowers held on stout stems; 'Scharlockii,' which is easily recognized by its small flowers topped by 2 spathes resembling a pair of ears; and 'Viridapicis,' with green tips to the outer and inner petals.

HERMODACTYLUS
Widow iris
Although not a showy plant, this bulb is well worth growing for interest's sake in a hot, sunny, sheltered place, such as at the base of a south-facing wall. In the fall, plant the fingerlike rhizomes about 2 in (5 cm) deep in well-drained soil, which may be acid to alkaline, although the latter is preferable. The rhizomes can eventually spread into patches over $3\frac{1}{2}$ ft (1 m) wide. Propagation is by division of established clumps in fall. Hardiness zone: 7.

H. tuberosus

H. tuberosus (**syn. Iris tuberosa**) (*above*)
This lone species of Hermodactylus resembles a small iris in flower shape, but the extraordinary translucent green color of its 3 large outer petals, each marked with a velvety black or brownish patch, give it its own distinctive character. The flowers have a delicate fragrance and last for a few days when cut so they are occasionally seen in florists' shops in winter or early spring. In gardens they flower later, in mid- to late spring. The stems reach 8-12 in (20-30 cm) in height and are produced separately from the long, narrow gray leaves that display a squarelike cross section.

HYACINTHOIDES or ENDYMION
Bluebell
Bluebells are very similar to scillas, with only slight botanical differences. They are very

good garden plants, suitable for naturalizing under shrubs or for planting in perennial borders that are relatively undisturbed. They tolerate a wide range of soil types but dislike hot, dry locations. The bulbs are best planted in autumn at a depth of approximately 2-3$^{1}/_{4}$ in (5-8 cm). Bluebells flower in mid- to late spring and grow 10-12 in (25-30 cm) high, spreading by bulb division into extensive clumps. Propagation is by division or seed in autumn. Hardiness zone: 4-5.

H. hispanica

H. hispanica (syn. H. campanulata) (*above*)
Spanish bluebell
This robust plant with fairly wide, shiny green straplike leaves and stout spikes of bell-shaped flowers arranged around the stem is useful for planting in perennial borders among herbaceous plants. The wild form is pale to midblue, but large-flowering selections offer bright blue ('Myosotis'), pink ('Rosabella'), and white flowers ('Alba').

H. non-scripta

H. non-scripta (syn. H. nutans) (*above*)
English bluebell
Smaller and more slender than the Spanish bluebell, this plant has ribbonlike leaves. It

can be invasive and is therefore best naturalized beneath deciduous trees and shrubs. A rich, deep blue color is most often associated with this bluebell, but there are pink and white forms.

HYACINTHUS
Hyacinth

Hyacinths have a sweet, pervasive fragrance. The colors and types available are descendants of the wild Middle Eastern *H. orientalis*, selected over generations from the time of the Ottoman Turks. They are naturally spring-flowering but are also ideal when cultivated in bowls for an indoor winter display. For early-winter flowering you must buy "prepared" bulbs; nonprepared, ordinary bulbs flower later and can be used for bedding displays or for permanent planting in borders since they are hardy and easily cultivated, requiring only a reasonably well-drained soil in sun or slight shade. In addition to the varieties with very large, solid flower spikes, there are some with smaller flowers in loose spikes, more like the wild species. 'Roman,' 'Cynthella' and 'Multiflora' hyacinths belong to this type. Hyacinths vary from 8-12 in (20-30 cm) in height when flowering. Propagation is by division of clumps in early fall. Hardiness zone: 4.

H. 'Borah'
A multiflora hyacinth, 'Borah' is distinguished by its loosely flowering spikes.

H. 'City of Haarlem'
A large-flowering variety, this hyacinth has lovely soft primrose-yellow blooms.

H. 'Delft Blue'

H. 'Delft Blue' (*above*)
This large-flowering blue variety has midblue blooms that are flushed violet on the outside.

H. 'Hollyhock'

H. 'Hollyhock' (*above*)
This hyacinth has deep red florets.

H. 'Jan Bos'
'Jan Bos' has dense, compact crimson spikes.

H. 'L' Innocence'

H. 'L' Innocence' (*above*)
This species is a good large white hyacinth.

H. 'Snow Princess'
A multiflora type, 'Snow Princess' has pure white flowers held in loose spikes.

IPHEION

The one and only species in general cultivation, *I. uniflorum*, sometimes listed as *Triteleia uniflora*, *Milla uniflora*, or *Tristagma uniflora*, is an excellent dwarf bulb for planting in perennial borders or around deciduous shrubs. It enjoys partial shade, and is best left undisturbed and allowed to build into clumps. The bulbs should be planted in autumn, in a reasonably well-drained soil that will not become too hot and dry, although it should not be too cool or damp either; a depth of about 1-2 in (3-5 cm) is sufficient. Propagation is by offsets removed in early fall when clumps are uprooted for splitting. Ipheions also make interesting subjects for small outdoor terrariums. Hardiness zone: 4.

I. uniflorum 'Alba'

I. uniflorum (*above*)

The blossoms of this little Argentinian bulbous plant have a mintlike scent, but the narrow, pale green leaves, when crushed, smell like onions. A single bulb sends up several stalks in midspring, 4-8 in (10-20 cm) long, bearing solitary upward-facing, flat, pale blue flowers, each about 1-1½ in (2.5-4 cm) in diameter. The color varies, and apart from the usual form, there are deeper violet-blues ('Wisley Blue' and 'Froyle Mill'), a clear midblue ('Rolf Fiedler'), and a lovely pure white ('Alba').

IRIS

Apart from the many beautiful and popular wild rhizomatous irises that appear in late spring and early summer, there are some excellent bulbous ones, some of which are among the earliest spring bulbs and may continue to the end of the season. Irises fall into two groups: the early and well-known Reticulatas, so called because the bulbs are covered with meshlike coats, and the much less well known Juno species, which flower later in the season and have leeklike leaves. The irises belonging to the Juno group are characterized by strange-looking flowers with very small, horizontal or even downward-pointing standards.

The cultivation requirements are similar for all irises: a well-drained, preferably alkaline soil and an open, sunny location. The best site is along a border or in a relatively undisturbed rock garden, since irises are best left alone for a few years to build into clumps, after which they can be lifted and divided in autumn. They also grow well in pots for an early display in an outdoor terrarium, but they require repotting every year and, in the case of some of the Reticulatas, especially *I. danfordiae*, new flowering-size bulbs should be purchased each year since they have a tendency to split into many small bulbs. Propagation is by division in the fall; Juno can also be propagated by seed sown in the fall. Hardiness zones: 4-5.

Reticulata

All the Reticulata irises are about 2-4 in (5-10 cm) high when in flower, although the leaves greatly exceed this later, before dying away for the summer. The narrow foliage is unlike that of other irises; it appears almost square or round in cross section.

I. bakeriana

I. bakeriana (*above*)

I. bakeriana has been used as a parent with *I. reticulata* to create many of the hybrid cultivars. The flowers have a pale blue background, the 3 hanging petals stained a deep violet-blue at the apex of the reflexed blade. This feature repeats in the offspring.

I. danfordiae

I. danfordiae (*above*)

This inexpensive iris blooms well the first season but is best planted afresh each year, since the bulb usually dwindles in size. It has lemon-yellow flowers spotted green in the center and is unusual because the standards are all but missing. Flowering in the second and subsequent years can sometimes be achieved by deep planting—4 in (10 cm) or more—and feeding with a potash-rich fertilizer in spring.

I. histrioides

This is one of the best of the Reticulatas because it withstands inclement weather. A robust grower, it blooms as soon as its leaves pierce the earth. Its large, rich blue flowers have conspicuous dark spots and blotches on the falls. 'Major' is particularly fine, with rich, deep blue-violet flowers.

I. reticulata 'Natascha'

I. reticulata (*above*)

By far the best known of this group, *I. reticulata* is available in a wide range of cultivars. It is good in a rock garden or at the front of a sunny border, and it is excellent in pots for an early display. It tolerates only gentle forcing; otherwise it goes "blind" (does not flower). The deep violet-blue flowers of the wild *I. reticulata* have an orange stripe down the center of each fall and emit a pleasant scent reminiscent of the primrose. Among the many excellent cultivars are 'J. S. Dijt,' with deep red-purple flowers; 'Joyce' and 'Harmony,' rich blue cultivars with yellow marks in the center of the falls; 'Clairette,' a paler blue, with dark blue-violet blotches on the tips of the falls; and 'Jeannine,' also pale blue, but with an orange-yellow ridge in the center of the falls, spotted darker blue toward the tips. At the lighter end of the color range is 'Cantab,' a lovely shade of pale blue with a yellow ridge on the falls, and 'Natascha,' almost white with a slight hint of blue.

I. winogradowii
This rare yellow-flowering Caucasian species is one of the hardiest of the Reticulatas. The bulbs do not have the same tendency to split as *I. danfordiae*, the only other yellow-flowering iris in the group. This iris flowers early, while the leaves are still very short, and is a beautiful soft lemon-yellow. It prefers a slightly cooler location, where the bulbs will not get too hot and dry over summer.

I. 'George' (above)
I. 'George' boasts large, deep red-purple flowers early in the Reticulata season.

I. 'Katharine Hodgkin' (*below*)
As one might expect of a hybrid between the blue *I. histrioides* and yellow *I. winogradowii*, 'Katherine Hodgkin' flowers in a curious mixture of colors, with a yellow background overlaid with blue veining. This extremely vigorous plant grows well in open gardens.

I. 'Katharine Hodgkin'

Juno
These bulbs, also known as Scorpiris, are covered with papery tunics and have rather thick, even swollen, fleshy roots that should be handled with care since they may break.

The gutter-shaped leaves initially resemble those of a small leek, until early spring, when they turn shiny green on the upper side, with conspicuous white edges. In mid- to late spring, flowers blossom in the axils of the upper leaves, although in some of the shorter, stockier species, they appear almost stemless in the center of the leaf cluster. All the following are good in alkaline conditions and can be cultivated in sunny borders in sandy, well-drained soil.

I. aucheri
This stocky plant, with leaves closely packed in a dense cluster at its base, grows only 6-10 in (15-25 cm) high when in bloom, with up to 6 pale blue flowers, each 2¼ in (6 cm) across.

I. bucharica

I. bucharica (*above*)
This somewhat taller plant, 8-16 in (20-40 cm) high, produces several flowers in the upper leaf axils. These are bicolored, white with erect petals and golden yellow hanging outer petals, or sometimes solid yellow, and are about 2¼ in (6 cm) across. The channeled leaves grow all the way up the stems.

I. graeberiana
Very similar to *I. bucharica* in habit, *I. graeberiana* ranges from 6-14 in (15-35 cm) in height, with several blue-lavender flowers produced in the leaf axils.

I. magnifica
As its name suggests, this is a particularly showy iris. A robust plant reaching 1-2 ft (30-60 cm) in height, it has many broad, glossy leaves and several large, pale lilac flowers in the upper axils. The blooms reach about 2¼-3¼ in (6-8 cm) across and are topped with an orange-yellow crest. 'Alba' is an excellent white form, with striking yellow-stained falls.

I. sindpers

I. sindpers (*above*)
A compact grower 4-6 in (10-15 cm) high, this iris produces a tuft of broad leaves with several large, pale blue flowers.

I. warlsind
I. warlsind is similar to *I. bucharica*, but the flowers are pale lilac-blue, with a darker stain on the falls and a yellow patch in the center.

IXIOLIRION
These unusual late-spring bulbs are seldom seen in private gardens. They are not difficult to grow, although only one type, *I. tataricum*, is readily available. The bulbs should be planted in well-drained soil in a warm, sunny site in autumn, at a depth of 3¼-4 in (8-10 cm). They are quite hardy, although they need a hot, dry period in summer while dormant. In cooler climates, either lift and store them or choose a site where they will bake. Hardiness zone: 3.

I. tataricum (I. montanum) I. pallasii (below)
This most common ixiolirion grows 1-1⅓ ft (30-40 cm) high, with long, narrow, grassy leaves and a loose head of blue, faintly fragrant funnel-shaped flowers, each 1-2 in (2.5-5 cm) long.

I. tataricum

LEUCOJUM
Snowflake

Closely related to snowdrops, snowflakes differ most noticeably from their better-known cousins in their bell-shaped flowers with 6 equal petals, which are borne on much longer stems. Most flower in spring, although a few of the less common ones flower in fall (see p. 208). All spring snowflakes have white flowers, usually tipped with green or yellow, although In some cases they are plain in color. *L. vernum* and *L. aestivum* are hardy, robust plants for growing outside in borders that do not become too dry in summer; a damp soil is best. *L. nicaeense* is a tiny plant more suited to pot cultivation in a small outdoor terrarium, where its minuscule charm can be better appreciated close up. Like snowdrops, leucojums can be planted or lifted and divided while in growth in spring or early summer, or in autumn before growth commences. Propagate by dividing clumps; or by seed that is freely produced, although it may be some years before the plants produce flowers. Hardiness zones: 4-5; 7 for *L. nicaeense*.

L. aestivum

L. aestivum (*above*)

This plant usually flowers in late spring. The flower stems of this tall, robust species reach $3^{1}/_{2}$ ft (1 m) or more in height and carry umbels of pendent flowers about $^{1}/_{2}$-$^{3}/_{4}$ in (1.5-2 cm) long. These are white with green-tipped petals. The leaves are long and strap-shaped, reminiscent of a daffodil, as are the bulbs, which require deep planting in damp soil, at a minimum depth of 6 in (15 cm). *L. aestivum* looks particularly attractive planted alongside a garden pond or stream, although it also grows well in grass. The cultivar 'Gravetye Giant,' with larger flowers, is more common.

L. nicaeense

This tiny species does best in a raised, well-drained part of a rock garden or in a pot, where it can be appreciated. It has very narrow basal leaves, often lying on the ground, and 2-4 in (5-10 cm) stems bearing 1-2 small white bells in late spring.

L. vernum

L. vernum (*above*)
Spring snowflake

This delightful snowflake is the earliest-flowering leucojum, appearing at the same time as snowdrops. Its long, glossy green, strap-shaped leaves, which die after flowering, are topped by 4-8 in (10-20 cm) long stems, each bearing 1-2 large, white, green-tipped bells. It does very well in dappled shade beneath deciduous shrubs but is fine in any cool, damp spot. *L. v. carpathicum* has yellow tips on the petals, and *L. v. vagneri* has 2 flowers per stem.

MUSCARI
Grape hyacinth

These small blue-flowering bulbs, with their dense spikes of tiny globular flowers, supply a wealth of flowers in the spring garden. While some species do not multiply rapidly and are even difficult to grow, others increase so rapidly that they create a blanket in the garden. Even the most invasive ones, however, are valuable garden plants if grown in the right place. They mostly flower in mid- to late spring, perhaps even early summer in the case of *M. comosum*. Some produce their leaves in autumn and are best planted as early as possible, about 2 in (5 cm) deep, in any reasonably well-drained soil in a sunny spot—although the common *M. neglectum* flowers in partial shade and is useful for naturalizing under shrubs. In general, muscari grows 4-8 in (10-20 cm) high and

may eventually expand into sizable areas by bulb division; *M. neglectum* can form extensive patches by bulblets and seed if left to spread. Outstanding selections of muscari include those with sky-blue flowers, as well as white, purple-green, and even unusual-looking bright yellow blooms. Hardiness zones: 3-6.

M. armeniacum (*below*)

One of the best garden plants in this group, the Armenian grape hyacinth has stout, showy spikes of oblong midblue flowers. Although it increases into clumps by bulb division, it does not become too invasive. 'Blue Spike' is a curious and showy variation with minute sterile flowers that bloom in a dense mass on fat spikes. It is good for spring bedding displays, mixed with yellow winter- or spring-flowering pansies and for naturalizing in borders as ground cover.

M. armeniacum

M. azureum (*below*)

This compact plant has bright blue, bell-shaped flowers produced in dense spikes on stems 4-6 in (10-15 cm) high with short leaves. It is ideal grown in a rock garden or left to naturalize in sunny or slightly shaded borders. It is very hardy.

M. azureum

M. botryoides

M. botryoides (*above*)
This grape hyacinth grows approximately 6–8 in (15–20 cm) high, with narrow, erect leaves and dense spikes of small, spherical flowers that are bright blue, with a white rim around the mouth.

M. comosum
Tassel grape hyacinth
M. comosum differs in appearance from the blue grape hyacinth; it has 8–12 in (20–30 cm) long, loosely flowering spikes of brownish flowers, crowned by a cluster of long-stalked, bright violet sterile ones. It needs a warm, sunny spot with good drainage and usually flowers after most of the other species in late spring or early summer. A sterile but showy curiosity with no flowers, 'Plumosum' ('Monstrosum') displays large heads of a mass of purple threads, hence the common name, feather grape hyacinth.

M. latifolium (*below*)
This unusual grape hyacinth has a broad, gray-green leaf per bulb and an 8–10 in (20–25 cm) long stem, bearing a dense bicolored spike of oblong flowers that have constricted mouths. Most of the flowers are deep black-violet, with the upper showing a paler blue. It is an attractive plant for a sunny rock garden.

M. latifolium

M. macrocarpum (*below*)
A delightful species but not the easiest to grow, *M. macrocarpum* requires a relatively undisturbed, hot, sunny spot since its bulbs produce fleshy perennial roots. It grows 4–8 in (10-20 cm) high and has dense spikes of oblong-shaped, bright yellow flowers, each with a brown rim around the mouth. The blooms send out a delicious fruity fragrance that is best appreciated when the plant is grown in a terrarium or conservatory. If it is planted in pots, they must be deep enough to accommodate the roots.

M. macrocarpum

M. muscarimi (**syn.** *M. moschatum*)
This version bears many similarities to *M. macrocarpum*, except that the flowers are gray or pale pearly blue, with brown-rimmed mouths and a musklike scent.

M. neglectum

M. neglectum (**syn.** *M. racemosum*) (*above*)
The most common species of muscari, *M. neglectum* produces long, narrow leaves in autumn that last right through to flowering time in midspring. The 4–6 in (10-15 cm) tall stems have dense spikes of oblong or egg-shaped, deep blue to black-blue flowers, usually with a group of fragrant, pale blue

sterile ones at the top. A ring of tiny white "teeth" encircle the mouth of each individual bloom. Although invasive in some gardens, it is an excellent plant for naturalizing in shrub borders beneath, for example, spring-flowering deciduous magnolias and azaleas.

M. tubergenianum
This grape hyacinth has dense, 6–8 in (15-20 cm) long, bicolored flower spikes of very bright sky-blue with a contrasting pale blue at the top. One of the best and most striking of its kind, this species is good for planting in a rock garden.

NARCISSUS
Daffodil

Daffodils are the mainstay of the spring garden and come in an ever-increasing array of colors and forms, thanks to the skill and patience of plant breeders. The true wild species are also very attractive, and many nurseries and catalogs offer a range of both species and cultivars.

Every narcissus flower has a cup or trumpet, known as the corona, that develops to varying degrees and is surrounded by 6 petals, called the corolla. The flowers may be solitary, as in most trumpet daffodils, or number several per stem, as in *N. tazetta* and *N. papyraceus*. Through extensive interbreeding, the combination of these features has led to the following horticultural classification based on the features of the species. Hardiness zones: 4-6; 7-8 for *N. tazetta*, *N. cantabricus*, *N. papyraceus* and *N. romieuxii*.

N. asturiensis

N. asturiensis (**syn.** *N. minimus*) (*above*)
This is the smallest trumpet daffodil, only 2–4 in (5-10 cm) high, with narrow gray-green leaves and small, solitary, deep yellow flowers barely $\frac{1}{2}$ in (1.5 cm) long.

N. bulbocodium 'Julia Jane'

N. *bulbocodium* (*above*)
Hoop-petticoat daffodil

This plant gets its name from its striking funnel-shaped trumpets about ³/₄-1 in (2-2.5 cm) long, which are surrounded by very narrow, rather insignificant petals. Because the dark green leaves are slender and threadlike and the plant is less than 6 in (15 cm) high, it is best grown in a rock garden or small outdoor terrarium, where it will not be swamped by other plants. However, it may thrive in some grasses; a sloping meadow of fine grasses through which water seeps in the early part of the year is ideal. In these conditions, *N. bulbocodium* seeds very freely to form large clusters. 'Julia Jane' is a good pale yellow-flowered selection. There are several variants, including *N. b. conspicuus*, with large, deep yellow flowers, and *N. b. romieuxii* (syn. *N. romieuxii*), a more tender, pale sulfur-yellow type.

N. canaliculatus

N. *canaliculatus* (*above*)

This plant, usually about 8-10 in (20-25 cm) high, requires a hot, sunny place where the bulbs will ripen over summer, as do all members of this Tazetta Mediterranean group. It bears clusters of sweet-smelling creamy white flowers with orange cups.

N. *cantabricus* (*below*)

This hoop-petticoat with white flowers is a more delicate plant, requiring protected cultivation, as in a small outdoor terrarium. Like *N. bulbocodium*, several variants exist, differing in corona shape and size.

N. cantabricus

N. *cyclamineus* (*below*)

One of the most delightful and distinctive of all the dwarf narcissi , *N. cyclamineus* has a long, slender trumpet, crinkled and flared at the mouth. This is all the more conspicuous because the petals are reflexed like those of a cyclamen. The whole flower is bright golden yellow, borne singly on a 6-10 in (15-25 cm) long stem and accompanied by shiny green leaves. It is a very good parent plant for breeding new hybrids, and a race of cultivars bearing similar characteristics has been raised, some of which are mentioned below under the Cyclamineus hybrids.

N. cyclamineus

N. *jonquilla*
Jonquil

Well known as a cut flower and for its delicious fragrance, the jonquil is also an excellent late-spring garden plant. The deep green leaves are almost rushlike, and the rich

yellow, long-tubed but small flowers, ³/₄-1¹/₄ in (2-3.5cm) in diameter, are carried in clusters on 8-12 in (20-30 cm) tall stems. It prefers sheltered spots and sandy soils.

N. *minor* (*below*)

Although this small trumpet daffodil is slightly larger than *N. asturiensis*, it is otherwise similar. The stems, 6-10 in (15-25 cm) high, bear solitary, deep yellow flowers. Also similar is *N. nanus*.

N. minor

N. *obvallaris*
Tenby daffodil

This is very similar to *N. pseudonarcissus*. It has deep yellow flowers, which are slightly smaller than those of the average daffodil, and it grows 8-10 in (20-25 cm) high.

N. papyraceus

N. *papyraceus* (*above*)
Paperwhite

This much-loved species with a delicious perfume is good for early forcing in bowls or as a winter cut flower. It requires no skill and flowers in pots of peat, soil, or gravel on a bright windowsill a month or two after planting. In warm locations, *N. papyraceus* can also be grown very successfully in a sheltered, sunny spot outdoors—at the base of a warm wall or fence. One of the cluster-headed species, it has up to 20 pure white, small-cupped flowers to a head and broad gray-green leaves.

N. poeticus

N. poeticus (*above*)
Poet's narcissus or pheasant's eye
The very small, yellow or green cup of *N. poeticus* has a bright orange or red rim staring out like an eye from the center of the large, flat white flower. This robust mountain plant from southern Europe is particularly hardy and wonderfully fragrant, flowering right at the end of the narcissus season in late spring. It is at its best when planted in grass.

N. pseudonarcissus

N. pseudonarcissus (*above*)
Daffodil
Most trumpet daffodil cultivars have been developed from this species. In its wild form, it is a small plant with bicolored flowers; the corolla is pale yellow and the ³/₄–1¹/₄ in (2-3.5 cm) long trumpet is deeper yellow and flared at the mouth. There are many variations of this daffodil in the wild that have been named separately. It is best when naturalized in semishade or grass.

N. pseudonarcissus moschatus **and**
N. alpestris
These Pyrenean plants are very similar and should be regarded as variations of one species. They are small trumpet daffodils with plain white or creamy flowers that hang downward on 6-10 in (15-25 cm) stems. Since the petals do not stand away from the trumpet, they have a droopy appearance. They do well in a cool, well-drained spot.

N. requienii (**syn.** *N. assoanus*)
This dwarf jonquil has slender, rushlike leaves and small-cupped, fragrant yellow flowers barely ¹/₂ in (1.5 cm) across; it has just 1-2 blooms per 6-8 in (15-20 cm) stem. Although hardy enough to be grown in a sunny, well-drained spot, it is easier to see and enjoy in a terrarium.

N. romieuxii

N. romieuxii (*above*)—See *N. bulbocodium*.

N. tazetta

N. tazetta (*above*)
The highly fragrant tazetta has formed the basis of several varieties, such as 'Soleil d'Or,' which is valuable as an early cut flower and for forcing. The wild form ranges 6-20 in (15-50 cm) in height and bears a cluster of up to 20 small white, yellow-cupped flowers on a single head. It varies considerably and there are several subspecies. It requires hot, sunny conditions and does not do well in cold gardens. Where climatic conditions permit, it is worth trying in a sheltered spot at the base of a warm wall.

N. triandrus 'Albus'

N. triandrus (*above*)
Angel's tears
One of the most delightful species for a cool spot in a rock garden, this narcissus can also be naturalized in the semi-shade of deciduous shrubs. It is only about 4-8 in (10-20 cm) high, with slender, dark green leaves and up to 6 pendent, creamy white flowers, which have prominent cups and reflexed petals. The usual form is 'Albus'.

N. watieri

N. watieri (*above*)
This small North African species looks too fragile to be grown outdoors, but it is fairly hardy and might be tried in a well-drained, sunny spot in a rock garden. It stands about 4 in (10 cm) high, with narrow gray leaves and a solitary flat white flower about 1 in (2.5 cm) in diameter with a shallow cup. It is best kept in a pot for the bulb to ripen.

Garden forms

In addition to the wild species, countless garden forms of narcissi exist, which have been classified into groups. A few of each are mentioned here; refer to current bulb catalogs for a fuller picture.

N. 'King Alfred'

Large-trumpet daffodils (*above* and *below*) These typical daffodils with long trumpets are available in a wide color range, including yellow (the old varieties such as 'King Alfred'), solid golden yellow ('Rowallane' is an excellent variety), pale lemon-yellow ('Spellbinder' ages to near-white with a yellow rim to the trumpet), and pure white ('Mount Hood').

Large-trumpet daffodils

Large-cupped daffodils (*next column*) These bear one large flower on each stem; the corona, which is shaped like a deep cup, must be more than one-third the total length of the petals to qualify as a Large-cupped daffodil. 'Ice Follies' flaunts white petals and a very widely expanded, pale lemon cup that fades to near-white with age. This highly attractive variety mixes well with plants like *Helleborus foetidus*. *N.* 'Ambergate' is very striking, with

an orange cup and golden petals that have a curious tint of peach. 'Pink Charm' is one of the so-called "pink" daffodils, with white petals and a pink cup.

N. 'Ambergate'

Small-cupped daffodils

The small cup that characterizes this group is less than a third the length of the petals because of the influence of *N. poeticus* in breeding. 'Barrett Browning' has a large, white flower, ruffled and crinkled at its rim, and is flat except for the small, shallow, orange-red cup in the center. 'Birma' has sulfur-yellow petals surrounding a small orange cup, and 'Verger' is white with a lemon-yellow, orange-rimmed cup. All have solitary flowers on tall stems.

N. 'Hawera'

Triandrus hybrids (*above*)

N. triandrus supplies the dominant characteristics. The hybrids are usually fairly compact, with more than 1 flower per stem, each with backswept petals. They require drier conditions than the Cyclamineus hybrids. 'April Tears' is a dwarf variety, about 6-8 in (15-20 cm) high, with several nodding yellow flowers per stem; it increases rapidly by offsets. 'Hawera' is an equally

popular dwarf narcissus 8-10 in (20-25 cm) high, with up to 6 small, long-tubed, fragrant flowers in a shade of lemon-yellow. This particularly graceful and delicate plant is a hybrid, having the small cup and long tube of *N. jonquilla* and the reflexed petals of *N. triandrus*. 'Liberty Bells' is larger, with several nodding lemon-yellow flowers per stem, and 'Thalia' has white blooms, also large with several flowers to each 8-12 in (20-30 cm) stem. Both have reflexed petals.

N. 'February Gold'

Cyclamineus hybrids (*above* and *below*)

These hybrids bear obvious similarities to *N. cyclamineus*, particularly in the backswept appearance of the petals. They are shorter than the majority of ordinary daffodils and are excellent plants for forcing and for growing in grass, since they do not mind a little more moisture than most narcissi. 'February Gold' and 'February Silver' are probably the best known, but many other varieties now exist in a wide color range. 'Dove Wings' is a delightful variety, with reflexed white petals and a pale yellow cup; 'Jetfire' has dramatic golden yellow petals and an orange trumpet; and the striking 'Peeping Tom' has golden yellow petals, and very long trumpets.

N. 'Peeping Tom'

Jonquilla hybrids

Members of this group have the upright, narrow leaves of *N. jonquilla* and several fragrant flowers per stem, with long, slender tubes. They readily form clumps in the garden and are excellent for cutting. 'Trevithian' and 'Sweetness' reach a medium height of 14–16 in (35–40 cm), with pale yellow flowers; the former has several per stem and the latter usually only one. 'Sundial' measures about 6 in (15 cm) high and has a few lemon-colored flowers tinged green. 'Pipet' (also spelled 'Pipit') has lemon-yellow petals fading to white at the base of the lemon-and-white cup.

N. 'Geranium'

Poetaz hybrids (*above*)

This group combines the scent of *N. poeticus* and *N. tazetta* with the cluster-headed characteristic of the latter and the larger flowers of the former. 'Geranium' is one of the best, about 14–16 in (35–40 cm) high, with 3–5 almost flat, fragrant white flowers and shallow orange cups.

N. 'Cheerfulness'

Tazetta narcissi (*above*)

This tender narcissus is not cold resistant. Although often planted in gardens or pots,

these half-hardy daffodils are mostly used for cut flowers or for forcing. As with the true species, the derivatives of *N. tazetta* have several very fragrant flowers grouped in a cluster. 'Cheerfulness' is aptly named, with its creamy double flowers, and the popular 'Soleil d'Or' has highly fragrant yellow-orange cups. The 'Chinese Sacred Lily' is sometimes available; it is like a large-flowering version of *N. tazetta*. Tazettas grown outside in the garden should be given a sheltered spot where they can bake over summer while dormant. However, the dwarf 'Minnow,' at 8–10 in (20–25 cm) high, seems to thrive in any well-drained, sunny spot and also grows in grass. It has lemon-colored flowers, with deep yellow cups.

N. 'Actaea'

Poeticus narcissi (*above* and *below*)

The most obvious characteristic of this narcissus is the deliciously fragrant, almost flat white flower with a tiny cup, 1 per stem. It often flowers in mid- to late spring. 'Actaea' makes a fine cut flower, very large and pure white, with a small yellow cup rimmed an orange-red color. The popular 'Pheasant's Eye' grows well in grass and has smaller, fragrant flowers, pure white or cream with orange or red cups.

N. 'Pheasant's Eye'

N. 'Cassata'

Split corona (*above*)
(Also known as collar and orchid-flowering daffodils)

In this comparatively recent development, the corona is split into segments that are pressed back against the petals, forming a flat flower, with two layers of "petals." This unusual shape is far removed from the classic daffodil. The various cultivars are mostly quite tall, $1\frac{1}{4}$–$1\frac{1}{2}$ ft (40–45 cm) high, and have only 1 flower per stem. 'Cassata' has white petals and the split corona segments are yellow; 'Baccarat' is a striking plant with orange corona segments flattened against yellow petals; and 'Orangery' has small orange segments and large white petals.

ORNITHOGALUM
Star-of-Bethlehem

Although this genus is a large group of spring-flowering bulbs, only a few of the familiar star-of-Bethlehems are in general cultivation. Many species are natives of Europe, western Asia and South Africa, some of which are not hardy. Since many are so alike, there is little point in growing more than a few types. In general, they have star-shaped white flowers with a green stripe on the outside of each of the 6 petals. The spring-flowering ones are all fairly low-growing and can be sited in a rock garden, at the front of a perennial border, or in the dappled shade of decid-uous trees and shrubs. While they will grow in shade, they need some sunlight during the day or they do not open, leaving ranks of closed green buds.

For most species, ordinary well-drained garden soil is acceptable, but avoid very hot, dry spots. These bulbs should be plant-ed in autumn about 2 in (5 cm) deep. Propagation is easy since the plants increase by division and seed, sometimes too abundantly. Hardiness zones: 4–6.

O. balansae (*below*)

This Turkish mountain plant is one of the earliest to flower and is a particularly choice species. It is a dwarf plant, only 2–4 in (5–10 cm) high, with 2–3 short, broad, glossy green leaves and a short raceme of white flowers about 1 in (2.5 cm) across. It is ideal for growing in a rock garden or an early display in an outside terrarium.

O. balansae

O. lanceolatum

Although not readily available, it is worth searching for this species. A rosette of wide leaves spreads out at ground level, with a cluster of white flowers nestled in the center, slightly higher than the leaves. The plant needs an open site in well-drained soil.

O. nutans

O. nutans (*above*)
Nodding star-of-Bethlehem

An excellent plant for the semishade, *O. nutans* is perfect for naturalizing under trees and shrubs. Unlike other species, *O. nutans* has spikes of drooping blooms. Its 6–10 in (15–25 cm) tall stems carry silvery white, pendent flowers, the pointed petals suffused with gray-green on the outside and elegantly curved outward at the tips.

O. umbellatum

O. umbellatum (*above*)
Star-of-Bethlehem

From Europe, this is the most common species of star-of-Bethlehem, producing dense clumps of narrow green leaves, each with a white stripe along the center of the upper surface. The flower stems are 4–8 in (10–20 cm) tall and, in mid- to late spring, bear flat-topped heads of shiny white flowers. These will not open in the shade and therefore the plant must be grown in a sunny location. This species is good for planting between and beneath shrubs where the sun filters through; it also does well in grass and may become invasive.

PUSCHKINIA

This relative of scillas flourishes in the mountains of the Middle East. Like the scillas, it requires a cool spot where the bulbs will not become too hot and dry in summer, and needs humus-rich soil that has grit or sand added to ensure good drainage. It is suitable for planting beneath deciduous shrubs in partial shade or in a not-too-dry place in a rock garden. The small bulbs are planted in autumn and should be buried about 2 in (5 cm) under ground. Hardiness zone: 5.

P. scilloides

P. scilloides (**syn. P. libanotica**) (*middle column*)

This plant grows 2¼–4¼ in (6–12 cm) high, with 2 leaves at the base and a raceme of fragrant pale blue flowers. These have a darker blue stripe along the center of each of the 6 petals. Each flower is about ½ in (1 cm) in diameter, with the segments joined into a short tube. 'Alba' is the white form.

ROMULEA

Romulea is a relative of the crocus. Although many species are widespread and sometimes common in the wild, they are scarcely known as garden plants. Unfortunately, some are not very hardy and others have less attractive flowers and require a sunny spring day before they will open. The spectacular species from South Africa can be tried in the warm climates of southern regions of North America, but gardens in cooler climates are restricted to the less striking Mediterranean species. *R. bulbocodium* is, however, worth trying in a warm, sunny, well-drained spot. The small corms are planted in autumn at a depth of about 2 in (5 cm) and may be left undisturbed for several years to increase into clumps, improving the flower display considerably. This is also a good plant for a midspring display in an outdoor terrarium. Propagation of romuleas is by division or seed in autumn. Hardiness zone: 7.

R. bulbocodium

R. bulbocodium (*above*)

This is the showiest of the hardier species. It reaches 2–4 in (5–10 cm) in height, with threadlike but tough leaves topping funnel-shaped lilac-blue flowers, which open to 1 in (2.5 cm) in diameter in the sun. The flower throat is usually yellow, but it is a variable plant, so there are many color forms.

SCILLA
Spring squill

Almost without exception, the spring species of scilla are blue-flowering, apart from a few selected color variants such as albinos. They are mostly hardy dwarf plants, flowering from early to late spring, and are generally inexpensive, making them particularly useful. Scillas vary in their cultural requirements, but all are best planted in autumn at a depth of 2-2³/₄ in (5-7 cm) in well-drained soil. Propagation is mainly by division of clumps in late summer or early fall since they tend to produce offset bulbs quite freely; seed is also produced, although this is much slower. Hardiness zones: 3-8.

S. bifolia 'Praecox'

S. bifolia (*above*)
This small early-spring bulb grows in semishade or full sun and is useful for naturalizing under shrubs or trees or for planting among early perennials such as hellebores. Each bulb produces 2 leaves and a 2-4 in (5-10 cm) high stem bearing a one-sided spike of small, deep blue-violet flowers that are flat and star-shaped when fully open. 'Praecox' is a vigorous, showy large-flowering form; 'Alba' is pure white and 'Rosea' has pale pink flowers.

S. bithynica
This is a good squill for naturalizing since it seeds freely and grows in full sun to partial shade, eventually forming sizable patches up to 3¹/₂ ft (1 m) or more across if it thrives. It will also grow in damp conditions and in cool spots in a rock garden. It grows as tall as 6 in (15 cm), with several narrow, straplike basal leaves and dense racemes of small, star-shaped medium-blue flowers, each about ¹/₂ in (1 cm) in diameter. It flowers late in spring, after *S. bifolia*.

S. greilhuberi
This scilla produces long racemes of lilac-blue flowers in midspring and grows well in the semishade.

S. italica (*below*)
A useful plant for a sunny spot in a rock garden or along a border, *S. italica* makes a good showing in midspring, increasing into clumps by bulb division and offsets. The thin leaves are accompanied in midspring by 6-8 in (15-20 cm) high stems; these carry flat-topped or conical racemes of pale to medium-blue flowers ¹/₂ in (1 cm) across and almost flat when fully open.

S. italica

S. lilio-hyacinthus
This squill has tufts of up to 10 broad, glossy green leaves. The 4-8 in (10-20 cm) stems carry racemes of small starlike flowers, pale to lilac-blue, or white as in 'Alba.'

S. amethystina

S. litardierei (*above*)
This scilla is better known by its incorrect name *S. pratensis* or its more vigorous form *S. amethystina*. It flowers later than most scillas, in late spring or early summer, and has narrow basal leaves. The dense, 4-8 in (10-

20 cm) long racemes display up to 30 small, star-shaped blue flowers, each ¹/₄ in (0.5 cm) in diameter. The plant grows best in a rock garden or along a sunny border where it can be left to grow undisturbed.

S. mischtschenkoana 'Tubergeniana'

S. mischtschenkoana (syn. *S. tubergeniana*) (*above*)
This species is invaluable for planting in groups in a rock garden, between hardy perennials or shrubs, or in the semishade of trees and shrubs. At flowering time in early spring, it has short, glossy, pale green leaves almost hidden by the pale blue flowers that open as soon as they push through the ground. The stems elongate and ultimately grow 4-6 in (10-15 cm) high when flowering is complete. The individual flowers are about ¹/₂ in (1.5 cm) in diameter, saucer-shaped, and pale blue with a dark blue stripe on each petal. 'Tubergeniana' is the best and the one most usually sold.

S. peruviana

S. peruviana (*above*)
This plant requires a hot, sunny spot where the bulbs can bake over summer when dormant. Plant them in autumn with their tips just beneath the surface. The large bulbs

start to produce rosettes of broad, pointed leaves that continue to grow until late spring, when they are accompanied by large conical heads of up to 100 steel-blue, flat, starlike flowers growing ¼ in (2 cm) across.

S. siberica

S. siberica (*above*)
Probably the most well known, this early-spring squill is inexpensive and worth planting in patches or clusters in the semi-shade of shrubs, where it provides a bold splash of color. It grows almost anywhere except hot, dry places and is reliably hardy. The glossy green leaves are topped by flowering stems that elongate through the season from 2-6 in (5-15 cm), bearing up to 5 bell-shaped mid- to deep blue flowers, each up to ½ in (1.5 cm) long. The form most often sold is 'Spring Beauty,' a brilliant deep blue; there is also an attractive albino form known as 'Alba.'

S. verna
Spring squill
Not as showy as the similar *S. italica* but nevertheless a charming plant, *S. verna* is well worth growing in a sunny rock garden or in a pot in an outside terrarium. It has narrow basal leaves and 2-4 in (5-10 cm) high stems that carry flat-topped racemes, each with up to 12 small lilac-blue to violet flowers. These are flat and star-shaped, barely reaching ⅜ in (1 cm) in diameter.

TECOPHILAEA
Chilean blue crocus
Although thought to be extinct in the wild, the Chilean blue crocus is propagated in cultivation and is obtainable from a few bulb nurseries. However, it is expensive since it does not increase very rapidly. Tecophilaea is not a difficult plant to grow, requiring well-drained soil and a sunny

spot, but in view of its rarity and cost it is probably best given the protection of an outside terrarium, cool conservatory, or cold frame. In summer, while the plants are dormant, the corms should be kept dry, but not allowed to bake, and repotted and watered again from autumn to the following summer. Propagation of tecophilaea is by seed sown in autumn or by offsets, which are sometimes produced. Hardiness zone: 9.

T. cyanocrocus (*below*)
The almost flat corms of *T. cyanocrocus* produce 2-4 in (5-10 cm) high stems with narrow, deep green leaves and 1-2 large, funnel-shaped flowers about 1 in (2.5 cm) in diameter. An intense deep blue, they rival gentians in color. *T. c.* 'Leichtlinii' is paler blue, with a large white center, and *T. c.* 'Violacea' is a deep purple.

T. cyanocrocus

TRILLIUM
Wake-robin
The first part of the Latin name aptly describes these gorgeous spring flowers: their stems have 3 leaves in a whorl, and the solitary flowers—1 per stem—have 3 sepals and 3 petals. Mainly woodland plants, the majority are from North America. Although hardy plants, young emerging shoots can be damaged by late frosts. The thick rhizomes rootstocks should be planted about 2-4 in (5-10 cm) deep, with the largest and most vigorous species buried deeper than the small ones. The types below are not difficult to grow, requiring partial shade in humus-rich soil. They are best if left undisturbed to establish clumps. The flowering period is mid- to late spring. Seed propagation is slow, but the clumps can occasionally be divided in autumn or spring. Hardiness zones: 3-6.

T. cernuum
Nodding trillium
About 10-12 in (25-30 cm) high, this trillium has white flowers, each with a maroon-colored ovary. The blossoms are held just below the rosette of 3 broad green leaves in a pendent position. For this reason, it is not easy to see the flowers, so plant it in a raised bed for the best display, where they can be fully appreciated.

T. chloropetalum (*below*)
This beautiful plant carries large flowers held upright, resting on top of the rosette of 3 mottled leaves carried on a 10-14 in (25-35 cm) tall stem. The flowers have erect petals 2-3¼ in (5-8 cm) long; among the numerous flowering colors, those most commonly seen have white petals.

T. chloropetalum

T. cuneatum (*below*)
(Also known as *T. sessile* of gardens)
This plant is very similar to *T. chloropetalum* in general appearance, but it has deep maroon petals over broad, handsomely mottled leaves. When growing well, it may reach 1⅓-1¾ ft (40-53 cm) in height and can form large clumps, ideal for wooded areas. The true *T. sessile* is rare in cultivation.

T. cuneatum

T. erectum (syn. T. pulchella)
The whorl of plain green leaves is held on stems 10-16 in (25-40 cm) high and is topped by the flowers on erect or oblique, slender stalks. There are several color forms, but the most commonly available are deep reddish maroon and white.

T. grandiflorum (*below*)
Wake-robin
Perhaps the best species, wake-robin is easy to grow and showy, with its snow-white flowers bearing petals up to 3½ in (9 cm) long. They are held on stalks well above the deep green leaves, which are carried on stems 8 in-1½ ft (20-45 cm) high. The flowers fade to purple-pink with age. 'Roseum' is a beautiful form with flowers opening soft pink, and 'Flore Pleno' has tight, double white flowers.

T. grandiflorum

T. luteum (*below*)
T. luteum has mottled leaves and erect, stemless, green-yellow flowers.

T. luteum

T. nivale (*next column*)
Snow trillium
This dwarf species is rarely cultivated and difficult to grow. It is only about 2-4 in (5-10 cm) high, with deep green leaves topped by small white flowers with petals 1-1¾ in (2.5-4.5 cm) long. It prefers an alkaline soil in sun or very slight shade.

T. nivale

T. ovatum
This trillium is similar to *T. grandiflorum*.

T. rivale

T. rivale (*above*)
An attractive dwarf species, this trillium does well in a cool spot in a peat garden or semishaded rock garden. It is only 2-3¼ in (5-8 cm) high, with a rosette of plain green leaves and a small flower only approximately 1¼ in (3.5 cm) in diameter. The flower is white or pale pink, spotted darker red to varying degrees and sometimes with a darker red eye in the center. Although a diminutive plant, it forms patches when growing well. It is an excellent choice for an outside terrarium or cold frame.

TULIPA
Tulip
If crocuses are the mainstay of the early-spring bulb display, and daffodils of the midspring period, then tulips provide the climax in late spring. As well as the many delightful tulip species that are readily bought, hundreds of selections and hybrids—from the dwarf early Kaufmanniana types to the tall late Darwins—exist thanks mainly to the skill and patience of the Dutch growers. Propagation is by division in autumn. Hardiness zones: 3-7.

T. acuminata (*below*)
For those who like curiosities, this strange tulip is tall, 1½-1¾ ft (45-53 cm) when in flower, and has slender flowers with long, tapering petals in a mixture of yellow and red. Although not showy enough for bedding displays, it is a fine plant for placing in small groups adjacent to neutral foliage that allows the flowers to stand out.

T. acuminata

T. batalinii (*below*)
This is a popular dwarf tulip for a rock garden or the front of a border. Given a warm, well-drained position, it is often persistent and may even increase into clumps. It is only 2-4 in (5-10 cm) high, with primrose-yellow flowers 2-2¼ in (5-7 cm) across, set amid narrow, gray, wavy-edged leaves. 'Bronze Charm' has an apricot-bronze flush to the flowers.

T. batalinii

T. clusiana chrysantha

T. clusiana (*above*)
Lady tulip

A graceful slender species up to 1 ft (30 cm) high, it has narrow gray leaves and elegant narrow-petaled flowers that open into a starshape 4 in (10 cm) in diameter. The flower is white with a dark crimson eye in the center and a strong pink-crimson stain on the outside. *T. c. chrysantha* is similar but with a yellow background color instead of white, whereas *T. c. stellata* has a white flower with a yellow central blotch. *T. aitchisonii* is almost identical to *T. clusiana*.

T. eichleri

T. eichleri (*above*)
This central Asiatic tulip reaches 10-12 in (25-30 cm) in height. It has broad leaves and large orange-red flowers, which are up to 4¾ in (12 cm) across when open, revealing a black center.

T. fosteriana (*next column*)
A vigorous red-flowering tulip that reaches 1½ ft (45 cm) in height, *T. fosteriana* has bold gray-green leaves and huge flowers that can measure up to 8 in (20 cm) across. Each bloom is flushed yellow-gold on the outside, with a black eye surrounded by a narrow yellow zone inside. The best of the group

includes 'Purissima,' creamy white turning pure white with age; and the striking 'Madame Lefeber,' brilliant glowing red.

T. fosteriana **'Madame Lefeber'**

T. greigii (*below*)
This early tulip is mostly grown for its attractive broad, purple-brown striped leaves. The true species is 8-16 in (20-40 cm) high, with bright red, black-eyed flowers.

T. greigii

T. humilis
A charming small tulip from the Middle East, this species flowers at the beginning of the tulip season in midspring. It is ideally suited to a rock garden, a warm, sunny border, or an outside terrarium. It is only 2-6 in (5-15 cm) high with narrow gray-green leaves clustered at ground level and pink-purple flowers with yellow eyes, about 2¼-2¾ in (6-7 cm) in diameter. 'Violacea' has rich purple flowers; 'Pulchella' is a paler purple-magenta with a deep blue eye; and 'Violet Queen' is another rich violet-red form.

T. kaufmanniana (*next column*)
Waterlily tulip
This stocky dwarf tulip from central Asia is about the earliest to flower, with broad gray-

green leaves that are fairly short at flowering time. It is a good candidate for growing in pots for an early display in a cool greenhouse but should not be forced with too much heat. In the wild, it varies a lot, but the most commonly seen variation has 4-8 in (10-20 cm) tall stems, with cream or pale yellow flowers flushed red on the outside of the petals. The leaves are all carried in a tuft at the base, making it a neat and compact plant when flowering. *T. kaufmanniana* has been hybridized; see Kaufmanniana hybrids p. 119 for details.

T. kaufmanniana

T. kolpakowskiana
This elegant species stands 4-8 in (10-20 cm) tall, with upright, gray-green wavy-edged leaves and a slender yellow flower flushed pink on the outside of its pointed petals.

T. linifolia

T. linifolia (*above*)
This dwarf tulip—4-8 in (10-20 cm) in height—can add a splash of color to a garden in midspring. It has narrow, wavy-edged leaves and scarlet flowers, each with a small black-purple eye in the center, opening out flat in the sun to 2¼-3¼ in (6-8 cm) across. In a hot, sunny spot, it can form clumps.

T. marjolettii
Unusually colored, this species has cream petals flushed purple on the outside and edged with pink. It generally reaches 14 in–1½ ft (35–45 cm) in height.

T. maximowiiczii
Similar to *T. linifolia* in general appearance, the bright red flowers of this tulip have a white-edged, dark eye in the center of them.

T. orphanidea
Although subdued when compared with some of the gaudy red species, color can nonetheless be this species' main attraction. It is effective with gray- or silver-leaved plants. It grows 10–12 in (25–30 cm) high, with up to 3 dull orange-brown flowers stained green on the outside and opening to approximately 1¾ in (4.5 cm) in diameter. *T. hageri*, with dull red flowers, and the attractive orange-bronze *T. whittallii* are closely related and sometimes available.

T. praestans

T. praestans (*above*)
The interesting feature of this central Asian tulip is that it produces up to 5 showy flowers on each stem and has played a part in the development of the 'bunch-flowering' tulips that have recently come onto the market. It has broad, upright, gray-green leaves and 12 in (30 cm) stems bearing several bright orange-red flowers up to 4 in (10 cm) across.

T. saxatilis
An unusual species from Crete, *T. saxatilis* requires the hottest, sunniest spot in the garden with room to develop, for it increases by stolons to form patches. It enjoys such sites as a border at the base of a warm wall and grows particularly well on alkaline soil, although this is not essential. The broad, glossy green leaves are accompanied by

8–12 in (20–30 cm) high stems bearing up to 4 pink flowers. Each bloom has a deep yellow eye in the center and reaches 2¼–3¼ in (6–8 cm) in diameter.

T. sprengeri (*below*)
This late-flowering tulip sometimes blooms in early summer. It produces small flowers that appear well after others have finished for a late splash of color—so late it almost qualifies as a summer bulb. It has erect, shiny green leaves and 1–1½ ft (30–45 cm) tall stems carrying solitary yellow-gold buds that open to reveal bright scarlet flowers. It does well in conditions ranging from full sun to partial shade, and also seeds very freely.

T. sprengeri

T. sylvestris (*below*)
With a height of 8–14 in (20–35 cm), this small-flowering tulip is not usually free-flowering. The yellow flowers are suffused green on the outside and about 2¼–3¼ in (6–8 cm) wide.

T. sylvestris

T. tarda (*next column*)
This is a popular dwarf tulip for the rock garden. The leaves are narrow and produced in a rosette at ground level, up to 5 of which

appear on each stem. The flowers open widely to about 2 in (5 cm) in diameter and are yellow with white-tipped petals.

T. tarda

T. turkestanica (*below*)
This slender species tulip from central Asia grows 4–10 in (10–25 cm) high, with narrow gray leaves and up to 12 small white flowers. Flushed green on the outside.

T. turkestanica

T. urumiensis (*below*)
T. urumiensis has yellow flowers diffused bronze on the outside.

T. urumiensis

Single early tulips (*below*)
Like the Double early tulips, these are short
and stocky in stature, mostly 8–12 in (20–30
cm) high, with single, rounded flowers on
sturdy stems, produced early in the tulip
season. 'Apricot Beauty' is a mixture of
salmon and orange and is recommended for
forcing in pots for an even earlier display;
'Bellona' has bright golden yellow flowers;
and 'Brilliant Star' is one of the first to
bloom, a short, weather-resistant variety with
bright scarlet flowers, suitable for planting or
for indoor forcing in midwinter.

T. 'Apricot Beauty'

Double early tulips (*below*)
These tulips flower at the start of the tulip
season and have tight double blooms. They
are stocky plants, usually 10–12 in
(25–30 cm) high, and are wind resistant,
making them good to plant in containers for
an early display on a terrace. 'Orange Nassau'
is a deep blood-red and orange-red mixture;
'Schoonoord' is pure white; 'Peach Blossom'
a deep rose-pink color.

T. 'Peach Blossom'

**Midseason tulips (including Mendel and
Triumph tulips)**
These tulip cultivars bridge the gap between
the very early types and the May-flowering
group. They have rounded flowers,
sometimes rather angular in bud, on stout,
short stems and are between 1¼–1¾ ft (40–53
cm) high, so they withstand inclement
weather quite well. A great range of these
tulips is available, including 'Lady Diana,' a
splendid shade of rose-red; 'New Design,'
very unusual and fairly new, with pink-edged
leaves and flowers that are yellow at first on
the outside, changing to pink-cream, and a
yellow interior flushed apricot; and 'African
Queen,' a deep wine color with a contrasting
narrow white edge on its petals.

T. 'Apeldoorn'

Darwin hybrids (*above*)
These plants also have large flowers that are
oval before they open fully. They are derived
from crosses between the red central Asian
species *T. fosteriana* and the Darwin
cultivars. Mostly about 2–2¼ ft (60–68.5 cm)
high, they flower slightly earlier than the
Darwin and Cottage types, in midspring.
'Golden Apeldoorn' is golden yellow
splashed with red on the outside, and when
open reveals a black eye in the center; it is a
persistent garden variety. 'Gudoshnik' is also
yellow but has more pronounced red spots
and streaks on the outside. 'Elizabeth Arden'
is a deep salmon-pink, with a darker red-
violet band in the center of each petal.
'Dawnglow' is a pale apricot, deep pink
outside and yellow within.

May-flowering hybrids (*next column*)
Also called Single late or Darwin tulips, these
varieties have large, oval to rounded flowers
on stout 2–2¾ ft (60–84 cm) high stems and
are very popular for bedding displays. 'Clara
Butt' is an old favorite with salmon-pink
flowers; 'Halcro' is bright red with the petals
edged orange-red; 'Queen of Night' has deep
velvet-maroon flowers; and 'Sorbet' is almost
white with a pink shading, becoming more
heavily striped and feathered orange-red with
age. A good yellow choice is 'Golden Harvest,'
with its lemon-yellow flowers.

T. 'Queen of Night'

Lily-flowering tulips (*below*)
These are among the most elegant tulips,
with tall stems 1½–2 ft (45–60 cm) high
carrying slender flowers with pointed petals
arching outward at the tips. They flower late
in the tulip season and are weather resistant.
'Maytime' has dull red-purple petals shading
at the edge to a narrow band of cream; 'China
Pink' is a fine shade of pink mixing well with
forget-me-nots in a border; 'West Point' is a
popular yellow with long, graceful, pointed
petals; 'Aladdin' is scarlet with yellow edges
to the petals; and 'White Triumphator' is a
pure white.

T. 'Aladdin'

Viridiflora tulips
This group contains curiously colored
varieties, all marked with green stripes or
bands to varying degrees. They are late-
flowering and stiff and stocky, about 1½ ft
(45 cm) high. 'Artist' has noticeably pointed
salmon-rose petals with a wide green band
along the center—an intriguing blend of

colors. 'Greenland' is predominantly pink with a narrow but conspicuous green stripe along the center of the rather broad petal. In 'Spring Green' the lower half of the flower is bright green fading to cream at the edges and upper half of the petals. 'Esperanto' has the added attraction of white-edged leaves, and its flowers are striking, with the petals deep rose at the edges and the tips shading to strong green in the center. 'Hummingbird' has yellow and green flowers.

Rembrandt tulips

These are the old single cottage-garden tulips with 'broken' flower colors—that is to say, the flowers are striped and feathered with contrasting colors. They flower in late spring and are 2-2¼ ft (60-68.5 cm) high. Few varieties are still commercially available, although mixed Rembrandts can be obtained. 'Cordell Hull,' a white flower with red flamelike markings, is sometimes available.

T. 'Black Parrot'

Parrot and Fringed tulips (*above*)

These are the exotic end of the tulip range, with the bizarre colors of the Parrot group and the crystal-fingered petals of the Fringed types. They flower late in the season and reach up to 1½-1¾ ft (45-53 cm) high. Of the Parrot types, 'Black Parrot' is one of the darkest, with black-purple flowers lacerated at the edges of the petals. 'White Parrot' is the pure white equivalent, and 'Flaming Parrot' is the extrovert with wavy, fringed pale yellow petals flamed with red on the outside and bold bright red stripes inside. The Fringed types are more like the May-flowering kind in flower shape, but the edges of the petals have a crystaline fringe. 'Blue Heron' is a blue-violet shade with a white fringe of needlelike crystals, and 'Burgundy Lace' is a deep rich burgundy-red with a very conspicuous fringe.

T. 'Mount Tacoma'

Double late tulips (*above*)
(Also known as Peony-flowered tulips)

This group of tulips flowers later in the season, coinciding with the May-flowering cultivars. They are noticeably taller than their Double early counterparts and need wind shelter, but compensate with showy, long-lasting blooms. 'Angelique' is a delicate pink in a blend of lighter and darker tones; 'Mount Tacoma' is a good pure white.

T. 'Stresa'

Kaufmanniana hybrids (*above*)

These hybrids descend from the waterlily tulip and are therefore compact plants standing 6-8 in (15-20 cm) high, with neat broad gray-green leaves only partly developed at flowering time. They flower early in the season and are very hardy and weather-resistant, making ideal container plants. Some are hybrids with *T. greigii* and have inherited the striped foliage. 'Stresa' is very popular, bright yellow with a smart red exterior to the outer 3 petals; 'Shakespeare' is a soft mixture of carmine and orange on the outside and yellow flushed pink-red inside; 'Gluck' has attractive mottled foliage topped by red flowers edged yellow, opening out to show a yellow interior; and 'Berlioz' is yellow with striped leaves.

Greigii hybrids (*below*)

These Central Asiatic tulips are easily recognized because of the attractive brown-purple striped foliage, a feature derived from *T. greigii*. They flower early and are short and stocky, making them ideal for a rock garden or along the front of a border; they are also well suited to container cultivation for patios or terraces. They are about 8-12 in (20-30 cm) high. 'Red Riding Hood' has bright scarlet flowers and beautiful purple-striped leaves; 'Corsage' has equally good foliage with flowers of a bright apricot-salmon shade; 'Cape Cod' has yellow-bronze flowers edges with yellow on the outside; 'Plaisir' has elegant pointed petals in carmine edged with pale cream-lemon; and the noteworthy 'Toronto' is a multiflowering variety of tulip with up to 3 pink-red flowers per stem.

T. 'Red Riding Hood'

Multiflowering tulips (*below*)

A few varieties of Multiflowering tulips that produce several flowers per stem are now on the market. This multiple flower characteristic was developed, in part, from *T. praestans*. These tulips flower late in the season. Apart from the red 'Toronto' (see Greigii hybrids), there is an excellent yellow variety available known as 'Georgette'.

T. 'Georgette'

SUMMER

Garden highlights

Bulbs provide exceptionally good summer highlights in a flower garden, and they can be used to fill awkward gaps in a border without disturbing surrounding plants. They can also be planted in corners among the roots of shrubs to supply mid- to late-summer color.

Of all the summer-flowering bulbs, lilies offer the greatest opportunity for spectacular displays. Indeed, they look so exotic that many gardeners think they are too difficult to grow. However, nothing could be further from the truth. Even though some are unreliable, many easy-to-grow lily cultivars are available.

Among the most widely grown lilies are Mid-century hybrids, an extensive range of cultivars with flowers that are equally good for border decoration and cutting. They are robust plants with strong stems that rarely need staking, and they can be combined in a number of ways for many different effects. For a bold look, grow a group of single-colored Mid-century hybrids in a border against a background of tall, spiky, soft yellow *Verbascum olympicum* (mullein), or mix the hybrids together in a colorful mass for a more informal look. Both *Lilium auratum* and *L. regale* have magnificent trumpet-shaped blossoms on towering stems up to 5 ft (1.5 m) high, which must be tied to stakes with garden string for support. They are among the most spectacular of the summer-flowering lilies and are especially effective when grown against a dark backdrop; dark green conifers, shrubby evergreen loniceras, or broad-leaved evergreens like *Osmanthus*, *Ligustrum* (privet), and *Cotoneaster* are all appropriate. For a terrace site, plant a mixture of *L. regale* and a low-growing shrub, such as *Viburnum davidii*, with a soft foreground planting of *Felicia* and a background of scented evergreen *Osmanthus*.

(previous page) *A bed of lilies is a dazzling sight, and on warm summer evenings they will perfume the air.*

(left) *In summer, nothing equals the majestic appearance of* Lilium regale, *with its deliciously scented white flowers.*

(below) *A striking effect can be achieved by mixing brightly colored lilies, such as this Oriental hybrid, with mixed nicotianas.*

Lilium candidum (Madonna lily) has an old-fashioned charm, as does the rich orange *L. lancifolium*. Both are easy-going species that look lovely in a mixed border in combination with unruly hardy annuals such as annual cornflowers, Virginia stocks, and toadflax. *L. speciosum* is another good choice, as its flowering season extends beyond summer into fall, sometimes continuing until the first frost. The fine crimson-and-white blossoms look their best when peeping out from shrubby evergreen ground cover such as *Sarcococca confusa* (Christmas box) and ivies like *Hedera helix hibernica*, both of which provide an attractive foil to the flowers. These lilies can also be grown among low-growing shrub roses and hardy fuchsias in a mixed border; fuchsias will act as a support to the lilies as well as lend color to the design.

Developments in storage techniques have greatly extended the planting period of lily bulbs, but the majority of gardeners still find spring is the best time. The only exception is *Lilium candidum* (Madonna lily), which must be planted in late summer in order to produce a rosette of leaves before winter. For the greatest impact, these lilies should be planted in a group, with perhaps a few architectural-looking foliage plants for contrast.

Galtonia (summer-flowering hyacinth) is good for a mixed border display. The showy white-flowered *G. candicans* provides an effective display; it is similar to a giant hyacinth but taller, with pendent creamy bells spaced farther apart. It does well when grown with bright red border plants; a pairing of *Galtonia* and *Lychnis chalcedonica* (Maltese cross) makes an excellent combination for a sunny corner. Galtonias also mix well with yellow-flowered *Hemerocallis* and *Lilium candidum*; alternatively, try them against a background of dark blue *Ceanothus*.

Allium (ornamental onion) provides some of the best examples of summer-flowering bulbs, producing brightly colored flowers from late spring until midsummer. Plant the bulbs in fall; they are not too demanding and prosper under most

(left) *Nothing is better than a cool, serene planting of white flowers. Use the white-flowered* Galtonia candicans *and phlox toward the back of the border, with African daisies grouped in front.* Gladiolus × colvillei 'The Bride' (top inset) *is another good subject for a white garden; it is more delicate in appearance than some of its relatives. For a completely different look, plant a clump of* Zantedeschia aethiopica (bottom inset).

conditions and soils, although the majority of the striking, colorful kinds need an open, sunny spot in order to perform well. They can be grown with any plants that do not require very damp soil, but because of their slightly ragged, faded foliage, they look best tucked away among other plants rather than grown as a feature.

Allium moly is the least expensive, most cheerful ornamental onion, with dense umbels of starry, bright yellow blossoms. It reproduces rapidly in most conditions and creates a perfect carpet beneath such summer-flowering shrubs as *Philadelphus* (mock orange), which produces deliciously scented white flowers; *Weigela*, with its red or pink trumpet-shaped blooms; and the bright-pink-flowered *Kolkwitzia* (beauty bush). *A. moly* does not tolerate a high degree of shade but quickly becomes established among the roots of mature woody plants.

Allium sphaerocephalon has a very different appearance from *A. moly*, and it is perfect for providing extra interest in a shrub border. With dense umbels of dark purple bell-shaped flowers 1-2 ft (30-60 cm) high, it is a versatile plant that prospers in sun or partial shade. Allow it to rise up through low-growing plants such as *Ajuga* and *Lysimachia nummularia* 'Aurea' (creeping Jennie) for especially good foliage contrasts. *Allium cernuum* can be planted on its own in a border, where it will spread freely, or it can be planted with lavender 'Hidcote' or *Santolina chamaecyparissus* (cotton lavender) for a pleasing display. *Allium aflatunense* can be grown in a sunny border with *Achillea taygetea* or the yellow Welsh poppy, *Meconopsis cambrica*.

Sun is the main requirement of *Allium rosenbachianum*, a large rose-purple-flowered onion with rounded heads of blossoms held on stout, upright stems. It is rather formal in character but excellent for filling gaps in the mixed or herbaceous border during midsummer. The enormous *A. giganteum* provides a startling addition to a mixed planting but is much better as a single focal point. It thrusts up bold flower stems 4 ft (120 cm) high topped with a large, perfectly spherical head of deep-lilac-colored blossoms 4 in (10 cm) in diameter. The leaves are long and straplike. It is best positioned at the end of a walkway or used as a highlight between

(top left) *The delicate blue of* Allium caeruleum *is brought out by striking pink-orange lilies and the pink rose* 'Queen of Denmark.'

(middle left) *Pictured here with pink phlox,* Allium sphaerocephalon *has dense umbels of pinkish-purple flowers held on tall stems.*

(bottom left) *In a charming cottage garden* Allium christophii, *with its loose umbels of starry flowers, mixes perfectly with roses.*

(right) *The pink flowers of* Allium aflatunense *are effectively complemented by the dark Parrot tulips growing in front.*

tall, shrubby plants. As the leaves are often fairly scruffy, plant the bulbs 1-2 in (2.5-5 cm) away from a dense shrub like *Potentilla* or a *Spiraea* like *S. japonica* 'Anthony Waterer.'

Dutch irises enjoy sunny, well-drained conditions. They are frequently used for cut flowers, and they can make a useful contribution to the border if carefully arranged. There are many different-colored hybrids to choose from. Plant a minimum of 20 bulbs in a group, allowing no more than 4 in (10 cm) between any 2 bulbs, and they will appear as a bold column of foliage and flowers in early summer, when the border is lacking interest. After flowering, the spiky foliage remains a decorative feature. Irises look particularly striking reflected in water and will tolerate the dry soil around the edge of artificial ponds.

Crocosmia, also known as *Montbretia,* is a striking summer-flowering bulb, with arching stems of brightly colored blooms. In southern regions and California, it, does not need protecting as even the more exotic modern cultivars, such as the bright red 'Lucifer' and soft yellow 'Solfatare,' are completely hardy. Crocosmias can be established almost anywhere, including a herbaceous border, where they add form as well as color, although few plants look finer than 'Lucifer' when reflected in water. However, that does not mean crocosmias enjoy wet soil; on the contrary, to obtain the best results, provide a well-drained medium that does not dry out completely during summer and incorporate plenty of well-decayed organic matter into the soil. Crocosmias also grow well among gladioli and can be used to intensify color schemes; *Crocosmia* 'Citronella' and the soft apricot-colored *Gladiolus* 'Tesoro' are good companions, as are *Crocosmia* 'Lucifer' and *Gladiolus* 'Black Lash.'

Tigridia is a beautiful orchidlike garden highlight, so bright and colorful that it does not blend very well with other flowering plants and thus should be planted against a green backdrop. These bulbs have vivid blossoms in almost every hue and combination imaginable, resembling tropical butterflies. Choose a bright, sunny spot and a well-drained soil for the best results, isolating the plants in a narrow border or pocket, or in a terrace flowerbed. The warmer and sunnier the spot, the better and more prolific the flowers. Under favorable conditions, the flowers will continue well into fall. Although individual blossoms last only a day, they are produced in such quantities that the plants seem to be flowering continuously throughout the season.

(top) *Mixed Dutch irises are versatile in border plantings. They are easy to grow and are a colorful and familiar sight in many gardens.*

(right) *Few flowers surpass crocosmia in dramatic impact. Its dazzling fiery orange-red blossoms always attract the eye.*

When *Tigridia* bulbs are planted in full sun, they give a creditable performance. However, the bulbs are rarely worth retaining for a second season. The same is true of the Ethiopian gladiolus, *Gladiolus callianthus*, which is often still listed as *Acidanthera bicolor* in catalogs. Producing slender spires of fragrant white blossoms with deep purple throats, these bulbs grow to a height of around 3 ft (90 cm). Acidantheras are extremely elegant, perfect for growing with soft gray foliage such as artemesias or santolinas.

Start these bulbs off in aquatic planting baskets or large pots early in the season, burying the pots in a border when the plants are well established. With such an early start, flowering can occur in late summer or early fall, avoiding the frost. If unseasonable cold weather threatens before the floral display is over, bring the pots indoors. While it is normal to dispose of both tigridias and acidantheras at the end of the season, if they are big enough, you can store them in a cool, frost-free place and they will last for several years.

Watsonia is a greatly underrated summer-flowering bulb. These elegant plants are similar in appearance and temperament to the small-flowered gladioli, but a little less hardy. They prosper in a warm, sunny spot in well-drained soil. Except for *W. pillansii*, they are likely to need lifting and storing during the winter, especially in cold climates. For good color combinations, plant the red, orange, and soft pink flowers among silver- and gray-leaved plants. Unlike other *Watsonia* species, *W. pillansii* tolerates the damp, although it must be grown in full sun. With a mostly unbranched stem reaching up to 3 ft (90 cm) high, it produces a dense spike of large apricot or orange-red flowers and makes a splash of color that gives the display a lift. It also looks very eye-catching when planted with leafy geraniums or billowing white masses of *Gypsophila* in a border.

The deep pink *Watsonia densiflora* is not as suitable for general border cultivation as *W. pillansii*. Nevertheless, it is well worth growing. The annually lifted corms should be planted about 3 in (7.5 cm) apart among gray-leaved plants like *Artemisia schmidtiana* and *Helichrysum angustifolium* (syn. *H. italicum*) to create a harmonious color combination of pink and silvery gray. White-flowering watsonias always look good alongside dark or evergreen foliage plants; small, dark green conifers, such as *Chamaecyparis lawsoniana* 'Forsteckensis' and *C. l.* 'Minima' are suitable. Unfortunately, few evergreens do well with the graceful, long-flowering *W.* 'Arderne's White' because it needs a well-drained, sunny spot. However, *Arbutus unedo* (strawberry tree) and *Laurus nobilis* (bay) will usually cope with such conditions and are the perfect companions for this particular watsonia.

The dappled shade under deciduous trees offers the opportunity to grow another summer-flowering highlight, the white lily *Cardiocrinum giganteum*. This hardy Himalayan plant loves a rich leafy medium in a woodland glade and grows well beneath a tree canopy where the ground is not too congested with roots. A single tree will suffice; birch, mountain ash, and flowering ash are good choices. A giant of a plant, it reaches up to 10 ft (3 m) high under perfect conditions, and it produces spectacular spires of pendent, trumpet-shaped white blossoms. Once the blossoms fade, the bulb dies, leaving a cluster of offsets that will not flower for another year or two. With this in mind, plant the bulbs every 3 or 4 years for a constant succession of flower spires.

Cardiocrinum does not mix well with other plants; it has a stately character that demands planting alone, perhaps at the edge of a winding woodland path. It looks especially attractive when emerging from a short, grassy area, but this is not always possible since quality grass does not always grow in the shade of trees. As an alternative, plant the bulbs among a shade-tolerant, low-growing scrambler like *Lysimachia nummularia* (creeping Jennie), where they will rise above the leafy ground cover.

(above) *Of all the gladioli available,* Gladiolus communis *supsp.* byzantinus *is one of the most attractive, with delicate-looking, vivid magenta flowers. It is a highly desirable member of the border because, flowering in early summer, it lends color and form to the area before the main show begins. It is also a hardy bulb—unlike other gladioli, which may need lifting over winter, the bulbs can be left in the garden the year round. If left undisturbed,* G. c. byzantinus *will grow into large patches.*

While the majority of summer-flowering bulbs demand hot, sunny conditions in well-drained soil, there are also plants for damp conditions; the beautiful *Nomocharis* represents one of the best. These high-mountain bulbs from Asia like rich, cool, damp soil that does not get waterlogged. To offset the exotic-looking blossoms, interplant them with delicately fronded hardy ferns such as *Athyrium filix-femina* (lady fern) and *Polystichum setiferum* (soft shield fern), and other finely cut foliage in different greens.

The easiest *Nomocharis* to grow is *N. mairei*, a lovely plant rarely reaching more than 2½ ft (75 cm) in height. Its drooping, saucer-shaped icy white flowers are liberally spotted with a deep rose-purple color. This plant looks most attractive when peeping out from a ferny carpet of the low-growing *Polystichum setiferum* 'Proliferum.'

Both *Nomocharis saluenensis*, with its bowl-shaped blossoms of pale rose-pink, and the pale pink, spotted *N. pardanthina* are bulky plants that look best when grouped together, especially when planted about 9 in (23 cm) apart in a sea of green fern fronds. The fern, *Athyrium filix-femina* 'Minutissimum,' is a fine companion, bearing a great profusion of very pale pea-green fronds.

(above) *For an informal display of contrasting but muted colors, the orangy-apricot* Gladiolus *'Perky' is here grown against a background planting of soft pink-flowered* Lavatera olbia. *The abundance of surrounding foliage provides a subtle color contrast.*

(left) *The main color in this border is supplied by* Gladiolus communis *supsp.* byzantinus *and* Iris *'Wild Echo,' along with the pink rose growing behind them. The introduction of red strengthens the color scheme and gives it some variety.*

Naturalizing

Most gardeners are familiar with a mass of spring-flowering golden daffodils standing proudly in the grass but may be less familiar with a carpet of naturalized summer-flowering magenta-crimson *Gladiolus communis* subsp. *byzantinus*. When grown in the appropriate grass, the effect is spectacular.

It is important to select the right grass when naturalizing summer bulbs since some types of grass can easily swamp the bulbs—something that is not a problem with spring bulbs. Ordinary coarse grasses in unkempt corners of the garden cannot be used for naturalizing; instead, the bulbs should be planted and fescue grass grown over the top so that the two root systems do not compete for space and nutrients.

A number of lilies can also be naturalized in fine grass, such as *Lilium martagon* (martagon lily). Although not the most striking lily, with its pinkish-purple or wine-red pendent Turk's cap blossom, it is still one of the easiest to grow, even if it is slow to mature from seed. Growing to a height of approximately 3 ft (90 cm), it is ideal for open spaces among trees; by the time the bulb flowers, the grass will have grown tall enough to mask the stems of the lily. In addition to the common species, there is an even lovelier white-flowered selection called 'Album,' which is of similar habit and disposition. Unlike many other lilies, it tolerates lime and, with a natural distribution including Siberia and Mongolia, is unusually hardy. Along with *L. duchartrei*, it prospers in a fine grassy area in the light shade of a few trees, lending itself well to woodland situations, perhaps interplanted with soft clumps of *Milium effusum* 'Aureum' (wood millet).

Lilium hansonii also responds well to naturalizing, although it is most frequently used in mixed plantings. The thick-petaled blossoms in deep yellow-orange are similar in appearance to *L. martagon*, although taller. Like *L. martagon*, *L. hansonii* is lime tolerant and after a year or two spreads freely to form sizable groups about 1-2 ft (30-60 cm) wide.

In damp areas *Lilium pardalinum* makes a good showing, spreading by means of a horizontal rhizomelike growth around which distinctive whitish bulbs are clustered. It flourishes in heavy damp soil but does not do well when waterlogged. In favorable conditions it produces bold flower stems up to 5 ft (1.5 m) high, which support nodding masses of pale reddish-orange blossoms in midsummer. Use *L. pardalinum* as a background plant among other tall plants such as meadowsweet and *Aruncus dioicus*.

A native of wet meadows, *Camassia* can also be naturalized. However, these plants suffer badly if they have to compete with vigorous grass. In the garden, only plant them among cultivated grass of a fine variety of fescues and bents. Several species can be grown, but *C. leichtlinii* is a strong grower, well suited to naturalizing. It has spikes of blue or violet-blue flowers, occasionally cream or white, and is commonly available.

The summer-flowering *Ornithogalum arabicum* can also be used for naturalizing, with its stout spikes of flower stems, sporting up to a dozen pearly white flowers, rising out of handsome dark green leaves. Given a well-drained soil and a sloping site in a sunny spot, without a heavy growth of grass, it should do well. For a shadier spot early in the season, grow *Nectaroscordum siculum* subsp. *bulgaricum*; the pendent, bell-shaped white flowers, flushed red and green are held on tall, thin stems and look particularly good when sited in dappled shade among other foliage.

(above) *The naturalized* Lilium martagon *looks better at the edge of a woodland than in a border, unlike* Lilium *'Pink Sensation' (above center),*

which is at home in either site. The delicate-looking Gladiolus papilio *(above right) holds its own in fine grass, where, if left undisturbed, it will spread.*

(right) *It is easy to create the impression of a naturalized flowerbed by growing hybrid lilies at random. Here they push up among lavender.*

Bedding displays

Summer-flowering bulbs can be used in bedding displays (see p. 25), planted close together to form a dense, colorful carpet or mixed with other bedding plants to add height to the flowerbed. Most bulbs need an open, sunny spot and well-drained soil. In the case of mass plantings, the soil should be even in structure and fertility to ensure uniform growth.

Tuberous-rooted begonias are the most useful and versatile plants for bedding. They are available in a wide array of strong colors, with blossoms that vary from the simple single and double kinds to the carnation type; attractive frilled varieties are also available. The strong, fleshy foliage provides an excellent foil for the blooms, and the plants completely cover the soil. The double tuberous begonias with smaller flowers, popularly sold by color, are perfect for summer beds. They have individual blossoms up to 3 in (7.5 cm) wide and are weather resistant. Different-colored begonias should come from the same series or strain. Among the most useful are the Non-stop color forms, because they are all of uniform height and stature.

Some cultivars grown by enthusiasts are expensive and not suitable for use in large quantities. The majority of these begonias have long, frilly flowers that are too heavy to tolerate life outdoors, as they are easily damaged by wind and rain; they tend to be favored by indoor gardeners, who grow them as house plants.

Single colors are the best for making an impact. Begonias of one color can be massed together, with an occasional highlight from a plant of a different color to give the display a lift. Color can also be used to create illusions. Mixed colors make a bed look bright, busy, and much smaller; the same bed planted with a single color looks much bigger. Tiny corners can be made to appear larger by a single light color such as a subtle shade of yellow or pink, but darker colors like red will make an area appear smaller than it is.

Dot plants in bedding displays of begonias should be selected with care. To avoid color clashes, brightly colored dot plants should be planted sparingly among vivid plants in spacious gardens. The best dot plants are those with foliage that complements the heavy leaves and blooms of the begonias. A well-grown *Kochia scoparia* (burning bush) is an ideal choice; it forms a mound of delicate foliage of very pale green, turning fiery red or purple in the fall. With its rounded form, it always looks good in a circular bed. *Grevillea robusta* (silk oak) is also recommended for mixing with begonias in any open bed. However, it needs to be a few years old before it is tall enough to have enough impact among other plants. With its finely divided, dark olive-green

foliage, it is worth retaining for four or five seasons, after which the plant should be replaced. For a large formal bedding display, plant *Canna* × *generalis* 'Black Knight' among deep crimson begonias, surrounded by scarlet-flowered begonias with copper-colored foliage. Lighten the shades of the begonias toward the edge of the bed: fade deep orange into clear yellow, finishing off the display with an edge of primrose-yellow. A more restrained combination consists of white-flowered begonias planted around the edge of a bed of *Crocosmia* 'Citronella' and white galtonias, with a centerpiece of deep golden *Gladiolus* 'Peter Pears' or *Lilium* 'Amber Gold.'

In shady formal gardens, tuberous-rooted begonias can be grown in the manner of annual bedding plants, arranged in fanciful shapes and surrounded by a neatly mowed lawn. For a more adventurous approach, plant a checkerboard of contrasting colors or create various motifs. Such complicated

(left) *Tuberous begonias are ideal for summer bedding displays, where their opulent flowers make a strong impact.*

(above) *With regular deadheading and feeding, begonias make a long-lasting focal point.*

designs work only with large, clearly defined arrangements, so do not be tempted by elaborate shapes; simplicity is the key. These patterns are best achieved with striking contrasting or complementary colors used in bold strokes; a design with strong central colors bordered by a band of a lighter hue is very effective. In fact, tuberous begonias often look more attractive when bordered by a different type of plant; neatly trimmed dwarf box edging is ideal. Alternatives include the blue-green 4 in (10 cm) high grass *Festuca glauca* (blue fescue) and the silver *Chrysanthemum hosmariense* and the gold *C. ptarmiciflorum*.

No other group of bulbs is as good for mass bedding, except perhaps some of the modern lilies, which can also be used as highlights or complementary plants to bedding annuals. However, lilies do not yield the same quality and continuity of flowers produced by tuberous begonias, and the cost of a large lily display is prohibitive.

The cannas or Indian shot plants, with their large green or bronze bananalike foliage, are popular and are often displayed in park beds. While they are noted for their handsome foliage, cannas also produce bright yellow, orange, pink, or red flower spikes that superficially resemble gladioli.

Although they are not really bulbous plants, having tough, fleshy rootstocks, cannas are regularly available from bulb

among a solid bed of red geraniums or salvias and a purple or bronze foliage type grown with lemon-flowered French marigolds. For a more Victorian touch, use a canna as the focal point in a bedding display of the purplish or blue-purple-flowered *Verbena* or *Calceolaria*, a slightly unruly but still formal plant that bears yellow or copper-colored flowers. *Heliotropium* (heliotrope) can be neatly clipped or left to take on its own shape; its flowers come in various shades of purple.

Zantedeschia aethiopica (arum lily) can take on the role of a dot plant in a summer bed, although it is usually associated with bogs or water gardens. As well as thriving in wet or damp

merchants during early spring and are worth considering. A few cultivars are available, but cannas are normally sold by flower and leaf color. A handful of plants is usually enough for a bedding display. As the foliage shrivels in frosty weather, planting should occur only in more clement periods, and since this also applies to companion bedding plants, both should be planted together.

Cannas grow well with most summer bedding plants. Two recommended choices include a bold green-leaved variety

(above) *To create an informal monochromatic bedding display, plant* Crocosmia *'Citronella,' antirrhinums, tagetas, and African marigolds.*

(right)*The familiar canna lily adds height to an otherwise uniform planting,* Canna × generalis *'Wyoming' is used here.*

conditions, if carefully cultivated, the arum lily prospers in the garden border. Use it in the same way as a canna, allowing the fine green leaves to give height and a hint of tropical elegance to a small bedding display. Mix arum lilies with the bright colors of French marigolds, impatiens, tagetes, or antirrhinums.

Rock gardens

Several small summer-flowering bulbs do well in a rock garden. These varieties need hot, sunny, well-drained locations. Either plant them in the soil or put them in pots and bury the pots in the rock garden.

Sparaxis is the most successful of the short-growing summer bulbs. Popularly known as the harlequin flower, it produces delicate, brightly colored blossoms on slender, wandlike stems. This delightful little plant, with a pink, peach, or reddish hue, often prospers in the open ground of the rock garden in a well-drained spot between the rocks. However, since it

Ixia (corn lily) is also unpredictable when planted directly in a rock garden and is more reliable first grown in pots and then plunged into a vacant space in the garden. These brightly colored African plants produce exotic star-shaped blossoms on strong, wiry stems that show up clearly against a background of fine gravel, but they do not perform well with sandstone. Since the flowers open only during the afternoon and evening, be sure to place them in a spot that receives sun at this time of day.

Rhodohypoxis can be grown the same way in pots. But if conditions are favorable outside and the soil is well drained,

grows quickly and the emerging growth is vulnerable to frost damage, it is more reliable when grown in a pot buried in the soil and removed later during winter.

Sparaxis is best displayed against dark, flat stones that provide some shelter. These bulbs are difficult to grow with other plants but can be interplanted with creeping thymes, such as *Thymus serpyllum* 'Coccineus' and the gray-leaved *T. lanuginosus*, or among the clump-forming ornamental onion *Allium narcissiflorum*.

you can plant it directly into the ground and it should grow from year to year. The very pale pink flowers mix well with the bluish purple of *Edraianthus pumilio* or, for a more subtle planting, a yellowish-green patch of *Hermodactylus tuberosus*. In more sheltered areas, *Anomatheca* will establish itself in an open rock garden in a hot, sunny spot, but it is much more reliable grown in pots. It is usually planted alone as it is easily swamped by other plants; it looks better when set against the hardness of rock, sand, or a fine mulch.

Containers, window boxes, and hanging baskets

Although there are fewer opportunities for growing bulbs in containers, window boxes, and hanging baskets in summer than in spring, plenty of imaginative summer plantings are still possible.

Begonias are the most useful group of plants for container planting. They are colorful plants available in white, pink, red, orange, and yellow. The pendulous

(above) *Begonias are available in a wide range of bright colors. Here, the tumbling red flowers create a soft, informal effect.*

kinds, either a single cultivar or a mixed variety, are especially well suited to hanging baskets due to their drooping flowers, particularly if grown alone or with other begonias such as the tuberous kinds. Used in a mixed planting, they never thrive, mainly because their soil requirements are too demanding. But, given a rich organic potting mixture, such as a peat-based soilless type, they will prosper. Grow a single cultivar in one color, pushing one or two tubers into the soil at the sides of the basket and on top. Pendulous begonias also look spectacular tumbling out of window boxes. In a large window box, the taller-growing, double-flowered tuberous begonia cultivars provide height and a good background, while the pendulous kinds can be used to fill the

foreground and spill over the edge. Each benefits from regular deadheading and removal of faded leaves.

In another window box, grow *Oxalis*, although avoid planting it in hanging baskets, which it dislikes. Its neatly mounded growth of cloverlike leaves and white, pink, or purple blooms is good for filling lower spaces and permits taller plants to grow through it. Brightly colored, upright antirrhinums grow well with oxalis, as do the various kinds of sweet-scented stocks. A group of oxalises on their own makes a handsome display; they are especially useful for narrow window boxes where there is little root room, or terra-cotta pots with limited soil space. Plant the fleshy rootstock in spring, ideally in a soil-based potting mixture. Although oxalis is a resilient plant, it sometimes rots—which can lead to complete defoliation in extreme cases—when it is planted in a soilless potting mixture.

(above) *A mixed group of icy white* Lilium regale *'Album' and cream-colored* Lilium *'Mont Blanc' highlight a dark corner.*

Sunny summer window boxes can be enlivened by the vivid purple, rose, and red tubular or funnel-shaped blossoms of *Achimenes* (or hot-water plant). Although usually regarded as an indoor plant, if given a little protection from the wind and grown in an organic growing medium, it will prosper. It does not mix well with other plants, apart from a few nephrolepis ferns.

While *Babiana* (baboon root) is normally planted in fall for spring flowering in greenhouses, in a window box it will flower in summer if planted during spring. Like begonias, babiana must have a sunny spot and ample moisture, although during the early stages of growth the soil must not become too wet. A vividly colored plant with exotic-looking bright blue, cream, or crimson blossoms, it is difficult to interplant with anything other than foliage; the various

(left) *Gladioli are ideal for a formal, elegant container display, here planted with begonias and trailing ivy.*

(right) *The exquisitely fragrant* Lilium regale, *with its purple-streaked white petals, is one of the easiest lilies to grow and propagate.*

gray-leaved helichrysums, if kept under control by regular trimming, are the most suitable companions.

Numerous bulbs are suitable for containers, including lilies, which are ideal for larger pots. 'Citronella' is a good one to try; it grows up to 5 ft (1.5 m) high and has bright yellow flowers. For the base of the display, plant the tender *Bidens ferulifolia* (bur marigold), an annual with fennel-like leaves that is liberally covered with yellow daisylike flowers and bushes out if pruned regularly. Highly scented varieties benefit from being grown on their own in pots—say, three bulbs in each container. 'Star Gazer' (crimson-pink trumpets), 'Black Dragon' (white, maroon on the outside), 'Imperial Gold' (shiny white flowers speckled with red and yellow stripes), and 'Pink Perfection' (bright pink) can all be relied upon to produce a heavy, sweet perfume. Gardeners new to lilies who want to try one fail-safe variety should opt for *Lilium regale*, an outright winner that never disappoints. At the other extreme, the splendid *L. duchartrei*, with white flowers flecked maroon, can be tricky; it needs damp, shady conditions and plenty of peat-enriched soil. If you prefer a slightly more unusual lily, then *L. × testaceum* (Nankeen lily) is both easily grown and rarely seen, producing nodding Turk's cap, light orange to brown-yellow flowers with a strong fragrance.

(above) *Warm shades of pink make this a charming summer window-box display, with begonias, dahlias, and dianthus in a simple terra-cotta container.*

Cannas are excellent for containers and, if placed on a patio or terrace, will create an exotic subtropical atmosphere. They look good in square or round terra-cotta pots. These plants' leaves are every bit as exciting as their spires of brilliantly colored red, orange, or yellow-edged blossoms. If the flower spikes are removed as soon as they appear, most of the plant's energy will be channeled into the foliage.

As cannas need a moist, rich growing medium and a warm, sunny spot, neighboring plants must be chosen with

(left) *This classical-style urn filled with yellow lilies and begonias needs a sheltered site to protect the lilies from any inclement weather.*

care. One of the finest combinations involves the blue *Scaevola* and the bronze-leaved canna; the tumbling succulence of *Scaevola* provides a particularly pleasing planting in a dark wooden tub. Bronze- or copper-leaved cannas also look good when planted with rosette-forming echeverias. These symmetrical, often olive-gray-leaved plants are technically succulents, and they do not grow well in the same heavy soil conditions as cannas. Bury them in their pots in well-drained soil around the stately dark foliage of the cannas, and they will form a pleasing base planting under the cannas.

Zantedeschia is too tall and bulky to rest easily in small containers but is a first-class plant for large pots. Boldly decorated terra-cotta pots and vases with deep, narrow necks are especially appropriate; choose those evocative of North Africa, the plant's homeland. These bulbs add a rich touch with their bold dark green foliage and contrasting snow-white spathes. The shorter-growing *Z. aethiopica* 'Crowborough' and the popular white species *Z. aethiopica* are very reliable when provided with a rich, heavy soil, plenty of water, and a

(below) *Daring in its simplicity, this planting relies on the perfection of the zantedeschias and a simple planter for a stylish effect.*

(above) *Pendulous begonias are ideal for hanging baskets, where their graceful drooping stems and flowers can be admired.*

sunny site. Mix them with *Lysimachia nummularia* (creeping Jennie), a moisture-lover with slender stems of bright green rounded leaves that are studded with yellow buttercuplike flowers in summer. This easily grown, tumbling plant has a softening effect but can also provide a good contrast with the golden-leaved *L. n.* 'Aurea.'

The large purple-flower *Allium giganteum* is a bigger, brasher plant that requires bold companion plants. Given its height and the architectural value of its rounded heads, the underplanting should be short and capable of dominating the container when the allium fades. Herbaceous tradescantias such as *Tradescantia virginiana* 'Isis' (spiderwort) are an excellent choice, providing short, bright green foliage when the allium is blossoming and continuing with bright blue flowers as the summer progresses. Later, tradescantias are equally pleasing when set against the dried, skeletonized heads of the allium.

A number of bulbous or tuberous plants grow best by themselves, not with other plants; their success partly depends on the design of the container they are grown in. The starker members of the arum family, such as *Sauromatum venosum* (voodoo lily) and *Dracunculus vulgaris* (dragon arum), have a sinister look; when planted in a bold group, their dark hooded spathes and gloomy leaves with boldly marbled stems call for the solidity of an antique lead container, perhaps a square solid tub with simple ornamentation. The same container can provide a different mood when the summer hyacinth, *Galtonia candicans*, is grown. This is a looser and more joyful-looking plant, which is a delight when growing through a carpet of the golden- or green-leaved helexine. *Dierama pulcherrimum* (angel's fishing rod or wand flower), excellent for a permanent planting, appears graceful, with its arching stems and pendulous pink or rose blossoms. It harmonizes well with either a soft green arrangement or a warmer silver-and-gray planting. This is a plant for a larger container with long-term plantings; it suffers when uprooted and moved.

Mixed tub plantings should utilize a number of bulbs that do not justify being grown as single specimens. They provide invaluable highlights for several weeks of the year, retiring gracefully among the foliage of their neighbors when flowering is over. *Nectaroscordum siculum*, a curious member of the onion family, is one of the most useful examples. Looking ill at ease in other parts of the garden, it is suitable for growing in a container. This bulb produces tall flower stems some 3 ft (90 cm) high and individual greenish-white and maroon blooms arranged in loose umbels. If allowed to remain after flowering, they turn into large seed capsules that are perfect for drying for winter flower arrangements. *Nectaroscordum* does not blend well with brightly colored plants and instead needs companions that are better known for their foliage, such as thyme, hyssop, horehound, and marjoram.

Indoors

A wide and interesting range of summer-flowering bulbous and tuberous plants grow well in greenhouses, sunrooms, or porches. Many also tolerate life on the windowsill.

The most useful and adaptable group of indoor bulbs are the achimenes, commonly known as hot-water plants. Grow these brightly colored plants in well-drained, richly organic soil, either in a pot on a windowsill or in a hanging planter. They thrive in bright spots but do not like direct sunlight. Provided they are not mixed with other plants, they will prosper; plant the strange-looking rootstocks during early spring in the warmth of a living room. Place several rootstocks in a single container or put them all in a tray of soil until they have sprouted and then replant them in pots or containers, pairing those of even growth for a uniform display.

(above) *This container planting of white begonias and cream-colored dahlias creates a cool, refined display.*

(right) *Arum lilies, here planted in a moss-lined container decorated with larch twigs, lend themselves well to dramatic arrangements.*

Once established in their pots, achimenes require little attention, but they must never be allowed to dry out because the wilted foliage is almost impossible to revive. During the growth period, a liquid fertilizer is beneficial and should be continued at regular intervals

until the flowering season comes to a close. Achimenes can be staked with twigs to support their drooping leaves, and if the twigs are positioned as soon as the shoots appear, the plants will naturally cover them. When growing achimenes in a hanging pot, however, allow them to tumble naturally over the edge.

Chlidanthus fragrans is a beautiful and richly fragrant bulb from Latin America that is easy to grow in a greenhouse or sunroom. The bulbs are similar to those of daffodils but require a shallower planting; the nose of the bulb should be sparingly covered. Use a soil-based potting mixture and plant the bulbs in pots during early spring. Staking is not necessary as the flower stems rarely exceed 1 ft (30 cm) in height and are borne in small, loose umbels.

Albucas also grow successfully indoors. The waxy white flowers are striped with red and have a distinctive fragrance. If given a late summer or early fall resting period, they provide a reliable display every year. The bulbs are sold during the fall and should be planted in a good soil-based potting mix in individual pots. When they start to grow, feed them regularly using a high-potash fertilizer; an application every 3 weeks or so is adequate. These bulbs do not normally require staking, although

(above) *Begonias make adaptable and effective houseplants; select a flower color to blend in with the color scheme of the room.*

(above) *The velvety blooms of assorted gloxinias are a familiar sight, and a long succession of flowers can be achieved with a little care.*

the tall *Albuca nelsonii* can become unruly and needs some support.

For an exciting indoor bulb during the summer months, choose *Haemanthus* for its tropical and exotic appearance. Best planted as a solitary bulb, it is simple to grow if planted in a free-draining potting mixture in a large pot. The most popular type is the shaving brush plant, *Haemanthus albiflos*. It has bold white or greenish flower heads with upright protruding stamens that resemble a shaving brush. The blossoms continue for a number of weeks, and where the bulbs are well established, a succession of flowers from daughter bulbs usually develop into congested groups. These need separating out periodically if the plants are to maintain their vigor. *H. coccineus* is different, with short, stiff, mottled stems supporting large heads of bright coral-red blossoms. These are followed by very showy strap-shaped leaves that lie flat against the surface of the soil. The blood flower, *H. katherinae*, has even larger, rounded heads of bright scarlet blossoms held on stems reaching up to 1 1/2 ft (45 cm)

high. Its leaves are not as coarse and leathery as *H. coccineus* and are carried separately from the flower stem. It is an excellent plant for a sunroom or greenhouse.

Hymenocallis can also be grown indoors, although it is not as showy as *Haemanthus*. The best species is *Hymenocallis narcissiflora*, known as the sea daffodil. Exotic pure white blossoms are carried on stout stems up to 1 1/2 ft (45 cm) high, and the plant looks its best when placed in a container with evergreen foliage. Unlike many other bulbs, it is easy to accommodate and will tolerate the soil and growing conditions of other indoor plants. In addition to the popular species, there is a hybrid called 'Sulfur Queen,' with blossoms of pale sulfur-yellow.

Sprekelia is a much-loved indoor bulb that can be grown almost anywhere, from the greenhouse to the windowsill. Popularly referred to as the Jacobean lily, it produces startling bright red orchidlike blossoms on strong stems 1 ft (30 cm) high. These are followed by dark green, narrow, straplike leaves. *Sprekelia* should be grown in a free-draining potting soil, in a container that is large enough to accommodate its extended root system; a pot 6 in (15 cm) in diameter is adequate for a single mature bulb.

Just as striking in appearance is *Gloriosa*, a genus of climbing lilylike plants. These bulbs can be grown, given enough support, in a pot, but are better when allowed to scramble up wires fixed to the wall of a greenhouse or conservatory. Plant the tubers during early spring in an organically rich potting mixture; a soilless mix is highly recommended. Put two or three tubers into a single 6 in (15 cm) pot about 1-2 in (2.5-5 cm) apart to ensure a good display and provide enough warmth—55-65°F (13-18°C)—to start them well into growth. Cultivation is simple; keep the plants moist, but not too wet, and regularly spray them with both a systemic fungicide and insecticide to prevent an outbreak of mildew as well as to control the spread of aphids.

Gloriosa superba is the most popular species that tolerates cool conditions.

(above) Lilium longiflorum, *with its exotic appearance and heady scent, is used here for a glamorous display.*

Its deep orange and red blossoms look similar to an exotic Turk's cap lily, but its petals are much thinner. *G. s.* 'Rothschildiana' is even finer, with crimson flowers marked with yellow. Both have narrow, shiny green leaves and tendrils that enable them to cling to supports. *Sandersonia aurantiaca* is closely related to the gloriosa and behaves in a similar way, producing scrambling stems some 2 ft (60 cm) high, which are sprinkled with soft orange, pendent, urn-shaped flowers.

Plant the tubers in pots filled with a rich organic soil, provide a simple plant support or twiggy stakes, and keep well watered. Unlike *Gloriosa*, *Sandersonia aurantiaca* can be grown in more modest surroundings if space is limited. The more tender *Littonia modesta* is similar in habitat although it can sometimes grow to a height of 6 ft (1.8 m) in favorable conditions. It tolerates a greenhouse in summer, provided it is started into growth by warmer conditions. Plant the bulbs in a rich organic medium and keep it moist; if given sufficient light, it will produce a continuous mass of bright orange-red bell-shaped flowers throughout summer.

Polianthes tuberosa (tuberose) is an underrated bulb that is now found only in the catalogs of specialist bulb growers. One of the finest florist's flowers, it has beautiful racemes of waxy white blossoms, which have a delicious sweet scent. Although a single-flowered bulb, the one usually offered to gardeners is the old-fashioned double cultivar called 'The Pearl.' In a greenhouse, summer cultivation is best for the tuberose. Plant the bulbs during spring in a soil-based potting mixture, several to a pot, and insert plant supports. When cultivated merely for cut flowers, the foliage can be allowed to grow unrestrained, the flowers developing naturally on strong, upright stems.

Cut flowers

There are several favorite summer-flowering bulbs which are excellent for cutting. For traditional cut-flower arrangements, the stems can be placed in a variety of vases, both ceramic and glass, or more informal everyday containers such as mugs and bottles. A more ambitious approach, however, might include summer fruits and vegetables worked into the floral display, ideal for a table decoration.

(above) *This harmonious arrangement in shades of purple consists of freesias, irises, scillas, Solomon's seal, and hosta leaves.*

Gladioli provide one of the finest summer cut flowers; the large-flowered cultivars represent a good example of plants that grow well away from a mixed border. Most gladioli need to be grown on their own because their large blossoms rarely fit the scale of a modest-size garden. However, as cut flowers they repay the extra attention given them with their colorful, long-lasting blooms.

There are innumerable varieties to choose from, but if a combination of garden decoration and cutting is required, select cultivars such as the scarlet 'Trader Horn' and 'Hunting Song,' the delicate pink 'Chanson,' and the rich orange-flowered 'Esta Bonita.'

Also recommended is the soft lemon-yellow 'Early Yellow,' the primrose-yellow 'Nova Lux,' 'Aldebaran,' with its bright yellow, deep red-blotched flowers, and 'Green Woodpecker,' an unusual gladiolus with lime-green, red-throated blooms. The pure white 'Lady Godiva,' 'Ice Cap' and 'White Friendship' are also popular. For a unique cut flower, look for the lilac-rose 'Vidi Napoli' or the cyclamen-purple 'Fidelio.'

Gladioli do not have to have large flowers and long stems to make good cut flowers; many of the shorter-stemmed and smaller-flowered cultivars make attractive mixed arrangements. For the small garden, they can serve a dual purpose—as cut flowers and as part of the mixed border display. If

(left) Gloriosa, lilies, gladioli and irises make up this impressive display, which is suitable for a large room or hallway.

planted close together, the stems will not even need staking.

With formally grown gladioli, a planting distance of 6 in (15 cm) between corms and $1\frac{1}{2}$ ft (45 cm) between rows is essential; with informally planted smaller-growing varieties, a planting distance of 3 in (7.5 cm) is adequate. Groupings in a mixed border require a minimum of 20 corms 3 in (8 cm) apart in an irregular patch, and this fairly dense arrangement not only helps produce a pleasing floral display but also permits every other flower spike to be cut without ruining the overall effect.

The best smaller-flowered gladioli for cutting come from the early-flowering Nanus group. The corms should be planted in pots of well-drained soil in fall

(below) Nectarines and grapes have been added to this colorful show of Gloriosa superba, Lilium 'Star Gazer,' freesias, and foliage.

to gain a late-spring or early-summer flush of blossoms. However, they are more frequently planted in spring at the same time as the large-flowered gladioli, blossoming slightly ahead, during mid- to late summer. There are innumerable proven and reliable cultivars to choose from: 'The Bride' (pure white), 'Peach Blossom' (shell-pink), and 'Amanda Mahy' (deep salmon-pink). But best of all, and a highlight of any summer garden or cut-flower arrangement, is 'Nymph,' a snowy white cultivar with a rich crimson throat.

Because gladioli are large and imposing, they are best used on their own or with complementary foliage so that their form can be fully appreciated. The white 'Ice Cap' looks particularly good with the smooth, silvery leaves of eucalyptus. For a more colorful arrangement, add the striking red blooms of 'Hunting

Song' as well as branches of dark red-leaved prunus. To create an impressive formal display, place the arrangement on a pedestal.

While gladioli generally hold court among the cut flowers of summer, many of the popular lilies are also excellent for cutting and will last up to 2 weeks indoors. When grown specifically for this purpose, they should be allocated their own corner, as nothing looks worse in a border than the basal remains of decapitated lilies. The plants do not need to be grown in rows for cutting but can be placed in a patch, where they can be picked at will. As they may be a permanent feature, ensure that the soil is in good condition to begin with, incorporating plenty of well-rotted organic matter, and eliminate perennial weeds.

Lilies are elaborate, decorative flowers with a sense of majesty and opulence. They are very adaptable and can be mixed with other summer blooms such as irises, gladioli, and Solomon's seal. For the greatest effect, use them on their own and put them in a simple container so they can be fully appreciated. The beautiful white *Lilium longiflorum* is raised extensively by commercial growers for the florist trade, but it is a short-lived, unpredictable bulb unless cultivated under glass; grown in the open it requires a very warm summer to perform well. There are innumerable cultivars of hybrid lilies to choose from, but Mid-century hybrids like the orange-red 'Enchantment' are highly popular. A number of seedling strains, including the Bellingham hybrids, are also useful, as are species and their varieties, such as *L. lancifolium*, *L. hansonii*, and the late-summer-flowering *L. speciosum* 'Album' (white) and *L. s.* 'Rubrum' (carmine).

Dutch irises can also be cut for indoor use, although they last only a maximum

of 5 days. Along with later-flowering English counterparts, they are easy to grow, requiring a constant supply of moisture and a weed-free environment. Few pests or diseases trouble them, although it is best to scatter some slug pellets around emerging shoots during spring. The bulbs can be planted at a depth of 3 in (7.5 cm) during the fall so that a root system can be established quickly, but in cold areas, especially with heavier soils, an early spring planting is preferable. If grown in a border, plant the bulbs at random 4 in (10 cm) apart; if specifically for cutting, plant the bulbs in rows 1½ ft (45 cm) apart, at 4 in (10 cm) intervals.

(above) *The fabulous Casablanca lily is thrown into relief by the finely etched lines of contorted willow in this candle decoration.*

The light blue 'Wedgwood,' dark blue 'Imperator,' 'White Superior,' and 'Yellow Queen' are the most frequently grown Dutch irises, while 'Blue Giant' and 'Mont Blanc' are among the best-known English irises. Although the beauty of the flowers is best appreciated when they are used alone, either in single colors or in various shades, irises also lend themselves well to mixed arrangements. Successful plant and color combinations include dark blue irises and yellow roses, mid- and light

blue irises with lime-green *Nicotiana* and variegated periwinkle or hosta leaves, or mixed white and yellow irises with yellow lilies. For a more informal look, combine blue irises with pink roses, mixed with sweet peas and creamy white honeysuckle.

Ornithogalum thyrsoides (star-of-Bethlehem) can be highly effective when grouped in a mixed border. It demands full sun and free-draining soil. Like gladioli, it must be lifted and stored to survive the winter in cooler climates. When used for cutting, the bulbs are only likely to be good the second year if the flower stems alone are removed, leaving the foliage to build up the next season's food supply.

Star-of-Bethlehem will last for up to 3 weeks indoors. Bearing dense conical spikes of delicate white flowers, it is rarely used on its own but adds much to a mixed arrangement; a colorful display might include cornflowers, dianthus, lavender, and *Alchemilla mollis*. The florists' *Ranunculus* copes with damper and shadier conditions than *Ornithogalum thyrsoides*. These gorgeous cut flowers should be planted in succession for near-continuous summer flowering. A clump will produce abundant blooms, so that individual stems can be picked without ruining a border display. Mixed strains of turban ranunculuses are usually available, including the large-flowered 'Accolade.'

Such colorful flowers should be used to make a bold statement; you can create a vibrant arrangement using ranunculuses, marigolds, and poppies. The addition of dark green or gray foliage will intensify the hues; try to select plain-shaped leaves like hostas to offset the blooms. Ranunculuses can also be used on their own.

(right) *White lilies, gladioli, and ornithogalum are combined here with various fruits and vegetables to create this treelike arrangement.*

ACHIMENES
Hot-water plant

These summer-flowering tubers, which are best suited for a windowsill or sun-room, produce a long succession of colorful tubular flowers. Of the many species, the most available are selections or hybrids. The tubers should be obtained in spring and potted in a commercial potting soil; they look best if planted several to a pot. Place the plants in a light spot and keep them moist and warm, at a temperature of 60-65°F (16-18.5°C). At the end of summer, they can be dried off for winter and repotted the following spring; most will produce extra tubers. They are easy to increase by division of rhizomes or by seed in spring. Hardiness zone: 10

A. longiflora 'Paul Arnold'

A. longiflora (*above*)
This species has been used as the parent for many hybrids. The violet-blue long-tubed flowers are held on hairy stems, which grow to a height of about 1ft (30 cm). The leaves are oval and toothed, with purple-stained undersides. The variation *A.* 'Paul Arnold' has large, rich purple flowers; 'Flamingo' is an excellent deep red; 'Tarantella' has lovely soft pink flowers; 'Snow White' is a good clean white; and 'Peach Blossom' has pale peach-pink flowers, stained darker toward the center.

ACIDANTHERA

Although found under the name of *Acidanthera*, this bulb is now regarded as a gladiolus, as it is very similar in growth habit. Hailing from tropical Africa, it is not a hardy plant, although the bulbs can grow successfully if they are planted in spring and then lifted and stored for winter in a dry, frost-free place. Propagation is by freely produced offsets. Hardiness zone: 7.

A. bicolor 'Murielae'

A. bicolor (syn. *Gladiolus callianthus*) (*above*)
This species grows to a height of about 3 ft (90 cm), with erect sword-shaped leaves and spikes of large white flowers that are about 3 in (7.5 cm) across. The blooms are very fragrant. Each flower has a purple blotch in its center and a curved tube 3½ in (9 cm) long. *A. b.* 'Murielae' is a slightly larger, more robust cultivar.

ALBUCA

This little-known African genus is grown more for its rarity than for its display. Although not frost hardy, the summer-flowering species can be planted in late spring and lifted and stored for winter in a dry, frost-free place. A sunny spot in well-drained soil is suitable, but it also grows in pots in a greenhouse or sun-room. Albucas have flower spikes that consist of 3 outer spreading petals and 3 inner ones that are held together to form a tube. Propagation is by seed in spring. Hardiness zone: 10.

A. canadensis (*below*)
Flowering in late spring or early summer, *A. canadensis* has narrow leaves and 6 in (15 cm) tall spikes of small yellow flowers. Each petal is marked with a green stripe along its center.

A. canadensis

A. humilis
A dwarf plant only 2-4 in (5-10 cm) high, this albuca has up to 3 white flowers, each petal having a green stripe on the outside. It can be grown outside year-round in mild areas.

A. nelsonii
This robust plant reaches a height of 3 ft (90 cm) at flowering time. The spikes carry large white flowers with a brown or green stripe on each petal.

ALLIUM
Ornamental onion

The very popular alliums have attractive, showy flowers and are easy to grow. Most of the species listed below can be grown in full sun, in well-drained acid or alkaline soil. The bulbs are best planted in fall at a depth of approximately 2-4 in (5-10 cm) according to size; those sold as pot plants should be planted in spring. There are also a few spring- and fall-flowering alliums (see pp. 87 and 203).

The small flowers are held in umbels on top of the stems, and the plants look most striking when planted in a group. The taller species are known as "drumstick" alliums because they lose their leaves by flowering time; these types look better planted among other low-growing plants so the basal part of the bare stems is hidden. Most of the plants smell of onions, but only if the bulb is cut or bruised. Propagation is by offsets, which in some species are produced quite freely, or by seed, which may take up to 3 years to produce flowering bulbs. Hardiness zones: 4-6.

A. aflatunense

A. aflatunense (*above*)
A. aflatunense grows up to 3 ft (90 cm) in height, with many tiny, rich purple flowers held in umbels about 4 in (10 cm) across.

A. altissimum
Very similar to *A. aflatunense* in general appearance, this species has purple "drumsticks" held on long, bare stems.

A. amabile
This Chinese species of allium has small umbels made up of a few funnel-shaped flowers, which are a rich, deep reddish-pink color. It grows in grassy clumps approximately 4–6 in (10–15 cm) high and is suitable for a rock garden.

A. atropurpureum
This species reaches up to 3 ft (90 cm) in height at flowering time. It has strap-shaped basal leaves and bare stems, which carry almost flat or rounded umbels of dark purple flowers. Each umbel is 2–3 in (5–7.5 cm) across. Due to its height, it is suitable for planting in a border.

A. beesianum (*below*)
A lovely blue-flowering species, *A. beesianum* is suitable for a cool spot in a rock garden. It grows to a height of approximately 6–8 in (15–20 cm), with wiry stems carrying small umbels of pendent bright blue bells. Grown in a group, these alliums form clumps of slender, bottle-shaped plants.

A. beesianum

A. caeruleum
Very similar to *A. caesium*, this clump-forming allium has narrow, erect leaves and an umbel which consists of 30–50 star-shaped, blue flowers. The umbel measures approximately 1½ in (4 cm) in diameter.

A. caesium
This unusual "drumstick" allium has dense umbels of blue flowers, each umbel growing 1¾ in (4.5 cm) in diameter. The wiry stem grows up to 2 ft (60 cm) in height.

A. cernuum

A. cernuum (*above*)
This allium is 1–2 ft (30–60 cm) tall and has red-purple, pink, or white flowers.

A. christophii

A. christophii (**syn.** *A. albopilosum*) (*above*)
This bulb produces a large, symmetrical spherical umbel that grows 6–8 in (15–20 cm) in diameter. The umbel is made up of star-shaped purple flowers held on a stout stem ½–1½ ft (15–45 cm) tall. At the end of flowering, the petals become dry and spiny and can be used for flower arrangements.

A. cyaneum
The pendent, deep blue bell-shaped flowers of *A. cyaneum* are held in small umbels. The stalks of this clump-forming bulb reach 5–10 in (13–25 cm) in height. It is a useful plant for the rock garden.

A. cyathophorum farreri
Another clump-forming plant, this 6–12 in (15–30 cm) tall allium is also suitable for the rock garden. It has reddish-purple bell-shaped flowers held in small umbels.

A. flavum (*next column*)
One of the few yellow-flowering alliums, *A. flavum* has slender, wiry stems that reach

up to 1 ft (30 cm) in height. The loose umbels of small flowers are held on long stalks; these are usually upright but arch downward with the weight of the flowers.

A. flavum

A. giganteum (*below*)
As its name implies, this is an enormous plant. It has broad basal leaves and a thick stem that grows up to 6 ft (1.8 m) high. The round umbels are made up of countless tiny, rosy purple flowers measuring 4–6 in (10–15 cm) across. It needs a hot, sunny spot.

A. giganteum

A. macleanii (**syn.** *A. elatum*)
Although similar to *A. giganteum*, this allium is usually slightly smaller.

A. macranthum
A clump-forming species, *A. macranthum* grows to a height of 10–12 in (25–30 cm). It has loose umbels of large purple bell-shaped flowers, each about ½ in (15 mm) long.

A. mairei
This slender dwarf allium forms grassy clumps of 4–6 in (10–15 cm) long stems. These carry small umbels of pink funnel-shaped flowers.

A. moly

A. moly (*above*)

This popular European woodland species is very easy to cultivate and enjoys both semishade and sun. In early summer its broad gray leaves are topped by umbels measuring 2-3 in (5-7.5 cm) in diameter. The star-shaped flowers are bright yellow.

A. nigrum (*below*)

This allium has broad, strap-shaped basal leaves and a stout stem that can reach 3 ft (90 cm) high; this carries a large umbel 3-4 in (7.5-10 cm) across. In the center of each white flower, there is a blackish ovary that produces a dark eye.

A. nigrum

A. pulchellum (syn. A. carinatum subsp. pulchellum)

A. pulchellum seeds freely but the seed heads can be removed to prevent it from spreading. It grows 1-2 ft (30-60 cm) high and has umbels of pendent, bell-shaped purple flowers.

A. ramosum

This clump-forming allium grows about 10-16 in (25-40 cm) tall. The umbels are 1-2 in (2.5-5 cm) in diameter and consist of white flowers; each petal is marked with a darker vein along its center. Although not as

colorful and striking as other alliums, this perennial is easy to cultivate in borders.

A. rosenbachianum

A. rosenbachianum (*above*)

This allium has 3 ft (90 cm) high stems and spherical umbels made up of small dark purple flowers.

A. schoenoprasum

A. schoenoprasum (*above*)
Chives

Although a useful culinary plant, this decorative allium is worth growing as an ornamental. It is a clump-forming allium, with many narrow cylindrical leaves and, in mid-summer, dense umbels 2 in (5 cm) across. The showy flowers vary in color, from shades of pale purple to pink. The selection known as 'Forescate' has rosy pink flowers and is a particularly strong grower.

A. schubertii

This is an unusual plant, with stout stems reaching 2 ft (60 cm) high. It carries a loosely flowered but enormous umbel expanding 1½ ft (45 cm) across. The star-shaped flowers are pale pinkish purple, and they can be cut and dried for flower arrangements. *A. schubertii* requires a hot, sunny site.

A. sikkimense

A. sikkimense (*above*)

A clump-forming plant, this species has very narrow, grassy leaves and 4-8 in (10-20 cm) long stems. These carry small pendent umbels of blue flowers in late summer. *A. kansuense* is very similar.

A. sphaerocephalon

An easy-to-grow "drumstick" allium, *A. sphaerocephalon* has long, wiry stems 2-3 ft (60-90 cm) high. The dense umbels, about 1½ in (4 cm) in diameter, are made up of many dark purple flowers. This allium can be dried for winter flower arrangements.

A. stipitatum

One of the tall Asiatic "drumsticks," this species has large umbels 3-5 in (7.5-13 cm) wide. The individual flowers are small and star-shaped; they are mostly pale purple, but a white form is also available.

A. tuberosum (*below*)
Chinese or garlic chives

A. tuberosum can be grown as a culinary or decorative plant. The 1-2 in (2.5-5 cm) wide umbels consist of attractive star-shaped white flowers, and at flowering time, the stems grow to a height of 1-2 ft (30-60 cm). It is a clump-forming plant.

A. tuberosum

153

ANOMATHECA

An interesting little South African plant, *Anomatheca* has freesialike corms that are planted about 2 in (5 cm) deep in spring for midsummer flowering. Although they will withstand a light frost in cold areas, in areas where the ground freezes for long periods, it is best to lift the dormant corms in fall and store them in dry, frost-free conditions over winter. The corms produce offsets, but it is just as easy to propagate the bulb by seed. Seeds are produced freely, and seed-raised plants may flower in the same season if sown in a greenhouse in early spring. A sunny spot in ordinary, reasonably fertile garden soil is suitable. Hardiness zone: 9.

A. laxa (syn. *Lapeirousia cruenta*)
This species has narrow, upright sword-shaped leaves and short spikes of bright red flowers, each with a long tube. The petals open to about 1 in (2.5 cm) in diameter, the lower ones being marked with a darker red blotch. The plant reaches 6–12 in (15–30 cm) in height when in flower.

ARISAEMA

These tuberous-rooted plants are related to the arums (see Spring Directory, p. 88), but unlike a number of arums, arisaemas have a pleasant smell. They are winter-dormant bulbs, and although many are very hardy, some of the Himalayan and eastern Asiatic species start to grow early in the year and may get frost-damaged. The more tender ones can be lifted in fall and kept frost-free over winter for planting outside the following spring. They require dappled shade and must be planted at a depth of approximately 6 in (15 cm) in a well-drained, humus-rich soil.

Like an arum, an arisaema has tiny flowers that are produced on a pencil-like spadix and enclosed within a hooded spathe. The spadix may have a long tail-like appendage hanging out of the spathe, and in some species the spathe itself has the "tail" at its apex. Spikes of red berries may be produced in fall. These plants are best sown in winter, although they may be easier to propagate by detaching the offsets that form on the tubers of some species. They do not require much space at flowering time, but many types develop large leaves, with a spread of up to 3 ft (90 cm). Hardiness zones: 4–8.

A. amurense
An Asian species about 1½ ft (45 cm) high, *A. amurense* has 5-lobed leaves and hooded spathes with purple, green, and white stripes.

A. candidissimum (*below*)
This Chinese species is one of the most attractive and is very hardy. Appearing above ground early in summer, it produces striped pale pink and white cowl-like spathes, approximately 6 in (15 cm) long, just before the leaves appear. The leaves, up to 1 ft (30 cm) across, consist of 3 broad leaflets. This plant tolerates full sun.

A. candidissimum

A. consanguineum (*below*)
This very robust plant may reach 3 ft (90 cm) in height. It has a stout dark-spotted or blotched stem that carries an umbrellalike leaf made up of 12–20 narrow leaflets. The 6–8 in (15–20 cm) long spathe is purple with white stripes. It has a tail-like tip.

A. consanguineum

A. dracontium
A. dracontium has a green spathe with a long, protruding whip-like spadix. The leaves are divided into 7–15 leaflets and carried on stout stems up to 2½ ft (75 cm) tall.

A. ringens
This species has a green or purple spathe with a pale purple stripe. A dark purple edge flares out into a wide hood at the apex and is topped by 3-lobed leaves. It may need protection from late frosts.

A. sikokianum

A. sikokianum (*above*)
This striking early summer-flowering Japanese species has a deep purple-brown tubular spathe out of which protrudes a thick, white clublike spadix. The whole plant is about 1–2 ft (30–60 cm) tall, and the leaves, which appear slightly after the spathes, divide into 3–5 leaflets.

A. tortuosum
This Himalayan species gets its name from its long spadix, which has an 'S'-shaped bend as it emerges from the green spathe. The plant grows 2–4 ft (60 cm–1.2 m) high, with leaves that divide into as many as 17 leaflets.

A. triphyllum
Jack-in-the-pulpit
A popular North American species, the 3-lobed leaves are held on 1–2 ft (30–60 cm) tall stems. The slightly shorter, green or purplish-flushed spathes are hooded at the apex. *A. atrorubens* is very similar and is regarded as synonymous with *A. triphyllum*.

BABIANA
Baboon root
These freesialike South African bulbs normally flower in winter or spring, but they are sometimes offered by mail-order catalogs for spring planting so they will flower in summer. However, if planted in spring, they will probably grow only during the first summer before reverting to their natural cycle of starting into growth in fall and dying down in spring. If planted in spring,

they require a sunny, well-drained site, with the corms buried at a depth of 2 in (5 cm). The bulbs are not frost hardy and must be lifted over winter, but in mild areas they can be planted permanently and are likely to behave as winter-spring growers. They are usually offered as a mixed collection of cream, yellow, blue, and violet. Propagation is by seed sown in fall. Hardiness zone: 9.

B. rubrocyanea (*below*)
One of the most colorful varieties, this plant has a short spike with funnel-shaped flowers that are 1½ in (4 cm) long. The blooms are red in the center and bright blue at the tips of the 6 petals. The plant reaches about 6-8 in (15-20 cm) in height at flowering time.

B. rubrocyanea

BEGONIA
Tuberous begonias are hardy in southern areas and slightly further north with a heavy mulch, but are suitable for planting only after the frosts are over. Tubers must be dug up before the frost or when flowering slows and stored over winter in peat moss at 40-50°F (5-10°C). For early blooming, start tubers indoors 2-3 months prior to outdoor planting time. Keep them barely moist in a greenhouse until the top growth appears. Propagation is by stem cuttings taken in summer or by division in spring. Hardiness zone: 10 for *B. grandis*; 9 for *B. sutherlandii*.

B. grandis (**syn. *B. evansiana***)
One of the hardiest of the tuberous-rooted begonias, *B. grandis* may be planted permanently in areas that receive only light frosts, provided it is given a sheltered position and humus-rich soil. This begonia grows 1-1½ ft (30-45 cm) high and has large pinkish-tinged leaves and pink flowers.

B. sutherlandii
This graceful begonia grows to a height of ½-1 ft (15-30 cm). It has leafy branches that spread out horizontally, reaching 1 ft (30 cm) or more across. The light orange flowers are produced over a long summer period. *B. sutherlandii* makes an attractive container plant when grown as a single specimen.

Tuberous hybrid groups
There are many types and cultivars, sometimes known as *B.* × *tuberhybrida*. A few of these are described below to give some idea of the range available.

Camellia-flowered begonias
These begonias are named for their tight, double flowers, which are similar in appearance to camellias. They produce upright stems, with large flowers in varying shades of pink, red, orange, and yellow; there is also a white version.

Double-flowered begonias
These begonias are upright in habit, producing very large double flowers in a range of colors and shades including red, orange, copper, pink, yellow, and white.

Nonstop begonias
These tuberous begonias are compact-growing hybrids, reaching 6-8 in (15-20 cm) in height. They start to flower earlier in the season than other types, continuing for a very long period. There are many colors to choose from, including orange, apricot, pink, yellow, and various shades of red.

B. 'Bertini'

B. 'Bertini' (*above*)
The hanging stems of this tuberous hybrid make it ideal for hanging baskets. The flowers are carried in loose clusters and are red or orange, with pointed petals.

B. 'Bouton de Rose'
This upright-growing begonia reaches up to 1½ ft (45 cm) in height. The white double flowers are edged with red.

B. 'Fimbriata' (*below*)
Of upright habit, this begonia has wavy-edged leaves and large double flowers. The petals are crimped at the edges, giving the effect of a double carnation.

B. 'Fimbriata'

B. 'Madame Helen Harms'
This is a double-flowering multiflora begonia, with large yellow flowers. It grows 1-2 ft (30-60 cm) tall.

B. 'Madame Richard Galle'
This upright multiflora begonia grows 1-2 ft (30-60 cm) high. It has large, double copper-colored flowers.

B. 'Marginata Crispa'
There are various color forms of this bicolored type, such as white with red edges and yellow with red edges. The petals are frilled or crimped around the edges. It grows 1-2 ft (30-60 cm) high.

B. 'Marmorata'
This tuberous begonia has carmine flowers with a white marbled pattern; each petal is waved and crimped at the edges. Growing upright, it reaches a height of 1-1½ ft (30-45 cm).

B. 'Pendula'
This type of tuberous begonia is good for hanging baskets because its slender stems hang down almost vertically, bearing clusters of large flowers throughout the summer. The flowers are usually semidouble, although some are singles; colors include red, pink, yellow, white, and orange.

BRIMEURA

A small, graceful bluebell-like plant, *Brimeura* flowers in late spring or early summer, depending on locality. The bulbs should be planted in fall in dappled shade, at a depth of about 2 in (5 cm), in humus-rich soil; several to a patch gives the best display. Seed is normally produced quite freely, and when growing well, the bulbs soon form a colony. Hardiness zone: 6.

B. amethystina (syn. *Hyacinthus amethystinus*) (*below*)

This aptly named bulb has a one-sided raceme of bright blue, pendent tubular bells. These are held on stems 6-8 in (15-20 cm) high, each flower reaching 1/2 in (15 mm) in length. 'Alba' is the pure white variant.

B. amethystina

BRODIAEA (including DICHELOSTEMMA and TRITELEIA)

These early summer bulbs are like alliums. Both types of bulb have star-shaped tubular flowers held in an umbel on top of a bare stem. Unlike the allium family, however, *Brodiaea* does not have the characteristic smell of onions.

A considerable number of species exist, but few are generally available. These North American plants are reasonably hardy and may be grown in sunny spots in soil that will dry out during the summer months. The corms, resembling those of the crocus, are planted in fall at a depth of 2-3 in (5-7.5 cm). Because the leaves look untidy and turn brown at flowering time, the bulbs look best when placed behind low-growing plants; small alpines or dwarf shrubs are suitable companions. Propagation is by digging up clumps in fall and removing the offsets or by seed sown in fall. Hardiness zones: 7-8.

B. ida-maia (*Dichelostemma ida-maia*) Californian firecracker

This very striking bulb is not as easy to grow as most species. It reaches a height of 1-1 1/2 ft (30-45 cm), and has a dense umbel of up to 12 tubular flowers, each about 1 3/4 in (4.5 cm) long. The lower half of the flower consists of a bright red tube; the upper part is made up of 6 reflexed green lobes.

B. ixioides

B. ixioides (syn. *Triteleia ixioides*) (*above*)

This well-known species, with a 4 in (10 cm) diameter umbel of star-shaped flowers, grows to a height of 1-1 1/4 ft (30-38 cm).

B. lactea (syn. *Titeleia hyacinthina*)

This bulb has dense, 2-3 in (5-7.5 cm) diameter umbels of white flowers, each about 1 in (2.5 cm) wide across the mouth. The stems grow 9-12 in (23-30 cm) high.

B. laxa (syn. *Triteleia laxa*) (*below*)

B. laxa has long-lasting large blue flowers. The wiry stems are 1-1 1/2 ft (30-45 cm) tall and carry loose umbels, each up to 6 in (15 cm) in diameter. The umbels are made up of funnel-shaped flowers that measure 1 in (2.5 cm) across at the mouth.

B.laxa

B. × tubergeniana

This begonia hybrid has large, lilac-blue flowers and is a vigorous grower.

B. 'Queen Fabiola'

B. 'Queen Fabiola' (*above*)

Again very similar to *B. laxa* in general appearance, *B.* 'Queen Fabiola' has rich, deep blue flowers.

CALOCHORTUS
Mariposa lily; cat's ears; globe lily, or fairy lantern

These beautiful North and Central American bulbs are not widely cultivated because it is difficult to grow them outside their native lands without protection. The flowers consist of 3 large inner petals and 3 much smaller, pointed outer ones. The mariposas have large upward-facing flowers, with gaudy zones of color in the center; the cat's ears have smaller upright flowers that have hair on the inside; and the globe lilies, or fairy lanterns, have pendent, almost globular flowers.

Although many are fairly hardy, they require a dry, warm period if they are to ripen after flowering in early summer, and are best grown in pots in a greenhouse or planted in a bulb frame. The bulbs are potted or planted in fall, in a sharply drained soil mix, at a depth of 3 1/2 in (9 cm). They require as much light as possible so that they do not become too elongated as they emerge in late winter.

Propagation is mainly by seed, which germinates very rapidly when sown in the fall, producing flowering bulbs in 3 or 4 years. Hardiness zones: 4-6.

C. albus

One of the fairy lanterns, *C. albus* has several pendent globes carried on a 1 ft (30 cm) high stem. The flowers are mostly a translucent

creamy white color, but are sometimes pinkish or reddish, each one measuring 1 in (2.5 cm) across.

C. amabilis

This calochortus is very similar in flower shape and size to *C. albus* but is deep yellow.

C. barbatus

C. barbatus (syn. Cyclobothra lutea) (*above*)
This Mexican species does not flower until late summer and is dormant in winter. The bulbs should be planted in spring. It grows to a height of 9–12 in (23–30 cm) and has pendent bell-shaped flowers that reach 1–1½ in (2.5-4 cm) across. These are a deep mustard color, with a hairlike lining inside.

C. luteus

C. luteus (*above*)
An upright-flowering mariposa, *C. luteus* has bright yellow flowers, often with brown marks in the center; they reach 2 in (5 cm) across. The stems are 10–12 in (25–30 cm) high.

C. splendens

Another mariposa, *C. splendens* has upright flowers 2 in (5 cm) wide. These are pale purple, with a darker blotch at the base of each inner petal.

C. superbus

Also a mariposa type, *C. superbus* has stems that are 2 ft (60 cm) tall, carrying upright flowers about 2 in (5 cm) in diameter. The color varies from white or yellow to lilac, with brown and yellow areas in the center.

C. uniflorus

This is one of the easiest species of calochortus to cultivate. It grows about 6–12 in (15–30 cm) high and has several erect lilac-colored flowers that measure approximately 2–2½ in (5-6.5 cm) in diameter and are held in an umbel.

C. venustus (*below*)

This mariposa has huge upturned flowers measuring nearly 3 in (7.5 cm) across. The white, yellow, purple, or red flowers are usually marked with a contrasting deep red blotch at the base of each petal. The plant may reach as much as 1½ ft (45 cm) in height in ideal growing conditions.

C. venustus

C. vestae (*below*)

Similar to *C. venustus*, *C. vestae* differs in the shape of the nectar area at the base of the petals. The flowers are white or pale purple, with dark brownish–red central patches.

C. vestae

C. weedii

The several erect yellow flowers, about 2 in (5 cm) in diameter, are speckled brown and hairy on the inside.

CAMASSIA

These native summer-flowering bulbs from North America have clusters of long, narrow leaves held in basal tufts and long racemes of star-shaped flowers. They require damp locations and enjoy growing in rough grass, between shrubs or alongside ponds. Propagation is by division or seed in fall. Hardiness zones: 4-5.

C. cusickii

C. cusickii (*above*)
The 2-4 ft (60 cm-1.2 m) high stems carry a raceme of many pale blue flowers.

C. leichtlinii 'Atrocaerulea'

C. leichtlinii (*above*)
A vigorous plant growing as high as 4½ ft (1.4 m), *C. leichtlinii* has striking racemes of large flowers, sometimes reaching as much as 3 in (7.5 cm) across. These flowers range in color from deep violet-blue to white. 'Alba' is a creamy white form that shows up well against a dark background. 'Atrocaerulea' is a deep purple.

CANNA

The showy cannas, from the warmer parts of North and South America, add a touch of the tropics to any garden. In many regions they are not hardy enough to be left out in the ground for the winter months and may need lifting and storing in a frost-free place. The flowers have a complicated structure and are somewhat orchidlike, being produced in spikes or racemes over large, bold ornamental foliage. Propagation is by seed in winter or division in spring. Hardiness zones: 9-10.

C. × generalis (*below*)

This name is given to a range of hybrid cultivars with varying flower and foliage color. 'King Humbert' (syn. 'Roi Humbert') is an old variety, with bright red flowers and brown leaves, reaching a height of 4-6 ft (1.2-1.8 m). 'Black Knight' also has red flowers and bronze-colored foliage, but is a shorter plant, growing up to 4 ft (1.2 m) tall. 'Lucifer' is a very striking red canna, with yellow-edged petals accompanied by purple leaves. It grows 3-4 ft (90 cm-1.2 m) high at flowering time. 'Wyoming' has bronze foliage with orange flowers and grows approximately 4 ft (1.2 m) high.

C. × generalis 'Lucifer'

C. indica

This wild species is more slender than the hybrids. It has green leaves and 5-6 ft (1.5-1.8 m) high stems that carry racemes of small, bright red or orange flowers. The lower lip of each flower is mottled and streaked darker red on an orange or yellow background color.

CARDIOCRINUM
Giant lily

These enormous plants are closely related to the true lilies. When flowering, they are very similar to the long, white trumpet lilies, although their broad, heart-shaped leaves are completely different. The very large bulbs are monocarpic, dying after flowering, but 2 or 3 small offsets are produced which can be grown and will flower 2 or 3 years later.

Cardiocrinums require deeply dug, humus-rich soil and a partially shaded area where they will not dry out too much in summer. They die down in winter and in cold areas are best given a mulch of loose straw to protect the resting bulbs from frost. They should be planted in fall or early spring, with the tips of the bulbs just beneath the surface. Each bulb can occupy a considerable space when in leaf; if planting more than one, space them a minimum of 3 ft (90 cm) apart. Propagation is by offsets in fall, or by seed in fall or winter; seed is very slow, and it may take up to 7 years to achieve flowering-size bulbs. Hardiness zone: 7.

C. giganteum

C. giganteum (*above*)

Growing up to 8 ft (2.4 m) tall when in flower, *C. giganteum* has broad, glossy leaves, some of which reach as much as 1½ ft (45 cm) across, diminishing in size all the way up to the flowers. Each flower stalk has up to 20 6 in (15 cm) long, semipendent, fragrant trumpets; these are each white, with a purple stain inside and a green flush outside.

CHASMANTHE

These robust perennials, resembling crocosmia, have large, almost flat corms that yield tufts of erect sword-shaped leaves and spikes of brightly colored tubular flowers in early summer. They are not very hardy, and in cold-winter areas they must be grown in a cool greenhouse, at a minimum temperature of 45°F (7.5°C), or in containers that can be moved outdoors after the last frost. They require a light, sandy soil and, if grown in containers, should be repotted each fall. The corms naturally increase quite rapidly; propagate by division in fall and replant the clumps at a depth of 3 in (9 cm). Hardiness zone: 9.

C. aethiopica (*below*)

The narrow leaves, up to 2 ft (60 cm) long, are topped by spikes of tubular red flowers. These are 2 in (5 cm) in length, and each has a long, hooded upper petal like a small gladiolus flower. All the flowers on the spike face the same way.

C. aethiopica

C. floribunda

Similar to *C. aethiopica* in flower shape, *C. floribunda* has much wider leaves and flowers that face in opposite directions.

CHILDANTHUS

The bulbs of this South American plant are usually sold in spring and are planted with the necks just protruding from the soil. It may be cultivated in the open garden in mild areas, but in regions with cold winters, it must be lifted and stored in frost-free, dry conditions. Alternatively, it can be grown in containers and brought into a greenhouse in fall, where it is dried off until spring. It is best grown in a sunny, well-drained spot. If grown in pots, use a loam-based potting medium with extra sand and feed the bulb once every 2 weeks with a liquid plant food formulated for acid-loving plants. In mild areas where they are placed permanently, the bulbs can be placed at a depth of 2-3 in (5-7.5 cm). Propagation is by division of separate bulbs in spring at repotting time. Hardiness zone: 9.

C. fragrans
These daffodillike bulbs produce strap-shaped grayish leaves and 4-12 in (10-30 cm) long stems, which carry umbels of 2-5 fragrant yellow flowers. These are funnel-shaped and 1½-2½ in (4-6.5 cm) long; the tips of the petals curl outward and back.

CROCOSMIA

This group of perennials from South Africa form tufts of erect, sword-shaped leaves, and their red, orange or yellow, funnel-shaped flowers are carried in branched, arching sprays. The modern hybrids have superseded the old cottage garden favorite *C.* × *crocosmiiflora* ('Monbretia'), although this is still a useful plant for difficult areas of the garden, since it tolerates a wide range of conditions which most other plants will not. However, the more highly developed cultivars can be tricky to grow in cold areas. Since the corms increase, the plants are easy to dig up and divide. Division is best in spring before growth starts, but the clumps may take a year or more to settle in. In very cold areas, mulch the plants with straw in winter. Hardiness zone: 7.

C. masonorum

C. masonorum (*above*)
This very robust plant grows up to 5 ft (1.5 m) high. Its arched stems bear many reddish-orange flowers. These are long-tubed, with spreading petals.

C. paniculata (syn. *Curtonus paniculatus*)
Similar to *C. masonorum*, the flowers of *C. paniculata* are carried on zig-zag stems.

Cultivars (*next column*)
The more highly developed cultivars are not always so hardy or easy to grow in cold areas. They require a well-drained sunny spot and

light, sandy soils rather than cold, heavy clays. But they are attractive, colorful plants for a mixed border: 'Bressingham Blaze' has wide, funnel-shaped, brilliant red flowers; 'Emily McKenzie' has deep orange flowers, each one with brown markings on the throat; and 'Lucifer' has deep, rich red flowers carried on 3 ft (90 cm) high stems over bold, swordlike foliage.

C. 'Lucifer'

CYPELLA

An irislike South American plant, cypella is worth growing outdoors in a sunny position in mild areas. In cold areas it needs to be lifted and stored over winter or grown in a frost-free greenhouse. Seed is produced freely and will produce flowering-size bulbs in only 1 or 2 years. Hardiness zone: 9.

C. herbertii

C. herbertii (*above*)
This cypella produces erect sword-shaped leaves and loosely branching flower stems, which carry upright mustard-yellow flowers. These resemble small irises, with 3 large outer petals and 3 smaller inner ones. Although each flower is short-lived, the bulb produces a succession over several weeks. It grows to a height of 9-12 in (23-30 cm).

DIERAMA
Angel's fishing rod or wand flower

These graceful perennials produce long, wiry stems that arch over at the apex so that the spikes of bell- or funnel-shaped flowers hang downward. The stalks grow from corms and have long, narrow leaves that are very tough and do not die back completely in winter, eventually forming sizable tufts when growing well. *Dierama* requires a sunny spot that is fairly moist but not waterlogged in summer, when the plant is in growth; it looks good when growing near water. Since it dislikes being disturbed, it is best to buy new plants or raise them from seed and place them in their permanent positions as young pot specimens. Hardiness zones: 7-9.

D. dracomontanum

D. dracomontanum (*above*)
This short, clump-forming plant offers bright pink flowers 1 in (2.5 cm) in length.

D. pendulum

D. pendulum (*above*)
Reaching 3-6 ft (90 cm-1.8 m) high, *D. pendulum* has branched, pendent spikes of wide, bell-shaped pale pinkish-purple flowers, each 1½-2 in (4-5 cm) in length.

D. pulcherrimum

D. pulcherrimum (*above*)
This bulb grows up to 6 ft (1.8 m) in height, and is similar in appearance to *D. pendulum*, but has narrower bells, approximately 2½ in (6.5 cm) long, in shades of deep reddish-purple or magenta.

DRACUNCULUS

This small group of arums has an enlarged cowl or saillike spathe enclosing a pencil-like spadix, which carries the minute flowers at its base. The spathe is tubular in the lower part and expands into a very large, flattened blade, leaving the thick, protruding spadix erect. It will tolerate either acid or alkaline soil as long as it is free-draining. The tubers are planted in fall, at a depth of about 6 in (15 cm), and covered with a layer of straw for winter protection. Offsets are produced readily, and when a clump has built up, it can be lifted and divided in late summer. Hardiness zone: 9.

D. vulgaris

D. vulgaris (*above*)
Dragon arum
The stout, blotched and striped stems of this plant reach nearly 3 ft (90 cm) high and are crowned by attractively divided leaves, some

of which have a spread of 1 ft (30 cm). The spathe can grow up to 1½ ft (45 cm) in length, and is a velvety deep maroon-purple, with a darker maroon projecting spadix.

Eucomis

EUCOMIS (*above*)
Pineapple flower
These bulbs are described in the Fall Directory (p. 207) because they often do not flower until this time. However, in mild gardens in zones 6 and above, they may start into growth earlier and be in full flower in mid- to late summer.

FREESIA

Freesias are naturally winter- or early-spring-flowering (see the Winter Directory p. 228). However, summer-flowering corms are sometimes available in spring for planting outdoors. If left in the ground, they will try to revert to their normal rhythm of growth, appearing in late fall and growing through the winter. Being tender plants, they will not survive in cold-winter areas. From a spring planting, it is possible to lift the corms in late summer after flowering, keeping them dry and warm for the winter to prevent growth. They can then be replanted the next spring. On the whole, they are best grown for their valuable fragrant winter flowers. Hardiness zone: 9-10.

GALTONIA
Summer hyacinth
These tall, graceful bulbous plants from South Africa have a cluster of long, strap-like basal leaves and loose racemes of bell-like flowers produced in mid- to late summer. They are very easy to cultivate, requiring a sunny site, adequate moisture, and fertile soil with a good humus content. The bulbs are planted in spring at intervals

of 3½ in (9 cm) at a depth of about 4 in (10 cm), or in cold areas they can be started into growth in pots in a greenhouse and then planted when the soil has warmed up. If the soil is likely to freeze deeply in winter, it is best to lift the bulbs in fall and store them in a frost-free place.

Propagation is by seed sown in spring, or by offsets removed from the parent bulb at planting time. Hardiness zones: 6-7.

G. candicans

G. candicans (*above*)
G. candicans has stems reaching 4-5 ft (1.2-1.5 m) in height. They carry a long raceme of pendent, short-tubed white flowers over 1 in (2.5 cm) in length.

G. princeps (*below*)
Although similar to *G. candicans*, this galtonia has slightly smaller flowers, under 1 in (2.5 cm) long, and its bell-shaped flowers have longer tubes. The blooms have a green tinge.

G.princeps

G. viridiflora
An attractive plant, *G. viridiflora* displays a spike of pendent funnel-shaped flowers in a soft green shade. It has shorter and broader leaves than *G. candicans* and *G. princeps*.

GLADIOLUS

Gladioli are very popular cormous plants. Most of those cultivated are hybrids derived from South African species, although a few Northern Hemisphere ones are worth growing; these are much hardier and need to be planted in fall. The South African species and their hybrids are planted in spring, when the soil has begun to warm up. There are very few gladiolus species in general cultivation, and most of those available are hybrids that have been classified into groups determined by height, flower size, and shape. To propagate gladioli, remove the young cormlets after lifting in winter or early spring, store them in frost-free conditions, and plant them later in spring. Hardiness zones: 9 for primulinus gladioli and the large-flowered hybrid and butterfly groups; 5-6 for *G. communis* subsp. *byzantinus* and *G. italicus*; 7 for *G. × colvillei* and *G. nanus* cultivars.

G. callianthus

In catalogs and books, this is much more likely to be found under the name of *Acidanthera bicolor* (see p. 150).

G. × colvillei and G. nanus

These two gladioli are very similar, if not synonymous. They are hardier than the large late-summer gladioli, flowering earlier in the season and only reaching about 1½-2 ft (45-60 cm) in height. They also have fewer wide, funnel-shaped flowers on each spike. In mild weather, the bulbs can be planted after purchase in fall. Sometimes corms can be obtained in spring, in which case they can be planted directly into the open garden.

G. 'The Bride'

G. (colvillei) 'The Bride' (*above*)
This has white flowers with green marks.

G. (nanus) 'Amanda Mahy'

This species has deep salmon-pink flowers with dark purplish splashes.

G. (nanus) 'Nymph' (*below*)

This species also has white flowers, but with pink markings on the lower petals.

G. 'Nymph'

G. communis subsp. byzantinus (*below*)

A hardy Mediterranean species for planting in fall, *G. communis* subsp. *byzantinus* produces robust, 2-3 ft (60-90 cm) high stems, with long spikes of bright reddish-purple flowers in early summer.

G. communis subsp. *byzantinus*

G. italicus (syn. G. segetum)

This slender species, common in Europe and Asia, is for summer and fall planting. It has pinkish-lilac flowers alternately facing in opposite directions up the spike.

Larger-flowered hybrids

These hybrids are derived from South African species and require spring planting. The flowers grow 2½-5½ in (6.5-14 cm) or more across when fully open. For show purposes, this type subdivides into groups based on flower width: Giant, Large, Medium, Small, and Miniature. The following is a limited selection of those available.

G. 'Trader Horn'

Giant (*above*)
'Trader Horn' is a rich, deep scarlet.

G. 'Peter Pears'

Large (*above* and *below*)
'Fidelio' is purple and 'Peter Pears' is a soft apricot orange color.

G. 'Fidelio'

Medium
'Aristocrat' has garnet-purple flowers; 'Green Woodpecker' is lemon-yellow.

Small

'Dancing Doll' has creamy-colored flowers that are suffused with pink and blotched red on the lower petals. 'Bluebird' is a rich blue-violet and appears early in the season; 'Claret' is rose-pink.

Miniature

'Greenbird' has sulfur-yellow flowers, which are tinged green, and red throats. 'Bo Peep' is much more subtle, with attractive almond-colored flowers with yellow flecks.

G. 'Camborne'

Butterfly hybrids (*above* and *below*)
This group of gladioli consists of small-flowered hybrids in dramatic hues, usually with contrasting patches of color on the lower petals. 'Camborne' has lilac flowers stained with deep violet; 'Avalanche' is a pure white form; 'Mykonos' has salmon-pink and yellow flowers with red markings; and 'Pamela' is a coral-pink gladiolus, with bright yellow and red centers.

G. 'Mykonos'

Primulinus gladioli (*next column*)
This group is partly derived from *G. primulinus* and has a similar flower form. The blooms are funnel-shaped, with the

arching upper petal forming a hood. The flowers are not so densely packed on the spike as in the larger-flowered types. 'Anitra' is deep red; 'Leonore' has bright yellow flowers; 'Lady Godiva' is white; and 'Columbine' has cyclamen-pink flowers, each with a white patch in the throat.

G. 'Leonore'

GLORIOSA
Fame lily or glory lily

Suitably named, this is very unusual among bulbous plants because it is a climber. The misshapen tubers of this winter-dormant plant are usually obtained in spring for summer growth and flowering. Occurring naturally in Africa and India, it is not hardy in cool areas of the country, but it makes an excellent container plant for a sun-room, as long as the tendrils are given plenty of support from twigs or a trellis.

One tuber requires a container that is at least 8 in (20 cm) in diameter; plant it about two-thirds of the way down, in standard potting soil. The plants are best started into growth in spring, at a minimum temperature of 55-60°F (13-16°C); once showing above ground, they should be given liquid fertilizer once every 2 weeks. In early summer, they can be placed outdoors if preferred, after which they can be dried off and stored in a frost-free place over winter. The tubers will increase slowly by division. Propagation by seed is also possible if it is sown in a greenhouse in spring and kept at the above temperature. Hardiness zone: 10.

G. superba (*next column*)
The weak stems grow up to 6 ft (1.8 m) high and bear scattered oval leaves with tendrils at their tips. A single flower is carried in each of the upper leaf axils; they are very striking, colorful blooms with 6 reflexed petals that are

wavy at the edges. Some forms have crimson-red petals with yellow edges and bases, while others are yellow, some plain, and some tinged orange-red. They may be listed in catalogs under separate names, such as 'Rothschildiana,' 'Carsonii,' and 'Lutea.'

G. superba

GLOXINIA (syn. SINNINGIA)

Although a genus of plants called gloxinia exists, few of the species are in general cultivation. The common name *Gloxinia* is used for a race of hybrids in the genus *Sinningia*, involving *S. speciosa* and others. These very tender, tuberous-rooted bulbs are usually treated as summer pot plants that should be dried off over winter and stored in a frost-free place. In early spring the tubers are planted in trays of damp peat and sand and started into growth at a temperature of approximately 60°F (16°C). When they start to sprout, plant them about 1 in (2.5 cm) deep in pots containing open potting soil consisting of loam, sharp sand, and leaf mold or old rotted compost in equal parts. Place them in a light spot but avoid direct sunlight. Throughout summer, they require liquid fertilizer twice a month; it is best to avoid wetting the hairy leaves when watering.

Propagation is by seed sown in spring, or by cutting up the tubers in spring before they start into growth, making sure that each division has a growing point. The following cultivars have a rosette of oval, toothed, soft, hairy leaves and short stems. They are compact plants, with clusters of showy, large, nearly upright funnel-shaped flowers. Hardiness zone: 10.

S. 'Tigrina' (*page 165*)
This name is given to speckled or dappled forms of gloxinia in pink, blue, or red. One variety is called 'Tiger Red' and has

cherry-colored flowers and white throats with red speckles. 'Mont Blanc' has pure white flowers that are frilled at the edges of the petals; 'Princess Elizabeth' is blue with a contrasting white throat; 'Blanche de Meru' is a rich red with a cream throat; and 'Emperor Frederick' has crimson flowers.

S. 'Mont Blanc'

HABRANTHUS

These bulbs can be grown only in mild, frost-free areas, so they are best treated as pot plants for a cool greenhouse or sun-room. They should be kept dry when dormant and started into growth in spring, by planting the bulbs halfway down a pot filled with well-drained loam-based soil. Plant approximately 5 bulbs in each 6 in (15 cm) diameter container and remove the surface layer of soil and top-dress with new soil. If growing them outoors, choose a warm, sunny spot and plant the bulbs about 3 in (7.5 cm) deep in well-drained soil. Propagate by offsets or seed sown in spring. Hardiness zone: 10.

H. robustus

H. robustus (*above*)
The large, funnel-shaped pale pink flowers are 2¹/₂ in (6.5 cm) long.

H. tubispathus

H. tubispathus (*above*)
This species will grow in areas of slight frost. It has small yellow flowers 1 in (2.5 cm) long, which are tinged a coppery or reddish brown on the outside of the petals. Propagation by seed takes 1-2 years to produce flowering-size bulbs.

HAEMANTHUS and SCADOXUS

This group is split into two genera, *Haemanthus* and *Scadoxus*, although most are found under the name *Haemanthus*. They are best treated as sunroom subjects, although they may be grown outside on a patio or terrace during warm summer months. The large bulbs produce broad leaves, either in a cluster or lying flat on the ground, and they have dense flower heads. The umbel is mainly spherical, but some are conical or brush-shaped, each consisting of 50-100 or more individual, small flowers. They should be potted in spring, with the tip of the bulbs just level with the surface, in a sandy, loam-based soil, and started into growth at a temperature of 55-60°F (13-16°C). During the growing season, they need plenty of water and a liquid fertilizer every 2 weeks; *H. albiflos* remains in leaf during the winter-dormant period and requires a little water from time to time.

Propagate by removing offsets when repotting in spring, although *Haemanthus* species are best left undisturbed for as long as possible since they seem to flower better when pot-bound. Hardiness zone: 9.

H. albiflos
An evergreen bulb, *H. albiflos* has broad, hairy, pale green leaves and small white flowers held in a dense brushlike umbel up to 3 in (7.5 cm) across. The stem reaches a height of 6-12 in (15-30 cm). This species is very easy to cultivate as a house plant.

H. coccineus (*below*)
This bulb has a spotted stem 1 ft (30 cm) high, carrying a dense umbel up to 4 in (10 cm) wide. The umbel is made up of small red or pink flowers, with the head surrounded by a whorl of broad pinkish-red bracts. This is followed by a pair of elliptical leaves, often spotted or banded purple, which lie flat on the ground.

H. coccineus

H. [*Scadoxus*] *multiflorus* (*below*)
Blood lily
The stout stem of *H. multiflorus* grows 1-1¹/₂ ft (30-45 cm) high and is crowned by a spherical umbel measuring 4-6 in (10-15 cm) in diameter. The umbel consists of up to 200 small red flowers with long protruding stamens. The erect basal tuft of broad, bright green leaves expands slightly later. *H. katherinae* is very similar but more robust, growing up to 3 ft (90 cm) high, each flower having wider petals and a longer tube.

H. multiflorus

H. pubescens
This bulb has red flowers borne in a dense umbel 2-2¹/₂ in (5-6.5 cm) in diameter, on a stout, 6-10 in (15-25 cm) tall stem, and are surrounded by red bracts.

H. [*Scadoxus*] *puniceus*
Royal paintbrush
The 1-1½ ft (30-45 cm) tall flower stem
carries a cone-shaped umbel, which grows
4-6 in (10-15 cm) in diameter. The small
flowers vary in color from pinkish red to
orange-red and are surrounded by red or
green bracts. The broad, upright leaves form
a separate cluster alongside the flower stem.
H. magnificus is a synonym of *H. puniceus*.

HERMODACTYLUS
Widow iris
A curious irislike plant with finger-shaped
tubers, the widow iris should be planted in
fall, at a depth of 3-4 in (7.5-10 cm) in well-
drained, preferably alkaline soil. It requires
a hot, sunny spot where it will sunbake
after its dormant midsummer period. The
tubers increase rapidly and, if left undisturbed, eventually form extensive patches
up to 3-4 ft (90 cm-1.2 m) across. Propagate by division in late summer or early
fall. Hardiness zone: 6.

H. tuberosus

H. tuberosus (syn. *Iris tuberosa*) (*above*)
This bulb produces 6-12 in (15-30 cm) tall
stems and long, narrow gray leaves with a
square-shaped cross section. Each stalk bears
a single iris-shaped flower; this is translucent
green or yellowish green, with a dark, velvety
blackish-brown tip to the 3 larger outer
petals. In mild areas, the plant flowers in late
spring rather than early summer.

HYMENOCALLIS
Spider lily, Peruvian daffodil
These 2-3 ft (60-90 cm) tall bulbous plants
of the amaryllis family have fragrant white
or yellow flowers which have large cups
and narrow petals. They are best treated
as pot plants for a heated sun-room or
greenhouse, with a minimum summer

temperature of 60°F (16°C). In warm areas
the hardier types may be grown outside,
either planted or in containers, and in a
cool greenhouse through winter. The large
bulbs are potted in spring, planted about
halfway down a 6-8 in (15-20 cm) diameter pot containing a light, open compost
of equal parts loam, sharp sand, and leaf
mold or peat, with a well-balanced fertilizer. During the summer, they need plenty
of water and should be given liquid plant
food formulated for acid-loving plants
every 2 weeks. They must then be dried
out over winter at a minimum temperature
of 50°F (10°C). The evergreen species
require a little water in winter. Propagation
is by removal of offsets at repotting time.
Hardiness zones: 9-10.

H. amancaes

H. amancaes (*above*)
A deciduous species, *H. amancaes* has an
umbel of large, fragrant yellow flowers with
frilly-edged cups and narrow petals.

H. × *festalis*

H. × *festalis* (*above*)
This deciduous *Hymenocallis* produces large,
fragrant white flowers which are about 6-8 in
(15-20 cm) in diameter.

H. × *macrostephana*
This has white, creamy, or green-yellow blooms.

H. narcissiflora

H. narcissiflora (*Ismene calathina*) (*above*)
H. narcissiflora bear up to 5 fragrant white
flowers with frilly-edged cups. This species is
a deciduous bulb.

H. speciosa
An evergreen, *H. speciosa* requires warm
conditions of 60-65°F (16-18.5°C). It has up
to 10 large, fragrant white or greenish-white
flowers, each with a funnel-shaped cup and
narrow, spreading petals. The flowers grow
7-12 in (18-30 cm) across.

H. 'Sulfur Queen'

H. 'Sulfur Queen' (*above*)
This deciduous bulb has loose heads of 2-5
fragrant primrose yellow flowers with a green
stripe inside the cup. The stems are
2-3 ft (60-90 cm) high.

IRIS
Most of the bulbous irises are associated
with spring, but the Xiphium group—com-
prising the English, Spanish, and Dutch
types—normally flowers in early summer
(although for cutting they can be forced

to bloom much earlier in a greenhouse). They all have long, narrow leaves, which are channeled on the upper surface, and 1-2 large flowers on top of strong stems. The bulbs are obtained in fall and need to be planted 3-4 in (7.5-10 cm) deep. They require an open, sunny site with well-drained acid or alkaline soil and look good placed in groups among herbaceous perennials. In areas without a warm, dry period in mid- to late summer, the Spanish and Dutch types are probably best lifted and stored dry until fall, whereas the English iris should be lifted and replanted in a moisture-retentive soil. Propagation is easiest by removal of offsets when established clumps are dug up for replanting in early fall, although dwarf irises can be divided. Hardiness zones: 5-7.

I. latifolia (syn. I. xiphioides)
English iris

In spite of its name, this plant is from the Pyrenees. It is a robust grower, reaching about 3 ft (90 cm) in height, with deep violet-blue flowers in midsummer. Each of the three outer petals—the "falls"—is marked with a yellow line in the center. These irises are usually available as mixed collections.

I. xiphium

I. xiphium (above)
Spanish iris

Growing 2-3 ft (60-90 cm) high, this slender-looking plant has slightly smaller flowers than *I. latifolia* and each petal is narrower. The flowers are a clear blue, yellow, or white, with a deep yellow band in the center of each of the outer petals. The Spanish iris is produced earlier than the English.

Dutch iris (next column)

This group name represents a wide range of hybrid Xiphium irises, which flower slightly earlier than the Spanish ones. They are frequently used for forcing to provide cut flowers in winter, but also make excellent garden plants. They grow to a height of 2-3 ft (60-90 cm) at flowering time. Good cultivars include: *I.* 'White Excelsior,' with white flowers and yellow marks on the falls; *I.* 'Bronze Queen,' a curious mixture of gold, bronze, and purple; *I.* 'Golden Harvest,' a deep yellow throughout; *I.* 'Wedgwood,' a clear midblue flower with a yellow stripe on each of the falls; and *I.* 'Professor Blaauw,' which has a rich gentian-blue stripe and is yellow on the falls.

I. 'Professor Blaauw'

IXIA
African lily

These colorful plants are South African in origin and not very hardy, since they naturally grow during the winter months and flower in spring. However, some nurseries keep the corms in storage and offer them for spring planting to flower in summer. This may work for the first season, but afterward they will try to revert to their normal growth cycle. They should be lifted for the winter and kept warm and dry until spring. Ixias are best planted in a warm, sunny position in well-drained, preferably sandy soil, at a depth of 3 in (7.5 cm). They grow best in a clump, with the corms $1\frac{1}{2}$ in (4 cm) apart. In areas with mild, frost-free winters, they can be planted and left in the ground.

Few species of ixia exist, the most likely being mixed, unnamed collections. They have slender, wiry stems with tough, narrow leaves and spikes of star-shaped, brightly colored flowers. Propagation is by offsets detached when the corms are dug up, or by seed, which takes 2-3 years to produce flowering-size corms. Hardiness zone: 8.

I. maculata

This corn lily produces stems that reach $1\frac{1}{2}$ ft (45 cm) high, with spikes of flat, 1-2 in (2.5-5 cm) diameter, star-shaped yellow or orange flowers with brown or black centers.

I.viridiflora

I. viridiflora (above)

A spectacular species, *I. viridiflora* has $1-1\frac{1}{2}$ ft (30-45 cm) long spikes of green flowers, each $1\frac{1}{2}-2$ in (4-5 cm) in diameter. The flowers are marked with a blackish-purple eye in the center.

LILIUM
Lily

Lilies are some of the most beautiful and stately bulbs, valuable for planting in borders among perennials or shrubs and in containers. The spectacular flowers come in a wide range of colors, from white through to red. There are many flower forms to choose from—for example, trumpet-shaped, Turk's cap, flattish, pendent, upright and horizontal (also known as "outward-facing").

They are easy to cultivate in the garden or as container plants for a patio or terrace. The bulbs are sold in both spring and fall; it is best to purchase them as soon as they are on the market and plant them immediately. Lilies dislike locations that are too wet, and extreme summer heat may make them fail to bloom in southern climates. Most lilies do well if their bases are shaded by other lower-growing plants, leaving their flowers to push up into the sunlight, but they will also grow in the dappled shade provided by nearby taller trees and shrubs.

Before planting, prepare the soil by digging in well-rotted compost or leaf mold, adding sharp sand if necessary to improve drainage and a well-balanced fertilizer.

For the larger-growing lilies, allow 2 ft (60 cm) in diameter for three bulbs, and plant them in a triangle at a depth of 4-8 in (10-20 cm), depending on size. *L. candidum* is the exception; these bulbs need to be only just below soil level. Most lilies can be grown in acid or alkaline soil conditions, but alkaline soil must have humus incorporated at planting time, otherwise the bulbs will not thrive.

Lillies can be propagated in many ways. Either lift and divide established clumps in fall, or pick the bulblets or bulbils produced by some plants on their stems or in their leaf axils in late summer, and plant them in pots or boxes or in a nursery bed of fertile soil for growth the following summer. They normally take 1-2 years to reach flowering size. Bulb scales can also be used to increase lilies; this is quite a simple and rapid method of propagation: break off a few scales any time between midsummer and early fall without harming the parent, and put them in a plastic bag of slightly damp perlite, vermiculite, or clean sharp sand, placing them in a warm room at about 70°F (21°C). In about 3-5 weeks, remove the small bulbs and grow them in the same way as the naturally produced bulblets and bulbils. Hardiness zones: 2-7

L. amabile luteum

L. amabile (*above*)
This Korean species grows 1½–3 ft (45–90 cm) high. It has many scattered narrow leaves and up to 10 pendent red flowers, which are usually spotted black; these have a Turk's cap shape, with rolled-back petals. *L. a. luteum* is yellow.

L. aurantum (*next column*)
Golden-rayed lily
This spectacular Japanese species has 1 ft (30 cm) wide, saucer-shaped, fragrant white flowers with a yellow band along the center of each petal and is also spotted red to varying degrees. There are usually 5-10 flowers per stem, the height of the stem varying from 3-5 ft (90 cm-1.5 m). *L. aurantum* performs best in a lime-free soil.

L. aurantum

L. bulbiferum (*below*)
Orange lily
This European species grows up to 5 ft (1.5 m) high, with upward-facing cup-shaped flowers. These are bright reddish orange, usually spotted brown inside. The leaf axils hold bulbils, although the variety *croceum* does not. *L. croceum* is similar in most other respects to *L. bulboferum*, although it has orange rather than red flowers.

L. bulbiferum

L. canadense
Canada lily or meadow lily
This very graceful North American species has a creeping rhizomelike bulb and stems up to 4 ft (1.2 m) high, bearing whorls of leaves. The pendent bell-shaped flowers have outward-curving tips and are available in a range of colors, from yellow to orange or red, often spotted darker inside. This lily needs moist rather than waterlogged soil.

L. candidum (*below*)
Madonna lily
A very distinct lily from the Mediterranean, *L. candidum* is the traditional symbol of purity. Unlike most lilies, it must be planted in early fall, since this is when it makes a new set of overwintering leaves. The 3-5 ft (90 cm-1.5 m) high flower stems appear in early summer. They carry many erect leaves and up to 15 white, wide, funnel-shaped, deliciously fragrant flowers. This lily needs a warm, sunny spot.

L. candidum

L. cernuum
An eastern Asiatic lily, *L. cernuum* grows up to 2 ft (60 cm) in height, with many narrow leaves and 1-7 pendent scented flowers. These Turk's cap blooms are pink-purple, spotted dark purple on the inside.

L. chalcedonicum (*below*)
Scarlet Turk's cap lily
A scarlet-flowered Turk's cap lily from Greece, *L. chalcedonicum* needs a sunny, well-drained spot and prefers alkaline soil. The 3-4 ft (90 cm-1.2 m) long stems have silver-edged leaves and are densely packed all the way up to the flowers. It is a striking brightly-colored border plant.

L. chalcedonicum

L. concolor

A Chinese species 1-3 ft (30-90 cm) high, *L. concolor* has scattered narrow leaves and up to 10 small flowers. These are almost flat and held upright; most are red with darker-colored spots, but some types are plain yellow in color and unspotted.

L. davidii (*below*)

This lily is a native of China. It has many very narrow leaves packed on to 3-5 ft (90 cm-1.5 m) tall stems, and up to 20 pendent Turk's cap flowers standing out horizontally on long stalks from the main stem. Each flower is bright orange, with black spots inside. The variety *willmottiae* is a more vigorous grower, with up to 30 reddish-orange flowers.

L. davidii

L. duchartrei (*below*)
Marble martagon

A beautiful but small-flowered lily from China, *L. duchartrei* has slender stems up to 4 ft (1.2 m) high, carrying scattered leaves and up to 12 pendent white flowers. The flowers have a Turk's cap shape similar to that of the martagon lily, and they are spotted and veined reddish purple, evoking the comparison with marble.

L. duchartrei

L. formosanum (*below*)

This tender trumpet lily from Taiwan grows up to 5 ft (1.5 m) tall. It has a few very fragrant funnel-shaped flowers 6-8 in (15-20 cm) long; these are pure white inside and flushed wine-purple on the outside. It is not a frost-hardy bulb and is best grown in a greenhouse. The variety *pricei* originates from higher altitudes and is much hardier; it is a dwarf plant, often reaching only 6-12 in (15-30 cm) in height.

L. formosanum pricei

L. hansonii (*below*)

A distinctive eastern Asiatic lily, *L. hansonii* has whorls of broad leaves held on a 3-5 ft (90 cm-1.5 m) high stem. The deep yellow Turk's cap flowers are spotted brown on the inside, and the reflexed petals are very thick.

L. hansonii

L. henryi (*next column*)

This Chinese lily is one of the easiest of all lilies to grow. It is a graceful plant reaching 7 ft (2.1 m) high, with broad leaves that diminish in size toward the top of the flowers. There are 10-20 or more pendent Turk's cap flowers. The blooms are bright orange, spotted darker toward the center, with prominent hairlike projections.

L. henryi

L. lancifolium (syn. L. tigrinum) (*below*)
Tiger lily

This familiar species is unfortunately susceptible to viral diseases. It reaches 5 ft (1.5 m) in height, with narrow, dark green leaves bearing bulbils in their axils. It has 10-20 or more pendent orange-red flowers that are spotted black in the center. The variety *flaviflorum* is a clear yellow variant.

L. lancifolium

L. langkongense (*below*)

This lily grows 3-4 ft (90 cm-1.2 m) high. It displays up to 15 large Turk's cap flowers; these are pale pink, spotted reddish purple.

L. langkongense

L. leichtlinii

An eastern Asiatic lily, the most common form of *L. leichtlinii* is the variety *maximowiczii* or *L. maximowiczii*. It grows stems 4-6 ft (1.2-1.8 m) high bearing Turk's cap flowers that are orange-red, spotted darker red inside.

L. longiflorum

L. longiflorum (*above*)
Easter lily or Bermuda lily

This well-known white trumpet lily comes from eastern Asia. It is so easy to grow that it is cultivated on a vast scale. A very tender species, it requires frost-free conditions. It may be raised from seed to flowering in just one growing season. The elegant, pure white funnel-shaped flowers are about 6-8 in (15-20 cm) long and are pleasantly fragrant; occasionally more than one per stem is produced.

L. mackliniae

L. mackliniae (*above*)
Manipur lily

A choice lily from Burma, this is suitable for growing outdoors in a cool, semishaded spot. A very disintct lily, it has 1-2½ ft (30-76 cm) high stems carrying 1-5 pendent bells about 2 in (5 cm) long; these are white, flushed pinkish purple on the outside.

L. martagon

L. martagon (*above*)
Turk's cap or martagon lily

This European lily is one of the oldest in cultivation. It is easily recognized by its racemes of up to 20 small, dull pinkish-purple flowers that are spotted darker in the center, with the petals rolled back to give the Turk's cap shape. It has whorls of broad leaves growing up the stems. A very hardy species, it is suitable for naturalizing beneath and between shrubs, or in grass. 'Album' is a lovely white-flowered form, and 'Dalmaticum' has almost black flowers.

L. monadelphum

L. monadelphum (*above*)

This large Turk's cap lily is about 4-5 ft (1.2-1.5 m) high, with stems carrying several large, pendent flowers of a lovely pale yellow, spotted dark purple on the inside. The petals are less rolled back than those of *L. martagon*. *L. szovitsianum* is very similar to *L. monadelphum*, with only slight botanical differences; for the most part, choice depends on availability.

L. nanum

A tiny lily from the Himalayas, *L. nanum* requires cool, damp growing conditions in summer and almost dry winters. It is usually only 3-12 in (7.5-30 cm) in height, with a solitary bell-shaped flower approximately 1½ in (4 cm) long. The bloom is normally a pinkish-lilac shade, although other color variants also exist.

L. nepalense (*below*)

A beautiful Nepalese lily, but unfortunately tender, this bulb requires cool greenhouse cultivation in cold-winter areas. It grows up to 4 ft (1.2 m) high and has 1-3 pendent funnel-shaped flowers with recurved tips to the petals. They are a curious greenish-yellow color, stained with purple on the inside. The stems may grow as much as 2 ft (60 cm) underground before emerging, so the plant may appear some distance from where it was originally planted.

L. nepalense

L. pardalinum (*below*)
Leopard lily

This very striking and easily cultivated western American lily requires a damp location. It has whorls of leaves on its 5-7 ft (1.5-2.1 m) high stems and several large, pendent Turk's cap flowers. These are a brilliant orange-red, shading to darker red at the tips of the petals, with deep brown spots toward the center.

L. pardalinum

L.parryi

L. parryi (*above*)

L. parryi has funnel-shaped yellow flowers.

L. pomponium

L. pomponium (*above*)

This very dramatic Turk's cap lily is best grown in a warm spot on alkaline soil. Its 2-3 ft (60-90 cm) high stems carry many narrow leaves and brilliant waxy red flowers in true Turk's cap fashion.

L. pumilum (**L. tenuifolium**) (*below*)

This lily is a red-flowered Turk's cap from eastern Asia. It is a small, slender plant, only 1½-2 ft (45-60 cm) high, with very narrow, grassy leaves and up to 15 small red flowers.

L. pumilum

L. pyrenaicum (*below*)
Yellow Turk's cap lily

Although not showy, this European Turk's cap is very hardy and easily cultivated. The stout, 2-4 ft (60 cm-1.2 m) high stems are densely clothed with many leaves and have up to 10 small greenish-yellow Turk's cap flowers. These have black spots and lines in the center; the more unusual variety *rubrum* has reddish-orange flowers.

L. pyrenaicum

L. regale (*below*)
Regal lily

Undoubtedly one of the best of all the white trumpet lilies, *L. regale* is hardy and tolerates a wide range of conditions in the garden. The wiry, 3-6 ft (90 cm-1.8 m) high stems carry many narrow leaves, and 1-20 outward-facing trumpets. Each one is approximately 6 in (15 cm) long, deliciously scented, and white on the inside with a purple-stained outside. 'Album' is a pure white version without the purple staining.

L. regale 'Album'

L. rubellum (*next column*)

This dwarf Japanese lily is quite hardy and worth trying in a peat-rich garden or in partial shade. It reaches only 1-2 ft

(30-60 cm) in height and has a few lance-shaped leaves. The 1-6 fragrant funnel-shaped flowers, about 3-4 in (7.5-10 cm) long, are a soft shade of rose-pink.

L. rubellum

L. sargentiae (*below*)

Very similar to *L. regale*, *L. sargentiae* has wider leaves and flowers slightly later. It is, however, less hardy.

L. sargentiae

L. speciosum

A fragrant Japanese lily, *L. speciosum* flowers later than most other species, often continuing into the early fall, and it can be caught by early frosts in cold northern areas. It is a stem-rooting lily and prefers a cool, well-drained, humus-rich spot. It usually grows up to 6 ft (1.8 m) high, and has thick, leathery leaves and up to 10 large, pendent flowers. The petals are rolled back like a Turk's cap, displaying long, protruding stamens and prominent hairlike projections on the inside. Several color variants exist, but typical flowers are white suffused with pink, with crimson projections. 'Album' is a pure white and 'Rubrum' a deeper carmine-pink, with pale edges to the petals; both have dark purple-colored stems.

L. superbum (*below*)
Swamp lily
This striking North American swamp lily grows up to 7 ft (2.1 m) high and flowers in late summer and early autumn. It has whorled leaves and a large head of many pendent Turk's cap flowers. These are orange, spotted maroon inside, with reddish tips to the petals. It needs a moisture-retentive, rather than waterlogged, soil.

L. superbum

L. × *testaceum* (*below*)
Nankeen lily
Probably the oldest hybrid lily, this cross between *L. candidum* and *L. chalcedonicum* exhibits soft apricot-colored flowers with a few red spots in the center. They are wide, open flowers with the petals rolled back; up to 12 are carried on 6 ft (1.8 m) high stems, which are densely packed with leaves. It prefers alkaline soil and a sunny position.

L. × *testaceum*

L. tsingtauense
This distinctive eastern Asiatic lily grows to height of about 3 ft (90 cm). It has whorls of leaves and upward-facing flat flowers that range from red to orange-red in color with darker spots in the center.

L. wardii
This Turk's cap from China has tough, slender, 4–5 ft (1.2–1.5 m) high stems, clothed with many deep green leaves. It bears up to 15 or more fragrant pinkish-purple flowers with dark center spots. The flowers are small and pendent and their petals are rolled right back. It is best planted in lime-free soil in light shade.

Hybrid groups
There are thousands of lily hybrids that have been grouped together for ease of reference into an internationally agreed-upon classification. This is largely based on the parentage of the hybrids, the flower shape, and the way in which the flowers are held on their stems. The most popular groups of hybrids are given below in the order recommended by the Horticultural Classification of Lilies.

Asiatic hybrids
These hybrids are derived from a group of mainly eastern Asiatic lilies and have given rise to a very popular range of hardy lilies including the Mid-century hybrids. These are much used as cut flowers as well as in the garden in borders. They subdivide into three groups: upright-flowered, outward-facing, and pendent.

L. 'Connecticut King'
Upright-flowered lilies (*above* and *next column*)
'Connecticut King' has plain, bright yellow, upright, almost flat flowers; 'Sterling Star' is a similar shape, but is white with conspicuous brown spots inside; 'Chinook' is upright and pale apricot; 'Enchantment' is very popular and has a bunch of bright orange upward-facing flowers that are spotted black inside; 'Destiny' is upright and yellow in color, spotted brown-red; and 'Firecracker' is deep red.

L. 'Sterling Star'

Outward-facing lilies (*below*)
'Corsage' has creamy white flowers, shaded to a pink tinge at the tips of the petals, and is spotted maroon inside with white centers; 'Fireking' is an intense orange-red, also conspicuously spotted.

L. 'Fireking'

Pendent lilies (*below*)
These tend to have Turk's cap flowers with reflexed petals. 'Discovery' has rose pink flowers with darker tips to the petals and spots inside; and 'Yellow Star' has graceful lemon-yellow flowers that are spotted black and brown.

L. 'Yellow Star'

173

Martagon hybrids (*below*)

These hybrids of the true Turk's caps involve either *L. martagon* or *L. hansonii*. Their flowers are generally small and their leaves are borne in whorls. Few are generally available, but 'Marhan' is sometimes found in catalogs; it has orange flowers with brown spots. 'Mrs. R.O. Backhouse' is also orange-yellow, with a few spots inside, flushed pink on the outside. 'Jacques S. Dijt' is a pale creamy yellow color, spotted purple.

L. 'Marhan'

American hybrids (*below*)

This group includes some of the most attractive lilies. They have tall stems bearing whorled leaves and large pendent flowers, which often have elegantly reflexed, pointed petals. The Bellingham hybrids are a vigorous mixed group, in colors ranging from yellow to deep orange, with a strong spotting of darker orange-red. 'Shuksan' is an individual selection from the Bellingham hybrids, with orange flowers flushed red and spotted darker red inside. It is one of the best-known forms and increases rapidly in ideal conditions. 'Lake Tahoe' is a lovely variety, with pinkish-red flowers and a yellow-and-white center, spotted deep red.

L. 'Lake Tahoe'

L. 'African Queen'

Asiatic trumpet hybrids (*above* and *below*)

This is one of the more important groups. It contains all the large, fragrant trumpet lily hybrids, which are spectacular and easily grown in the garden or containers. They are 4-6 ft (1.2-1.8 m) high, with large funnel-shaped flowers, each approximately 6 in (15 cm) long. 'Green Magic' is white on the inside, with a lemon-yellow center and a green flush on the outside; 'Pink Perfection' has large trumpets in varying shades of pinkish-purple; 'African Queen' is a soft orange, flushed pinkish bronze on the outside; and 'Golden Splendor' is a deep golden yellow, flushed purple outside. 'Bright Star' differs from the majority of the trumpet group because the flowers open wider and the tips of the petals are recurved. The flowers are white, with orange-yellow bands radiating from the center along the middle of each of the 6 petals.

L. 'Golden Splendor'

Oriental hybrids (*next column*)

These are mostly derived from the Japanese species *L. auratum* and *L. speciosum*, but some may involve *L. henryi* and other eastern Asiatic species. Their flowers, almost flat or with recurved petals, usually have prominent projections on the inside. They are especially

fragrant. 'Black Beauty' has deep red reflexed petals edged with white; 'Casa Blanca' has enormous, almost flat, white flowers with contrasting brown stamens; 'Star Gazer' is unusual with its upward-facing flowers in a rich crimson, spotted darker maroon; and 'Journey's End' has deep crimson flowers, with the white-edged petals reflexed at the tips. The white flowers of 'Imperial Gold' are large and almost flat, with a yellow band along the center of each petal.

L. 'Journey's End'

LITTONIA

This bulb is rarely seen, although it is very easy to cultivate. It is tender, requiring greenhouse or sun-room cultivation in cold areas, but since it is winter dormant, it can be grown outdoors in a container for the summer. The elongated tubers should be planted in spring at a depth of approximately 4 in (10 cm), in a medium-strength loam-based soil, and started into growth by slight watering. They require a minimum temperature of 55°F (13°C). Sticks or a trellis should be provided since this climber can reach up to 6 ft (1.8 m) in height during summer growth. After flowering, it is kept growing until the leaves begin to die back in fall, when the tubers can be dried and stored in a frost-free place for winter. In areas with mild winters, it can be grown outdoors as a permanent planting, at the edge of a supporting shrub. Propagation is by division at repotting time, the tubers naturally producing offsets. Hardiness zone: 9.

L. modesta

This slender-stemmed plant has lance-shaped leaves with tendrils at their tips and bell-shaped orange flowers in the axils of the upper ones. These are pendent and about 1-1½ in (2.5-4 cm) long.

MONTBRETIA (see CROCOSMIA)

MORAEA

These bulbs are the African equivalent of irises. The flowers have 3 large outer petals, or "falls," and 3 smaller inner ones, the equivalents of the "standards" of an iris. The plants have a corm rather than a rhizome or bulb; the leaves are usually narrow and flat, or channeled on the upper surface. They are much less hardy than irises, and most require a frost-free climate or cultivation in a greenhouse or sun-room. However, there are a few species from the eastern Cape region that are winter dormant and fairly hardy. They should be planted in spring at a depth of 3 in (7.5 cm); the soil should not be waterlogged or allowed to dry out too much during the summer growing season. In very cold areas, where the ground freezes to a considerable depth (zones 5-6), the corms are best lifted over winter and stored in a frost-free place. Propagation is by seed sown in spring, which takes about 2 years to produce flowering-size corms. Hardiness zones: 7-8.

M. huttonii

M. huttonii (*above*)

Growing to a height of 3 ft (90 cm), the stems of this bulb carry several flowers. These are initially encased within tight bracts and afterward produced one after the other. The flowers are yellow, marked with brown in the center of the 3 larger outer petals, and grow 2-3 in (5-7.5 cm) in diameter.

M. moggi and M. spathulata

These types are very similar to *M. huttonii*.

NECTAROSCORDUM

This small group of bulbous plants from southern Europe and Turkey is related to the onion family (*Allium*). They release a similar but much more pungent smell if crushed. The bulbs grow well in ordinary garden soil; they should be planted in fall, in a sunny or partially shaded spot where they can be left to self-seed, although the seed heads can be cut off before the seeds ripen. After flowering in early summer, the plants die down, but they may be left in the ground since they do not require particularly warm or dry conditions during the dormant season. The dried seed heads make attractive cut flowers for winter decorations. Propagation is by division of clumps or seed in fall. Hardiness zones: 6-7.

N. bulgaricum

This species grows to a height of 3-4 ft (90 cm-1.2 m) and has long, channeled basal leaves and a bare stem. It is crowned by an umbel of bell-shaped flowers that are held on long, drooping stalks; each flower is white with a green tinge and reaches ¾-1 in (2-2.5 cm) in length. After flowering, the stalks turn upward so that, in the fruiting stage, the umbel is cone-shaped.

N. siculum (syn. *Allium siculum, N. dioscoridis*) (*below*)

Similar in overall shape and size to *N. bulgaricum*, *N. siculum* has green flowers that are strongly flushed with purple, although some are almost entirely red-purple.

N. siculum

NOMOCHARIS

These beautiful Himalayan and Chinese relatives of the lily are not as easy to grow, except in cool northern gardens with damp summers. The scaly bulbs and leafy stems are similar to those of the lily, but the flowers tend to be almost flat, with fringed edges to the petals, often with a darker eye or prominent blotches on a paler background. Plant the bulbs in partial shade in fall at a depth of 4-5 in (10-13 cm); they require humus-rich soil. Propagation is best from seed, but it will take 3-4 years to produce flowering-size bulbs. Hardiness zones: 5-6.

N. aperta

N. aperta (*above*)

This nomocharis grows 2-3 ft (60-90 cm) high, with scattered or paired leaves and up to 6 nodding saucer-shaped flowers. Each flower is about 3-4 in (7.5-10 cm) in diameter, with a pale pink background and a dark purple eye in the center, surrounded by reddish-purple blotches.

N. farreri

Similar to *N. aperta*, *N. farreri* has whorls of leaves and up to 10 near-white flowers, which have fringed edges to the petals.

N. mairei (*below*)

This very showy species grows to a height of 2-2½ ft (60-76 cm). It has whorls of leaves and almost flat, nodding flowers that are heavily blotched and spotted reddish-purple on a white background. The 3 inner petals are strongly fringed at the edges.

N. mairei

N. pardanthina

N. pardanthina (*above*)

This nomocharis has up to 10 almost flat flowers; these are pink, each with a slight purple spot and a dark purple central eye.

N. saluenensis

N. saluenensis (*above*)

The leaves of this nomocharis are held in pairs rather than in a whorl. It has from 1-6 saucer-shaped flowers that grow 3-4 in (7.5-10 cm) in diameter. These are mostly pink or red in color, although off-white forms are occasionally found, with a dark eye in the center and a light sprinkling of dark spots.

NOTHOLIRION

A small group of bulbous plants, notholirions are related to lilies, but most have bulbs enclosed within brown papery coats, smaller flowers, and long, narrow basal leaves. After flowering, the bulb dies down, having produced offsets that carry the plant on to the next generation. These bulbs are best planted in fall, in a sheltered spot near shrubs that provide winter protection for the leaves. The soil needs to be well drained but moisture-retentive in summer, with a good humus content. Propagation is by growing on the offsets. Hardiness zone: 7.

N. bulbuliferum (**syn.** *N. hyacinthinum*)

This plant has long basal foliage and scattered leaves growing on its 2-3 ft (60-90 cm) tall stems. The raceme is made up of 10-30 funnel-shaped pale lilac flowers that flare out at the mouth. They are 1½ in (4 cm) long, with green tips to the petals.

N. campanulatum

This notholirion has drooping, 2 in (5 cm) long bells that are crimson, tipped green.

N. macrophyllum

N. macrophyllum (*above*)

A shorter species reaching only 2 ft (60 cm) high, this bulb has only a few wide, funnel-shaped flowers that are pale lavender and spotted with purple on the inside. They reach 1-1½ in (2.5-4 cm) long, opening to 2 in (5 cm) across at the mouth.

N. thomsonianum

This bulb produces its leaves in early fall and requires a sunny, well-drained site that will dry out slightly in late summer. It has long basal leaves and leafy stems up to 3 ft (90 cm) high, which carry up to 25 flowers, each about 2-2½ in (5-6.5 cm) long. These are funnel-shaped and pale lilac in color.

ORNITHOGALUM
Star-of-Bethlehem

This very large group of bulbous plants hails from Europe, western Asia, and South Africa. Many *Ornithogalum* species are spring-flowering. Dormant in summer, most of these plants grow in winter but a few, such as the popular *O. thyrsoides* (chincherinchee), can be treated as summer growers. The majority of the Northern Hemisphere species are much hardier than the South African ones and can be planted in fall at a depth of 2-3 in (5-7.5 cm) in any reasonably well-drained garden soil. They grow in sun or slight shade but need a certain amount of sun at flowering time or the flowers will not open. The more tender species can be kept dry and frost-free over winter, and planted out in spring for summer flowering. In most cases, propagation is easy since they produce offsets quite readily; alternatively, seed takes up to 3 years to make flowering-size bulbs. Hardiness zones: 6-8.

O. arabicum

A striking and unusual species, *O. arabicum* has broad basal leaves and 2-3 ft (60-90 cm) high stems crowned with a dense head of almost flat, upward-facing cream-colored flowers. Each of these is approximately 1½-2 in (4-5 cm) in diameter, with a dark eye in the form of a black ovary. This species needs a warm, sheltered spot.

O. narbonense

O. narbonense (*above*)

Producing a cluster of long, narrow gray basal leaves and tough, 1-2 ft (30-60 cm) high stems, this star-of-Bethlehem bears a raceme of many star-shaped white flowers, ½-1 in (1.5-2.5 cm) in diameter. Each petal has a pale green stripe along its center on the outside. For best results, plant the bulb in full sun.

O. pyrenaicum
Bath asparagus

Of similar habit to *O. narbonense*, Bath asparagus has smaller, pale greenish-yellow flowers; when in bud, they look like thin asparagus shoots. The plant grows up to 3 ft (90 cm) high and requires a sunny or partially shaded spot.

O. thyrsoides (*next column*)
Chincherinchee

A South African species, chincherinchee is

naturally winter-growing, but in cold-winter areas, planting can be delayed until spring to provide flowers in summer. In winter it can be grown in a frost-free greenhouse or sunroom. It grows 1-2 ft (30-60 cm) high, with dense conical racemes of many white flowers, each cup-shaped and approximately 1 in (2.5 cm) in diameter. They are popular cut flowers and last a long time in water.

O. thyrsoides

OXALIS

An extremely large group of plants, many oxalis have swollen rootstocks and can be bought from bulb catalogs. The majority have attractively divided leaves and buds that unfurl like umbrellas in the sun, opening into rounded, showy flowers with 5 petals. Plant them in fall or, if purchased as pot plants, in spring, at a depth of about 2 in (5 cm) unless otherwise stated. They require a well-drained site that receives sunshine for the greater part of the day. Propagation is by division once clumps have formed. Hardiness zones: 7-8.

O. adenophylla

O. adenophylla (*above*)
A native of Chile and Argentina, this oxalis has an unusual bulb resembling a ball of felt, which should be planted just below the surface of the ground in gritty soil. It is only 2-3 in (5-7.5 cm) high and forms a clump of gray leaves, each consisting of several small leaflets. In early summer it produces many short-stemmed, pale pink-lilac flowers that are almost flat, each growing about 2-2½ in (5-6.5 cm) in diameter.

O. enneaphylla
From the Falklands, this species is similar to *O. adenophylla* but has a more elongated, rhizomelike rootstock.

O. tetraphylla

O. tetraphylla (**syn.** *O. deppei*) (*above*)
This easily cultivated species can grow up to 4 in (10 cm) high. It has tufts of cloverlike leaves consisting of 4 green leaflets, with a reddish-brown zone near the base. The light carmine flowers are carried in small umbels in early summer. It will grow in a rock garden or a border in sun or slight shade.

PANCRATIUM

A small genus of the amaryllis family, *Pancratium* has beautiful fragrant flowers resembling large white daffodils, each consisting of a cup surrounded by narrow petals. The Mediterranean species begin to grow in fall after a summer dormancy and should be kept in growth until the leaves die away in midsummer, after which the bulbs should be kept as warm and dry as possible. Although they are not hardy, it is worth trying them outdoors in mild areas, planted at the foot of a sunny wall or in containers that can be moved under cover during cold periods. They are best left undisturbed to develop into clumps. Propagation is by seed sown in fall, which takes up to 5 years to produce a flowering-size bulb, or by offsets detached in early fall. Hardiness zone: 8.

P. illyricum
A beautiful plant from Corsica, this is the hardiest species of pancratium and will flower reliably if given a warm rest period. It has gray-green strap-shaped basal leaves and 1-1½ ft (30-45 cm) high stems. In early summer these carry an umbel made up of 10-15 fragrant white flowers; each is about 3-4 in (7.5-10 cm) in diameter, with a fairly small central cup.

P. maritimum (*below*)
Sea lily or sea daffodil
P. maritimum is much less hardy than *P. illyricum*. In late summer it produces up to 6 flimsy flowers per umbel, each with a large cup. It seldom flowers in cultivation and is often found growing on the beach at sea level in the Mediterranean.

P. maritimum

PARADISEA

Although related to many of the bulbous members of the lily family, this is a herbaceous plant with fleshy roots that cannot be dried off to the same extent as bulbs. Since it is usually obtained as a pot-grown plant, it can be planted at any time, preferring a sunny, well-drained spot. The single cultivated species is a clump-forming perennial, which can be lifted and divided in early fall or spring, before new growth commences; young plants can be raised from seed. An established clump may reach 6-12 in (15-30 cm) in diameter. Hardiness zone: 4-5.

P. liliastrum
St. Bruno's lily
A hardy plant, *P. liliastrum* grows 1-2 ft (30-60 cm) high with long, narrow, grassy leaves and racemes of up to 10 funnel-shaped white flowers in early summer, each 1½-2 in (4-5 cm) long.

POLIANTHES

Although belonging to a small genus of Mexican plants, *Polianthes tuberosa* is cultivated in many parts of the world, mainly for its scented white flowers. The large bulblike rootstocks should be planted in spring, in a warm, sunny spot in rich soil, but in cold areas they are best started in pots ready for planting when the soil has warmed up. Alternatively, grow them in a greenhouse in larger containers and move them outdoors during summer. They die down over winter and should be kept warm and relatively dry until spring, after which they are repotted. Except in very mild areas, those planted outdoors should be lifted for winter storage. Propagation is by division of the bulbs at repotting or replanting time. Hardiness zone: 9.

P. tuberosa

P. tuberosa (*above*)
Tuberose

The tuberose has long grayish-green leaves and a 2-2½ ft (60-76 cm) high stem that bears a raceme of fragrant, waxy white flowers. These have a narrow funnel-shaped tube a minimum of 1 in (2.5 cm) long, which opens out into 6 flat lobes at the mouth. 'The Pearl' is a double form.

RANUNCULUS
Buttercup

Since most ranunculus species do not have swollen rootstocks and cannot be dried off during their dormant season, they are not sold by bulb nurseries. However, one species, *R. asiaticus*, has been developed from its original wild forms.

R. asiaticus comes from the eastern Mediterranean and has fleshy clawlike roots that lie dry and dormant over summer, before starting into growth during fall and winter. It should be planted in fall, in a well-drained, sunny spot sheltered from severe weather, at the foot of a sunny wall or near a group of evergreen shrubs, for example. The tubers are planted at a depth of 2 in (5 cm), spaced 4 in (10 cm) apart, with the "claws" pointing downward. In cold-winter areas, they should be kept dry over winter and then planted in spring for flowering in summer; they are sometimes found in spring catalogs. These plants are not suitable for areas where spring is short and hot. Propagation is by division of the tubers into separate crowns at replanting time. Hardiness zone: 8.

R. asiaticus

R. asiaticus (*above*)

The wild form has a basal cluster of long-stalked, lobed leaves, and 1-2 ft (30-60 cm) high stems that carry erect saucer-shaped flowers in a range of colors, from red and pink to yellow, orange, and white. Each flower has a single row of petals and a large central mass of stamens, but some of the highly developed cultivated forms, such as the Turban- and Peony-flowered types, have tight double blossoms.

RHODOHYPOXIS

These delightful dwarf bulbs come from South Africa and produce a long succession of flowers from early to late summer, which range in color from white to various shades of pink and red. They are dormant in winter and will survive freezing conditions of 23°F (-5°C), but in very cold areas they are best lifted over winter and stored in peat in a frost-free place. Planting takes place in spring in a light soil with a good sand and peat content; small tubers should be planted at a depth of 1 in (2.5 cm), spaced 1 in apart. They require sunny or partially shaded sites in hot, dry climates, but do not like to be too sunbaked in the growing season. They are also suitable for shallow pots or pans in a terrarium or sun-room. Propagation is by offsets and stolons in spring. Hardiness zone: 7.

R. 'Susan'

R. baurii (*above*)

Growing 2-4 in (5-10 cm) high, *R. baurii* has narrow, hairy leaves and slender stems. Each bears a solitary flat flower with 6 petals meeting in the center, completely closing off the eye of the flower. The flowers are about 1 in (2.5 cm) in diameter and come in a wide range of colors: 'Ruth' has large white flowers; 'Fred Broome' is a large-flowering strong pink; 'Pictus' has white flowers with pink tips to the petals; and 'Albrighton' is a deep pink version. The popular 'Susan' is a red-pink color.

SANDERSONIA

A genus of just one species, this is a climbing plant from southern Africa that may be grown outdoors in mild-winter areas, but elsewhere is best treated as a greenhouse or sun-room plant. The fingerlike tubers are planted in spring at a depth of 4 in (10 cm), in well-drained, sandy potting soil in a sunny spot; they need watering to start into growth. Feed them every 2 weeks with a liquid fertilizer, and provide them with a trellis or thin stakes to climb up. They should be lifted and stored in a frost-free place during winter dormancy. The tubers increase naturally and propagation involves division at repotting time. Hardiness zone: 9.

S. aurantiaca

This bulb grows up to 3 ft (90 cm) high and has scattered lance-shaped leaves, with solitary orange pendent flowers in the axils of the upper ones. The urn-shaped flowers are about 1 in (2.5 cm) long.

SAUROMATUM

Like most other plants in this family, these tuberous-rooted members of the arum family carry their tiny flowers on a pencil-like spadix surrounded by a large spathe, which is tubular at its lower part. The spathes are produced before the leaves, and the bulbs will flower unplanted if placed on a windowsill. However, the bulbs must be potted or planted if they are to be kept. In cold areas, grow them in a greenhouse in humus-rich potting medium. Feed them with a liquid fertilizer during the growing season and dry them off in winter. If planted outdoors, plant the tubers about 4 in (10 cm) deep, in well-drained, rich soil in a sheltered, partially shaded spot; in areas where the ground freezes, they will need lifting over winter. Propagate by offsets at replanting or repotting time. Hardiness zone: 10.

S. venosum

S. venosum (syn. *S. guttatum*) (*above*)
Voodoo lily or monarch of the east
This is a Himalayan plant whose tubers produce a 1-2 ft (30-60 cm) long spathe, with a tubular, bottlelike lower part that widens into a coiled blade in the upper half. It is yellowish-orange, green, or purple with large purple blotches. The flower is followed by a single leaf with several finger-like lobes, which may reach a height of 1½ ft (45 cm).

SCADOXUS (see HAEMANTHUS)

SPARAXIS
Harlequin flower

Although these colorful bulbs normally begin to grow in the fall and flower in early spring, the corms are often kept dry through winter and sold for spring planting and same-year summer flowering. In such cases, it is necessary to lift the corms in late summer and dry and store them in a frost-free place over winter; otherwise they will revert to their normal habit of starting into growth in fall. While not a problem in very mild-winter areas, in frosty-winter regions they will not survive. These plants do well in sandy soil but require plenty of moisture during their growing season. The corms should be planted about 2-3 in (5-7.5 cm) deep. Propagate by division or seed in fall. Hardiness zone: 9.

S. elegans (syn. *Streptanthera elegans*) (*below*)
This sparaxis has fans of upright lance-shaped leaves and 1 ft (30 cm) tall stems. These carry spikes of up to 5 almost flat flowers, each 1-1½ in (2.5-4 cm) across. The blooms are orange or white, with a purplish-black area surrounding a central yellow eye.

S. elegans

S. grandiflora
Similar in general appearance to *S.elegans*, *S. grandiflora* has deep purple flowers.

S. tricolor (*below*)
This has large flowers 2-2½ in (5-6.5 cm) in diameter, which come in a range of colors, from red and orange to purple and pink.

S. tricolor

SPREKELIA
Jacobean lily

A lovely Mexican bulb of the amaryllis family, the Jacobean lily is often treated as a pot plant for a greenhouse or sun-room; however, in mild areas, it can be grown outdoors in a sheltered spot. The bulbs should be planted in a well-drained, loam-based potting soil in spring, 1 per 5 in (13 cm) pot, with the tip of the bulb just protruding. Start into growth by gentle watering and keep the bulb at a minimum temperature of 60°F (16°C). During the growing period, apply a liquid plant food formulated for acid-loving plants. When the plant dies back in fall, withhold water and keep dry and frost-free over winter, repotting in spring. Propagate by removing offsets at repotting time. Hardiness zone: 9.

S. formossisima (*below*)
With the narrow, strap-shaped leaves held in a basal cluster, the stems of this plant reach a height of 6-12 in (15-30 cm) in early summer. Each stalk bears 1 large, deep red flower made up of 6 petals; the upper 3 are wide-spreading and the lower ones are pendent, held close together to form a lip.

S. formossisima

TIGRIDIA
These bulbs can be grown outside in areas that have only slight winter frosts; where the ground freezes, they are best lifted in fall and stored in dry peat in warmer conditions. The bulbs are planted in spring, requiring a sheltered, sunny site and well-drained soil. In areas with a cold, late spring, it is better to start them off in pots and plant them when the soil has warmed up. Propagation by seed sown in spring will produce flowering plants only in the first or second flowering season. Named

varieties should be propagated by division of clumps since they will not breed true from seed. Hardiness zone: 8.

T. pavonia

T. pavonia (*above*)
Tiger flower
This species has erect sword-shaped leaves with prominent veins and 1-2 ft (30-60 cm) high stems bearing green spathes that enclose several buds. They emerge in succession to give a long flowering period, but each flower is very short-lived, lasting only one morning. The blooms reach 4-6 in (10-15cm) in diameter and are somewhat irislike in appearance, with 3 large outer petals. The most frequently seen form is a deep flame-red, with a heavily red-blotched center on a near-white background. There are, however, many forms: 'Alba' has pure white flowers; 'Aurea' is a yellow-flowered type; 'Liliacea' has reddish-purple flowers that are variegated white in the center; and 'Canariensis' is a deep yellow color, although a pink form is sometimes offered under this name.

TRITONIA
A small genus of southern Africa cormous plants, some tritonias are winter-growing, while others flower in summer. The former are normally planted in fall, in frost-free conditions, for spring flowering, but some are kept dry over winter and sold in spring. These must be lifted in late summer and dried off again or they will revert to their normal behavior and try and grow through winter. The summer-growing species are hardier since they die down over winter and are protected underground. They need ordinary, reasonably fertile garden soil and a sunny spot in which to grow. Propagation of both types of *Tritonia* is by division at replanting time. Hardiness zones: 7-8.

T. crocata (*below*)
A winter-growing species, *T. crocata* can be kept dry for a spring planting and summer flowering. It grows from 1-1½ ft (30-45 cm) high, with a loose spike of up to 10 flowers, each 1-2 in (2.5-5 cm) in diameter. The rounded flowers narrow to a short tube at the base; they are usually orange.

T. crocata

T. rubrolucens (syn. *Crocosmia rosea*)
This summer-growing species flowers late in the same season. It grows up to 2 ft (60 cm) high, with narrow leaves and loose spikes of 5-8 pink funnel-shaped flowers.

VALLOTA
Although most likely to be found in catalogs under this name, *Vallota* is now botanically regarded as a *Cyrtanthus*. It is a tender bulbous plant from South Africa that, after flowering in summer, has a period of winter rest. However, since it is evergreen, it does not die down and should never be dried out completely. The bulbs are potted in early spring, 1 per 5 in (13 cm) diameter container filled with a loam-based potting medium. Start the plant into growth by lightly watering it and keep it at a temperature of 60-65°F (16-18.5°C). It is best left undisturbed for several years, with monthly feeds of liquid fertilizer during the growing season. In areas with very mild winters, it can be grown outdoors in a sheltered, sunny spot, provided the bulbs are planted at a depth of 4-6 in (10-15 cm). Propagation is by offsets, detached without disturbing the larger bulbs. Hardiness zone: 10.

V. speciosa (syn. *Cyrtanthus purpureus*)
Scarborough or George lily (*next column*)
This species grows to a height of 1-2 ft (30-60 cm) and has wide, straplike, semierect bright green basal leaves and large, wide, funnel-shaped scarlet-red flowers. They reach 3-4 in (7.5-10 cm) across and are held several to an umbel at the top of a stout stem.

V. speciosa

WATSONIA
A large South African genus, watsonias have dense, symmetrical spikes of brightly colored funnel-shaped flowers. They are mostly tender but are very easy to grow in sunny spots that experience only slight winter frosts. Elsewhere, they can be grown in large containers and moved to a greenhouse over winter. On the whole, they perform best if left undisturbed, although they can be lifted and dried over winter. The large corms should be planted 6 in (15 cm) deep in a light soil; in areas of heavy, badly drained soil, add sand. Propagation is by division of clumps or by seed, which may take 3-5 years to produce flowering-size corms. Hardiness zone: 8.

W. angusta

W. angusta (*above*)
Growing 3-6 ft (90 cm-1.8 m) high, this watsonia has tough, narrow leaves and branched flower spikes that bear several narrow, tubular red flowers.

W. densiflora (*below*)

This is an aptly named bulb because its unbranched flower spikes bear up to 40 funnel-shaped pink flowers that are packed tightly together; each measures about 2 in (5 cm) long and 1½ in (4 cm) across at the mouth. The stiff, tough swordlike leaves are erect, and the whole plant may reach 4 ft (1.2 m) or more in height.

W. densiflora

W. meriana

This watsonia measures 2-6 ft (60 cm-1.8 m) high and has broad, tough sword-shaped leaves. The stems are mostly unbranched, although some have 1-2 branches. The loose flower spike is made of tubular orange, red, or pink flowers that open 1½-2 in (4-5 cm) wide at the mouth. There is also a form that produces bulbils on the flower spike, known as var. *bulbillifera*.

W. pillansii (**syn.** *W. beatricis*) (*below*)

This plant reaches 1½-3 ft (45-90 cm) in height, and has tough, narrow, erect leaves. The densely flowered spikes of up to 30 bright orange or red flowers are usually unbranched; each narrow bloom is funnel-shaped and about 3 in (7.5 cm) long, opening out 1½ in (4 cm) wide at the mouth.

W. pillansii

ZANTEDESCHIA
Calla or Arum lily

These showy members of the arum family are well known for their large, upright funnel-shaped spathes and are often used by florists throughout the year in cut-flower arrangements. In a warm greenhouse they can be brought into flower at almost any time of the year, but they can also be grown outdoors in mild climates for summer flowering, in which case they are usually evergreen. In colder areas they make good container plants: start them into growth in spring and move them outside in early summer; they should be returned to a frost-free place and dried off over winter. The tubers should be planted at least 6 in (15 cm) below soil level in deep containers, in a well-drained, rich potting medium, and given liquid fertilizer at 2-week intervals during the growing season. For the majority of the species and varieties, a minimum winter temperature of 50°F (10°C) is necessary, but *Z. aethiopica* is hardier and may be grown outdoors in areas where the ground does not freeze, if planted at a minimum depth of 2 in (5 cm). It can also be grown as a water plant, with up to 12 in (30 cm) of water covering the tubers. Propagation is by removal of offsets at repotting or replanting time. Hardiness zones: 8-9.

Z. 'Crowborough'

Z. aethiopica (*above* and *next column*)

This South African species has dark green arrow-shaped leaves and 2-3 ft (60-90 cm) high stems, each carrying a large white spathe up to 8 in (20 cm) long that encloses a yellow club-shaped spadix. The variety 'Crowborough' is considered a hardier version, and the attractive 'Green Goddess' has green spathes, splashed green on a white background in the center.

Z. 'Green Goddess'

Z. rehmannii (*below*)

Pink arum

This is a much shorter plant, about 1-1½ ft (30-45 cm) high, with pink to reddish-purple spathes about 3 in (7.5 cm) in length.

Z. rehmanni

Z. 'Black Eye Beauty' (*below*)

This cultivar has striking cream-colored spathes, with a black central eye.

Z. 'Black Eye Beauty'

Z. 'Solfatare'

One of the yellow-spathed varieties, 'Solfatare' is a paler sulfur-yellow.

FALL

Garden highlights

Fall-flowering bulbs make outstanding additions to the garden, whether planted individually or mixed with other plants. They are prized because they flower toward the end of the season, when many annuals and perennials have finished their main burst of color. All are adaptable, and with careful placement, most areas of the garden benefit from their presence because little else is in flower at this time.

Colchicums are good fall-flowering bulbs, but take care because the bulbs are poisonous and some people get a rash from touching the stems. A small group of about five bulbs planted in the gap between two shrubs can make a startling difference on a dull fall morning. The white-flowered forms, including *Colchicum autumnale* var. *album* and *C. speciosum* 'Album,' are ideal, particularly when planted in a straight, narrow strip in front of a conifer hedge, a row of evergreen such as *Viburnum davidii*, or a few small-leaved

hollies, such as *Ilex crenata* (Japanese holly). For a white theme, grow white colchicums at the base of a white-berried shrub like *Gaultheria cuneata* or *Symphoricarpos albus* 'White Hedge' (snowberry), or plant it beneath the lovely *Sorbus cashmiriana*. White-variegated hollies can also be used, with white-variegated ivies as ground cover. Large-flowering colchicum hybrids, however, produce large leaves in the spring and can swamp their smaller neighbors, particularly squills or anemones.

The exotic *Amaryllis belladonna*, an impressive fall bulb, needs a sunny spot, ideally at the base of a fence or wall. It can either be planted on its own for a bold display or grown among climbers and wall shrubs that are nearing the end of their season and are beginning to lose their color. With its heads of beautiful pink or white trumpet-shaped blossoms, *A. belladonna* looks stunning pushing up its flowers through

(previous page) *Naturalized clumps of* Colchicum speciosum *'Album' show up well among the carpet of golden-brown autumn leaves.*

(below) *The brilliant color of this* Colchicum speciosum *hybrid when used in a bold grouping makes an unforgettable impact.*

(right) *During flowering, the goblet-shaped colchicums open wide to reveal their orange stamens, as shown here.*

a fading, tangled mass of *Clematis orientalis* with its feathery seed heads. It also mixes well with the almond-scented, creamy white late-flowering *C. flammula*. For a bold combination of strong colors, mix *A. belladonna* with *Ceratostigma willmottianum*, a shrub with bright blue flowers produced from late summer and continuing into fall. Wall-trained espalier apple and pear trees also provide an unusual backdrop for *A. belladonna*. For a simple but effective display, plant the bulbs in gravel-topped soil at the base of a fence or wall, which will act as a uniform background against which the elegant beauty of the leafless flowers will stand out. To reap the full benefit of the plant's architectural shape, space the bulbs approximately 1½ in (3.5 cm) apart in a line rather than leaving them in a clump.

Nerine bowdenii is a delicate-looking plant, with slender, bright pink blossoms. Being taller than *Amaryllis belladonna*, it needs to be planted much closer to a fence or wall. Unlike the majority of bulbs, it prospers only when crowded; plant the bulbs almost touching and leave them to grow. The choice of companion plants for *N. bowdenii* is limited, but the flowers look good against a fence or wall covered with the

climber *Trachelospermum jasminoides* 'Variegatum,' which in some weather conditions develops pinkish edges on its leaves. The *Agapanthus* Headbourne hybrids are recommended, especially for narrow borders in enclosed areas, against a backdrop of large-leaved ivy. These vigorous, exotic-looking plants have umbels of bright blue flowers that start to open before the nerines but fade around the same time. The fall-flowering *Liriope muscari* (lily turf), with its spikes of rounded lavender or purple-blue flowers and narrow, glossy dark green leaves, creates a bold, colorful display when mixed with *N. bowdenii*. More formal companions include yucca and the coppery-leaved *Phormium*.

The tropical appearance of *N. bowdenii* can be fully utilized to create an exotic-looking garden. Where they are hardy plant it beneath the upright spring growth of *Rosa moyesii* or its variety 'Geranium,' both popular shrub roses that have butter-yellow foliage and masses of crimson red hips in fall. Alternatively, *Rosa glauca* (syn. *R. rubrifolia*) provides an attractive background punctuated with bright red hips. In a more confined space, you can insert *N. bowdenii* between the spreading branches of the herringbone *Cotoneaster horozantalis*, so the blossoms peep up through the partially defoliated branches of the shrub, when it is heavily laden with colorful fruit from late summer onwards.

(left) *Soft pink* Nerine bowdenii *grouped alone in a leafy spot create a subtle, airy effect.*

(below) *Vibrant crimson and purple asters frame pink nerines in a bold and vibrant border planting.*

Crinums are among some of the most attractive of the fall-flowering bulbs. They are large, showy plants with umbels of funnel-shaped flowers. Some are tender and need a warm, sunny spot ideally against a wall. However, *Crinum × powellii* is the hardiest of the group and can be grown outside in a border in temperate climates. With its soft drooping flowers in white or shades of pink, it is ideal for providing early-fall color. Crinums are best planted in clumps on their own as they tend to swamp any nearby plants with their leaves.

Another good plant for autumn is the eucomis, commonly known as the pineapple flower. They are not very showy bulbs, and their tall spikes of star-shaped white, pale green or

(left) Crinum × powellii *is ideal for a large-scale planting. Here, they are used boldly, generously massed together in parallel borders beneath a walk of apple trees. The foliage of the crinums overhang the edge of the path, softening the effect and inviting the visitor to walk slowly along the path to admire the plants. Crinum's leaves can swamp other plants and therefore they are best planted in clumps on their own. A largely frost-free site with plenty of sun is essential for crinums, or they will not perform well. For a good show of flowers like this one, they must have a plentiful supply of water in summer during the growing season and during flowering.*

(right) Eucomis comosa, *commonly known as the pineapple flower, needs a sheltered site, ideally against a wall, to produce a healthy display of flower spikes like these.*

pale pink flowers and rosettes of basal leaves are best appreciated when seen against a background planting of dark foliage. They enjoy sheltered conditions provided by walls and fences, which also provide a backdrop against which the plants show up.

Schizostylis coccinea 'Grandiflora' has spikes of gladiolus-like red flowers and can be used as a colorful border highlight when mixed with late-flowering red dahlias and *Sedum spectabile* (ice plant), which has fleshy gray-green leaves and vibrant pink flowers. If the border is big enough, plant *Anaphalis triplinervis* (pearly everlasting) at the back. This can form a clump up to 2 ft (60 cm) across, of neat gray foliage, topped by masses of star-shaped white flowers that hide the otherwise straggly foliage of the schizostylis.

(above left) *Although it may be a year or two before* Sternbergia lutea *flowers, if it is left undisturbed, it will grow into clumps.*

(above right) *Despite its fragile appearance,* Colchicum speciosum '*Album*' *will naturalize under trees and shrubs, and even in rough grass.*

(right) *Both the pink and white forms of* Cyclamen hederifolium *are happy growing in a cool, semishaded spot like this one.*

Naturalizing

There are many superb opportunities for naturalizing some of the smaller fall bulbs, but great care must be taken with their positioning. The two small fall crocuses, *Crocus speciosus* and *C. sativus*, can be naturalized in grass. They cannot be raised in a regularly mowed area because the flowers may be decapitated before they have a chance to open. A sparse grassy patch under the edge of a tree canopy is the perfect spot for naturalizing crocuses, as are areas of turf around shrubs, where the grass can be left to grow without being mowed until the bulbs have died down. Instead of grouping an individual species, mix a number of different varieties together at planting time for an eye-catching multicolored effect. All will flower during fall, over a period of several weeks rather than simultaneously. In more open ground, autumn-flowering crocuses look sensational when mixed with the steel-blue short-growing grass *Festuca glauca* (blue fescue). This is a mound-forming plant rather than a spreading grass, so the crocus corms can easily be planted around it. A different but equally appealing combination involves the golden-leaved grass *Milium effusum* 'Aureum' (wood millet).

Crocus sativus (saffron crocus) is one of the most popular autumn crocuses for naturalizing. It has rosy lilac or deep purplish blossoms, which look pretty when sprinkled at random in a grassy area. *C. sativus* can also be planted among a clump of *Viola labradorica* 'Purpurea,' a violet that has dark purple-green kidney-shaped foliage. *C. kotschyanus*, also a popular choice, does not spread as quickly in open grass as when planted beneath trees and shrubs or in the bare earth. It is a delicate-looking yet robust crocus; the masses of rosy lilac chalicelike blossoms contrast superbly with the foliage of brightly colored fall plants. For the best effect, select a shrub with branches that spread horizontally across the ground, touching it, and plant 15 to 20 bulbs in the soil among the shrub's foliage.

Fothergilla major (syn. *F. monticola*) is an especially fine companion shrub, with clusters of fragrant white flowers in spring and fiery orange-red leaves that coincide with the appearance of the autumn crocus. *C. kotschyanus* can also be planted among the rugged stems of *Rhus typhina* (stag's-horn sumach), which has fiery fall foliage.

Crocuses mix well with ground-cover plants, particularly ajugas, many of which have strikingly colorful leaves. *Ajuga reptans* 'Multicolor' is a first-class choice, with its rose, cream, and purple foliage, as is the dark purple-copper *A. r.* 'Atropurpurea.' Even the ordinary green *A. pyramidalis* becomes an appealing feature when interspersed with *Crocus speciosus*. The almost evergreen, rounded foliage of *Lysimachia nummularia* (creeping Jennie) can be enlivened with a sprinkling of autumn crocuses for a fine display. Although its golden-leaved cultivar, *L. n.* 'Aurea,' fades as fall moves into winter, it remains sufficiently colorful to make a first-rate companion. The golden yellow *Thymus* × *citriodorus* 'Aureus' (lemon-scented thyme) and *Trifolium repens* 'Purpurascens' (a purple-leaved clover) also provide suitable ground cover for naturalized crocuses.

Sternbergia lutea makes an attractive fall highlight, requiring a free-draining soil in a raised bed or rock garden. A waxy crocuslike plant, it is one of the few bright yellow fall flowers. Possible companion plants include *Thymus vulgaris* (common thyme), *T.* × *citriodorus* (lemon-scented thyme), and *T.* × *c.* 'Aureus,' a golden-leaved relation.

The colorful fall-flowering cyclamen deserves a place in any garden. The best choice of hardy cyclamen is *Cyclamen hederifolium*, which has pink or purplish-rose flowers and contrasting dark green and silver-marbled foliage. Since it enjoys partial shade, it can be naturalized beneath a fine ornamental specimen tree like one of the Japanese maples. An excellent alternative to Japanese maple is *Betula utilis* var. *jacquemontii* (Himalayan birch). This tree has a white trunk against which the rose-pink cyclamens look especially striking. Cyclamens can also be planted under any of the mountain ash group of *Sorbus*. For a vibrant display, underplant *Sorbus* 'Joseph Rock' with *Cyclamen hederifolium* or *C. h.* 'Album'; the mahogany-red leaves and brilliant yellow fruit of the tree look marvelous with the show of deep rose pink or cool, icy white flowers beneath.

With careful placing, colchicums can also be naturalized successfully. However, they produce enormous basal leaves the following spring, which may be a handicap unless the bulbs are naturalized in soil beneath shrubs and trees—in which case the foliage is an enormous advantage since it covers otherwise bare earth.

The best shrub for mixing with colchicums is the rhododendron, with its broad, straplike glossy foliage. This combination is not only visually satisfying, enlivening the rhododendron before it flowers, but useful, since few other plants grow well in close proximity to rhododendrons, which produce a dense shade and have extensive surface roots. Colchicums, however, can be grown under the edge of the foliage canopy for a fine planting. Rhododendron hybrids grown in a formal garden combine well with hybrid colchicums such as 'Lilac Wonder' and 'The Giant.' If the rhododendrons are species plants or primary hybrids, then they should be underplanted with lilac-pink *Colchicum autumnale* var. *album*.

Other mixtures involve colchicums and herbaceous plants such as *Hosta glauca* (plantain lily), *Bergenia purpurascens*, and peonies. These plants are useful because their new growth hides the fading early summer foliage of the bulbs.

(below) *Autumn-flowering colchicums need careful siting as they produce large foliage in spring. They are ideal for naturalizing in the light shade of tree canopies, and the more vigorous types grow well in grass.*

(above) *The unusual-looking* Gladiolus papilio *is very hardy and will spread into sizable patches in free-draining conditions.*

(above) *Sternbergias enjoy free-draining conditions, as provided by this sunny gravel bed, and the flowers show up well against the pale chips.*

(above) Colchicum bivonae *thrives in well-drained soil. For the greatest impact, group the plants together in large clumps.*

Rock gardens

A selection of fall-flowering bulbs can add color and interest to a rock garden at a time when few other alpine or dwarf plants are producing attractive displays. Crocuses are especially valuable because they can be planted among established alpines without interfering with their lifestyles. Unlike many other bulbs, crocuses present few problems when dying back as they discretely fade into the associated plant cover without smothering nearby growth.

The hardiest of the fall crocuses, *Crocus speciosus* and *C. kotschyanus*, thrive among most of the popular mound-forming rock plants such as aubrieta and arabis. *C. speciosus* has produced some fine cultivars that can be planted in tiny niches in the rocks where mound-forming plants cannot establish themselves; plant two or three corms together in a group and top-dress with a layer of fine mulch to form a pleasing background. The bluish-lavender 'Cassiope' and pale violet-blue 'Pollux' are the nicest to grow, although the blue 'Oxonian' is reputedly the most difficult to establish. *C. speciosus* shows up well against soft gray-green plants like *Artemisia schmidtiana* 'Nana,' but it also mixes well with brightly colored plants, such as *Polygonum vacciniifolium*, which has deep pink flowers held on red stems.

The lilac-colored *Crocus longiflorus* is another good choice for a rock garden, along with the deep purple *C. nudiflorus* and creamy white *C. ochroleucus*. Each is best grown alone in an isolated position between two rocks, without competition from permanent plants. But there is no reason why small-growing annuals, such as *Limnanthes douglasii* (poached-egg plant or meadow foam) and night-scented or Virginia stocks, should not be sown over the top to provide summer color. However, take care when removing the plants at the end of the season not to disturb the awakening crocus corms.

Just as valuable as crocuses in the rock garden, cyclamens thrive when planted in pockets of free-draining soil that is rich in organic matter. *Cyclamen hederifolium* is the most decorative species; it has attractively patterned, ivy-like foliage with a velvety feel to it and pale to deep pink flowers that are stained darker around the mouth. *C. graecum* is also handsome, with pink or white flowers that are stained purple around the mouth and silver-marked dark green leaves that have reddish undersides. The pink- or white-flowering *C. cilicium* has dark green, silver-blotched heart-shaped leaves, and the smaller, more delicate, fragrant flowers are charming. They are appropriate for a small rock garden, where it is easier to cultivate the more refined species. *C. hederifolium* starts to flower in early fall and continues into winter.

The much-neglected fall-flowering snowdrop, *Galanthus reginae-olgae*, grows well in a sheltered corner of the rock garden, in rich, free-draining soil. Closely allied to the common snowdrop, *G. nivalis*, it requires drier summer conditions than its more familiar cousin.

Containers and window boxes

The majority of fall-flowering bulbs are too transient for use in window boxes, where a constant and colorful display is vital. However, autumn crocuses are well suited to this type of cultivation because they provide an excellent show in the first year. Plant them among established plants like pansies, primroses or *Bellis* (cushion daisies) for some late-fall color. After flowering, the crocus corms can be dug up and returned to the garden; they will continue to grow in the open ground provided the corms are planted immediately.

Colchicums are also useful for window box displays, despite their brief flowering period. Choose the hybrid types, particularly the double lilac-pink 'Waterlily,' the magnificent 'Lilac Wonder,' and the rose-pink 'The Giant.' All flower for about 3 weeks, before their large basal leaves appear, after which they can be planted outdoors and the window boxes filled with plants like pansies and spring bulbs.

Even some of the taller-growing bulbs are suitable for containers. Some, such as *Eucomis comosa* (pineapple flower), can be grown alone for a really

(above) *This unusual container demands dramatic but not overpowering planting, as provided by these hardy cyclamen and the trailing ivy.*

dramatic feature. Plant three to five bulbs in an antique-looking container positioned in a corner of a courtyard, set against a brick or stone wall draped in ivy. This will show them off to best advantage. Stone and terra-cotta look particularly good with the purple-spotted stems and greenish-white flowers.

Nerines grow well in containers, looking best in terra-cotta pots. Planted alone, they produce a fabulous display for approximately 4 weeks, after which they should be put away in a frost-free place such as a garden shed or basement; if the soil in the container freezes solid, the bulbs will quickly perish. They can also be mixed with other plants for a more varied show. Generally, *Nerine bowdenii* is the best choice for mixing because it is the hardiest and most reliable. Choose companions with plenty of verdant foliage, as the flowering spikes of the bulbs look most attractive when seen pushing up through a mass of greenery. In a large tub, *N. bowdenii* combines well with hardy ferns, such as *Athyrium filix-femina* (lady fern), with its dainty lance-shaped, much-divided arching fronds, or *Polypodium vulgare*, with its herringbonelike fronds.

The moisture-loving *Schizostylis coccinea* and its various cultivars, usually seen in large patches near ponds or streams, can also be grown in large, deep containers, provided they are given a rich organic soil. Plant them with hostas and evergreen ferns like *Polystichum acrostichoides* (Christmas fern) or *Vinca minor* (lesser periwinkle).

(above) *Pink nerines (*Nerine bowdenii*) and bright green ferns complement one another, and the fern fronds help mask the bare stems of the nerines.*

The last combination works particularly well in a large stone trough; by the time the bulbs flower, the periwinkle will be finished flowering, leaving a carpet of lovely dark green foliage around the base of the tall stems.

Large urns and vaselike containers, especially those that are shallow and have broad bases, are suitable for displaying *Crinum powellii* and *C. × p.* 'Album.' These giant bulbs, with long, straplike leaves and bold heads of pink or white trumpetlike flowers, create a luxuriant tropical impact on a sunny terrace or patio. In cold winter areas, they must be grown in a well-drained soil with winter protection because, while they are hardy enough to cope with life in the open ground, in a container they are more vulnerable because their roots are very near the freezing air. Plant them on their own rather than mixing them with other plants, so the full splendor of the bulb is displayed.

(below) *A simple terra-cotta window box is ideal for this combination of lilies, cyclamen, skimmia, and ornamental cabbage.*

Indoors

Indoor bulbs can be planted in pots and bowls and forced into early growth for fall-flowering displays. Colchicums are the easiest to grow; they can flower as unplanted bulbs because they have substantial food stores, together with embryo flowers, within their large, fleshy bulbs. Prop up the bulbs or place them in a square glass vase or goldfish bowl on a windowsill. In a light spot they will flower without any assistance. Immediately after flowering, the bulbs should be planted outside in the garden so that they can build up their food reserves for the next year. If you are considering using the smaller-flowered *Colchicum autumnale* choose the white var. *album,* the large double-flowered 'The Giant,' 'Waterlily,' or the beautiful 'Lilac Wonder.'

(above) *The purple-green continus leaves used to cover this container blend beautifully with the pink flowers of this autumn-flowering cyclamen.*

Some of the tender nerines also make lovely fall-flowering pot plants, especially the bright pink *Nerine sarniensis,* which is considered the most attractive. Although all these nerines naturally flower at this time of the year, the main benefit of a year-long indoor cultural regime is that plants blossom in perfect condition, without being damaged by the weather. Pack approximately five bulbs into a 6 in (15 cm) diameter pot or bowl filled with soil for the best results.

N. masonorum is a much shorter species, ideal for small pots, rarely growing more than 6 in (15 cm) high. It sports small, undulating crimped blossoms of the softest pink. The closely allied *N. filifolia* is also short, with its loose umbels of rose-pink blossoms held on stems no more than 1 ft (30 cm) high. It has narrow, rush-like leaves that, unlike most other nerine leaves, are evergreen in areas with mild winters. If regularly watered, *N. filifolia* can become a permanent colorful indoor feature, continuing to show off its leaves after flowering.

Of all the fall-flowering indoor bulbs, *Eucharis amazonica* is the most difficult to grow, demanding a consistently high temperature of around 70°F (21°C) if it is to perform well. It can rarely be cultivated to perfection without a heated

greenhouse, but it is well worth considering for a modern sun-room. A magnificent plant with a stout stem up to 2 ft
(60 cm) high, it is studded with large, icy
white flowers of the richest fragrance. It
is such a magnificent plant it is suitable
for a polished brass or copper vessel, or
even an Italian-style terra-cotta pot.
Plant a single bulb in a pot with a 5-6 in
(13-15 cm) diameter.

(right) *These soft apricot-colored begonias are
particularly appropriate for a mellow autumnal
indoor display.*

(below) *Autumn-flowering cyclamens make
excellent indoor plants, provided that they can be
kept at a constant cool temperature and are not
exposed to direct sunlight. They will also grow well
in cool conservatories. Interest is added here with
spiky, lichen-encrusted twigs, which provide a
contrasting shape to the plant yet pick up the silvery
green of the cyclamen leaves.*

Cut flowers

There are relatively few fall-flowering
bulbs suitable for cutting, but those that
are tend to be colorful, stately charac-
ters. They are best displayed on their
own or mixed with a few branches of
fall foliage to bring out their color. More
ambitious arrangements suitable for cel-
ebrating harvest time, however, might
include a variety of berries, as well as
other fruits, grains and vegetables.

Fall-flowering nerines, especially the
hardy pink *Nerine bowdenii*, make
excellent long-lasting cut flowers, as do
Crinum and *Amaryllis belladonna*. None
of these bulbs requires special cultural
treatment to be suitable for cutting, but
if they become congested, the stems
are sometimes shorter than they would
otherwise be. Carefully lift the clumps
from the soil using a hand fork, split
them into a number of smaller clumps,
and replant the smaller clumps. This will
reduce overcrowding and produce
longer flower stems.

Nerines come in a wide variety of colors, from white through pink to scarlet.
Because they are such intricate flowers,
they look good in plain vases, especially
glass ones. For added color, include
some orange-red-leaved *Prunus*, small
branches of copper beech, or stems
of pink fall-flowering sedums. The belladonna lily, however, looks best on its
own; either bunch several together in a
colorful mass, or for a simpler arrangement, place a few stems on their own in
a glass container.

use. The delicate-looking yellow or white flowers, suffused with violet, have hooded upper petals and darker yellow patches on the lower petals. Plant the bulbs approximately 3 in (7.5 cm) apart, and once the flower spikes appear, feed the plants with liquid fertilizer to strengthen the spikes. When cutting the stems, remove as little foliage as possible so the corm will be replenished for the following year. These blooms look best on their own in a vase.

(left) *A jar of shiny conkers provides a seasonal solid foundation for this bunch of exotic-looking amaryllis blooms.*

(below) *The elegance of* Lilium longiflorum *demands simple arrangements in which their shapes can be admired without distraction.*

(far left) *For a harvest-time display, mix* Gloriosa *'Rothschildiana,'* Anemone *'Mona Lisa,' and* Crocosmia *'Emily McKenzie' with fruit and foliage.*

All the popular varieties of *Schizostylis* are good for flower arrangements. The flower spikes resemble red gladioli and look very effective on their own or mixed with glossy, dark green, trailing ivy stems, which show off their color. For an especially vibrant display, include brightly colored dahlias.

Because they flower so late in the fall and they are quite tall, *Schizostylis* varieties are vulnerable to weather damage, particularly buffeting winds, and must be grown in a sheltered spot. In order to ensure quality flowers and long stems, the bulbs need lifting and dividing every 3 or 4 years; congested plants growing in a border will make a better overall display but will not produce good individual blooms that are suitable for cutting.

The unusual-looking *Gladiolus papilio* can also be cut for decorative indoor

ALLIUM
Ornamental onion

Most alliums are dealt with under the Spring and Summer Directories (see pp. 87 and 150), but one small species, *A. callimischon*, is well worth growing in autumn. Although not showy, it is delightful when viewed up close. Allium grows best in a sunny spot in well-drained soil; it is perhaps best treated as a terrarium plant. If planting outdoors, choose a sheltered spot where the soil is unlikely to freeze deeply for any appreciable time. Propagation is by offsets, which in some species are produced quite freely, or by seed, which may take up to 3 years to produce flowering bulbs. Hardiness zone: 8.

A. callimischon (*below*)
The best form of this allium is the Cretan subspecies *haemostictum*, which is only 2-6 in (5-15 cm) high and has umbels of small, papery, white flowers with red spots on the petals. When it grows well, it may form clumps up to 4 in (10 cm) across. It is a suitable bulb for planting in a sheltered spot in a rock garden.

A. callimischon

AMARYLLIS
Cape belladonna or Jersey lily
The hardy amaryllis from South Africa should not be confused with the tender South American hippeastrums (see p. 228), which are often sold as house plants during winter under the erroneous name "amaryllis." The true amaryllis flowers in autumn before the leaves appear, having lain dormant during summer. To do well, it requires a hot, sunny, well-drained spot. It also needs protection from severe winter frosts, which can damage the leaves and lead to a loss of vigor. Given these conditions, the Cape belladonna is capable of

developing into clumps 1-1½ ft (30-45 cm) across in 3-5 years. Large clumps can be divided by lifting and pulling them apart in late spring; replant as soon as possible and water the bulbs to encourage new root growth. Established clumps benefit from a light dressing of a potash-rich fertilizer in fall or spring. Hardiness zone: 8.

A. belladonna

A. belladonna (*above*)
In autumn the very large bulbs of this plant produce stout, leafless flower stems 1¾-3 ft (50-90 cm) tall, and bear up to 6 or more large, fragrant, bright pink funnel-shaped flowers with petals that curl out gracefully at the tips. Once the flowers are finished, bright, glossy strap-shaped leaves appear and remain green until the following summer. There are several named cultivars in slightly different shades of pink or carmine, with varying amounts of white or pale yellow in the flowers' throats. There is also a lovely but uncommon pure white cultivar called 'Hathor.' The hybrid × *Amarcrinum* looks similar to *A. belladonna* but bears leaves throughout the year; it is a hybrid with the seldom cultivated *Crinum moorei* and is an attractive plant for a sheltered, sunny spot.

COLCHICUM
Meadow saffron
Colchicum are fall corms that are incorrectly referred to as fall crocuses; they are more closely related to lilies than true crocuses. The two can easily be distinguished —colchicums have 6 stamens and crocuses only 3. The leaves also differ: those of most colchicums are much larger than those of crocuses, which are narrow, with a white stripe along the center. The name meadow saffron is also confusing, since the well-known culinary saffron is obtained from a true autumn crocus, *Crocus sativus*;

moreover all colchicums are poisonous.

Most of the fall colchicums produce large, showy flowers in late summer and early fall. The leaves emerge in winter and spring, and they last until early summer. Although they do not require a hot, sunny spot to thrive, they look best when the flowers receive as much available autumn sun as possible, encouraging them to open into a graceful goblet shape. A well-drained soil, acid or alkaline, is suitable; the robust ones also do well in heavy clay if it is not too dense and wet. Because colchicums are leafless at flowering time, they look best planted close together in clumps or between plants that provide foliage interest, such as the purple- and gray-leaved sages. However, the leaves of colchicums are large when fully developed and swamp small plants that are planted too close. Although the flowers may be only 4-6 in (10-15 cm) high, the foliage can grow up to 1-1½ ft (30-45 cm) tall, and even a small clump of corms may have a spread of 1½ ft (45 cm) when fully developed. Colchicums look good when planted in rough grass; this compensates for the bare appearance of the flowers and the grass provides some support in inclement weather.

Seed propagation is possible but very slow, and it is more practical to dig up and divide established clumps in late summer. The corms must be planted with a minimum of 4 in (10 cm) of soil above the top of the bulb. Hardiness zones: 4-8.

C. × *agrippinum*

C. × *agrippinum* (*above*)
This excellent early-flowering hybrid has wide, funnel-shaped flowers that are strongly checkered purple on a pale background. It is best planted in a sunny spot. The foliage is much smaller than that of other colchicums.

C. autumnale (below)

This is the common meadow saffron that produces a succession of small, long-tubed, goblet-shaped pink flowers in early fall. It is weak and does not stand up well to wind and rain, so plant it in grass or with a ground cover of other plants for support. It produces large, glossy green leaves in spring. There is a white form known as *C. a.* var. *album* and a double version with many-petaled, pink-lilac flowers called var. *pleniflorum*; the white double form is called *alboplenum*. *C. autumnale* is good for naturalizing in grass and in soil among shrubs.

C. autumnale **var.** *album*

C. bivonae **(syn.** *C. bowlesianum***)** *(below)*
This colchicum has elegant goblet-shaped flowers with a purple tesselated pattern on a pale pink background. The flowers are much larger than those of *C. autumnale*. This species grows best in a sheltered, sunny spot.

C. bivonae

C. byzantinum
The blooms are similar to the small pink-purple flowers of *C. autumnale* but slightly larger. Many are produced by each corm to provide a good show in early autumn. The leaves are very large when fully expanded.

C. cilicicum

C. cilicicum (above)
An excellent species for a sunny, well-drained spot, *C. cilicicum* produces many rosy-purple, wide, funnel-shaped flowers.

C. speciosum

C. speciosum (above)
This is the showiest species, having large, goblet-shaped flowers held well above ground on strong tubes. It comes in various shades of purple and usually has a large white zone in the flower's throat; the bold leaves are a shiny green and quite attractive. It is extremely hardy and does well in sun or partial shade so long as the soil is well drained. If left undisturbed, it will increase into sizable patches. The pure white form, 'Album,' is one of the best autumn bulbs.

C. variegatum
This is a species rare in cultivation that requires a sheltered, sunny spot. It has a short tube and flat, wide, funnel-shaped flowers conspicuously marked with a purple tesselated pattern on a pale background. This coloration has been passed onto the hybrid *C. × agrippinum*, which is much easier to obtain and cultivate. The leaves of *C. variegatum* are small, gray-green, and they usually display wavy edges.

Cultivars and hybrids *(below)*
In addition to the species, a large number of cultivars and hybrids are available. 'Lilac Wonder' is a vigorous hybrid with lilac-pink flowers; 'The Giant' has large, well-formed, goblet-shaped flowers in mauve with white centers; 'Waterlily' is a double-flowering colchicum with many rich pink-lilac flowers produced together in a bunch; and the hybrid 'Conquest' has attractive checkered flowers that are a deep purple-pink, tesselated darker purple.

C. 'Waterlily'

CRINUM
Although mostly tropical, several South African crinums are hardy enough to be cultivated in cooler temperate regions of the country. They are large, showy plants with umbels of funnel-shaped flowers similar to those of an amaryllis. In warm, sheltered gardens, it is possible to grow them in a border with other perennials to provide a display in late summer or early fall, but in colder areas, a warm, sunny spot against a wall is necessary. Crinums also make attractive subjects for large containers, which can be moved into a frost-free greenhouse or shed over winter, when the bulbs are dormant. The very large bulbs are normally planted with the neck just protruding from the soil, but in containers it is necessary to leave the upper half exposed because of the limited soil depth. Propagation is best by division of established clumps in spring. Hardiness zones: 6-8.

C. bulbispermum
This is a striking species with stems about 2-3½ ft (60 cm-1 m) high, each with up to 12 long-tubed, funnel-shaped flowers that are white with a pink-red streak along the center of each petal.

C. moorei

This crinum reaches $3\frac{1}{2}$– 5 ft (1–1.5 m) in height at flowering time. Each of its stout stems carry several fragrant, white or pale pink funnel-shaped flowers.

C. × powellii 'Album'

C. × powellii (*above*)

The hardiest hybrid of the group makes a good herbaceous border subject; it is also the most readily obtainable. Up to 10 large, funnel-shaped flowers are produced in an umbel on $3\frac{1}{2}$ ft (1 m) high stems in a soft shade of pink or white in the variety known as 'Album.'

CROCUS

The true autumn crocuses should not be confused with the meadow saffrons (see *Colchicum*). They are ideal for providing a splash of fall color but need to be sited where they will receive as much available sun as possible to open up the flowers. With a few exceptions, those mentioned here require an open, sunny spot in well-drained soil.

Since these crocuses are short at flowering time, they are best planted in a rock garden, at the front of a border, or in grass, grouped close together to provide a vivid display. The corms should be planted about 1-2 in (2.5-5 cm) deep. When clumps have built up, they can be lifted and divided in late summer, or new stocks can be raised from seed, although it takes about 3-4 years to produce flowering corms. Most of those mentioned here have no leaves when in flower. Hardiness zones: 4-6.

C. banaticus (*next column*)

This crocus is an exception to the general rule because it requires damp soil that does not become sunbaked in summer, although it still needs autumn sun to show off the flowers. It is pale to mid-violet-blue and long-tubed with 3 large outer petals and 3 small inner ones, resembling an iris flower.

C. banaticus

C. cancellatus

This Turkish species has pale lilac or white flowers striped with violet on the outside. It needs a sunny spot in a rock garden.

C. cartwrightianus

A beautiful Greek plant, this species is worth growing in a terrarium where the large, wide-open, fragrant flowers can be appreciated. It will also grow outside in a well-drained, sunny spot. The blooms are either purple with darker centers or white. Both forms have red stigmas like the saffron crocus.

C. goulimyi

C. goulimyi (*above*)

This crocus has long-tubed, goblet-shaped lilac flowers, which appear with the leaves. It needs a sheltered, sunny spot.

C. hadriaticus

Another of the saffron crocuses with bright red stigmas, this has creamy white flowers with a yellow zone in the throat.

C. kotschyanus (**syn.** *C. zonatus*) (*below*)

An excellent Turkish species, this crocus rapidly increases into clumps and is one of the first to flower in early fall. The pale lilac flowers have a yellow zone or blotches in the throat, but the variation known as *C. k. leucopharynx* has a white throat.

C. kotschyanus

C. longiflorus

One of the most fragrant of the autumn crocuses, *C. longiflorus* has deep lilac flowers with darker veins on the outside and a yellow zone in the throat. The flowers appear with the leaves.

C. niveus

Needing a sheltered, sunny spot, *C. niveus* is one of the largest-flowered of all crocuses. Goblet-shaped flowers appear with the leaves and are white or pale lilac with a yellow zone in the throat.

C. nudiflorus (*below*)

This crocus is best planted in grass or partial shade where it will not get too hot and dry in summer. The elegant long-tubed flowers are rich purple with an orange stigma. This species is stoloniferous, so large patches build up when it grows well.

C. nudiflorus

C. ochroleucus

C. ochroleucus (*above*)
This seldom seen crocus has white flowers.

C. pulchellus

C. pulchellus (*above*)
This excellent autumn crocus has pale blue flowers with deep yellow throats and darker veins.

C. sativus

C. sativus (*above*)
Saffron crocus
The large, wide-open purple flowers of *C. sativus* appear with the leaves in mid- to late autumn; each bloom has 3 long, deep red stigmas, the source of saffron. In cold areas, this crocus is not free-flowering, and the best

chance for success is to plant the corms deeply, about 4-6 in (10-15 cm) below ground, in a well-drained alkaline soil where they will bake in summer.

C. serotinus
This Spanish crocus has sizable lilac-blue flowers appearing with the leaves. The best and most readily obtainable variant is *C. s. salzmannii*, which is easily cultivated.

C. speciosus

C. speciosus (*above*)
This is the best known of all the autumnal species. Inexpensive, it is suitable for naturalizing among deciduous shrubs or in grass. Its large blooms come in shades of lilac or blue-violet, with a network of darker veins. 'Albus' is an attractive white form and 'Oxonian' one of the darkest blues.

C. tournefortii

C. tournefortii (*above*)
This beautiful late autumn crocus hails from the Greek Islands. It will grow outside in a warm, sunny spot, but does best when protected in an outside terrarium or cold frame. The blooms, which accompany the leaves, open out almost flat and are soft lilac-blue with a large, frilly orange stigma.

CYCLAMEN
The florists' cyclamens, sold annually in huge quantities as winter house plants, are developed from the frost-tender scented species *C. persicum*. Much less well known are the hardier small-flowered species from the Mediterranean and Near East, which make an excellent addition to the garden and produce an interesting autumn display. Most require sheltered places in partial shade, with well-drained soil that has a good humus content, preferably in the form of leaf mold rather than acid peat. They are dwarf plants, not more than about $3^1/_4$ in (8 cm) high, and are ideal for a rock garden or cultivation in pots in an outside terrarium. The tubers should be planted just below the surface in fall, or at almost any time of year if they are purchased as growing pot plants. The only practical method of propagation is by seed, which can produce flowering-size tubers in 2-3 years. Apart from the small, graceful flowers with their back-swept petals, cyclamens have attractive silver-mottled and zoned foliage. Each tuber produces many leaves, giving the plant a total spread of 4-6 in (10-15 cm). Hardiness zones: 6-8.

C. cilicium
C. cilicium displays rounded or heart-shaped leaves, with pale green and silvery zones. The white or pink flowers have a dark purple-red stain around the mouth.

C. cyprium

C. cyprium (*above*)
This is best grown in a pot in an outside terrarium or greenhouse, where the small, fragrant flowers can be appreciated. The white blooms have a carmine ring around the mouth and are accompanied by dark green triangular leaves with silvery green zones.

C. graecum

C. graecum (*above*)

A Greek species, this cyclamen has pale to deep pink flowers with a darker stain around the mouth and heart-shaped leaves. The leaves have a satiny appearance with green and silvery patterns. Provide a hot, sunbaked spot in a rock garden or against a sunny wall.

C. hederifolium

C. hederifolium (syn. **C. neapolitanum**) (*above*)

This Mediterranean species is the best and hardiest garden plant among the autumn cyclamen; it is also very free-flowering. The ivy-shaped leaves have attractive patterns and form a ground cover from flowering time in early fall through to late spring, so it is well worth planting a patch in the dappled shade of deciduous shrubs. It also does well under pines, provided it receives winter moisture. Seed is produced freely and if growing conditions are suitable the plant will naturalize. The flowers are either pale pink with darker mouths or pure white.

C. mirabile

This is an unusual species, similar to *C. cilicium* but with tooth-edged petals and heart-shaped leaves with scalloped borders. The foliage is stained deep red underneath.

C. purpurascens (syn. **C. europaeum**)

A fragrant species, this cyclamen produces a succession of flowers over a long period, from summer into fall. The blooms are pale to deep pink- or red-purple and accompany rounded leaves varying from plain to a silvery-patterned deep green.

EUCHARIS

This group of South American bulbs, mainly tropical, may be grown in containers outdoors in summer and returned to a heated greenhouse for the winter. However, in cool areas it is best to treat them as greenhouse plants throughout the year. Use a well-drained, loam-sand-leaf mold medium, and the bulb requires a minimum winter temperature of 50°F (10°C). On the whole, the bulbs are best left undisturbed for as long as possible, but if repotting becomes necessary through overcrowding, this should be done in spring, when the bulb clumps can be divided. Flowering is in midsummer to early fall. Hardiness zone: 10.

E. amazonica

E. amazonica (*above*)
Amazon lily

This plant produces tufts of broad, oval, deep green leaves and 1½–2 ft (45–60 cm) high stems. The stems carry several fragrant white flowers like large daffodils, each about 3¼–4 in (8–10 cm) in diameter with a cup-shaped corona in the center.

EUCOMIS
Pineapple flower

These South African plants are mostly from the eastern Cape region, where they remain dormant and dry in winter and grow during the rainy summer season. In cultivation, they behave the same way, flowering in late summer or early fall. They

all have a basal tuft of broad leaves, with a spread of 1 ft (30 cm) or more in the larger species. From the center, a stout flower spike appears with densely packed, almost flat flowers, topped by a further tuft of small leaflike bracts, which is why it is called the pineapple flower. The large bulbs should be planted in spring, about 4 in (10 cm) deep in well-drained soil that will not become too dry and sunbaked in summer, since they require plenty of moisture in the growing season. Eucomis also grow well in containers but should be moved to a frost-free shed in winter. Propagation is best by clump division, but seed is formed, taking about 3 years to produce flowering bulbs. Hardiness zones: 4-5.

E. bicolor

E. bicolor (*above*)

This is the most readily available eucomis. It has 1 ft (30 cm) tall spikes of green flowers, with each petal edged in purple. The flower stem is also heavily blotched purple.

E. comosa (*below*)

An attractive species up to 1½ ft (45 cm) high, *E. comosa* has long spikes of pink flowers, made more colorful by a purple ovary in the center of the flower.

E. comosa

E. pallidiflora

This large plant, with leaves up to 2-2¼ ft (60-68.5 cm) long. These are semi-erect and sword-shaped, with wavy edges. The green-white flowers are 1¾-2 ft (53-60 cm) tall.

E. undulata (syn. *E. autumnalis*)

E. undulata is a robust species that reaches 1½ ft (45 cm) in height, with long, wavy-edged leaves and a spike of green-white-colored flowers.

E. zambesiaca

E. zambesiaca (*above*)

This dwarf form seen in gardens is a delightful little plant, with 8 in (20 cm) tall spikes of white flowers and a compact rosette of wavy-edged leaves.

GALANTHUS
Snowdrop

Autumn-flowering snowdrops may come as a surprise, but the Greek *G. reginae-olgae* produces fall blooms almost before the leaves appear above ground. It is uncommon in cultivation and therefore expensive, although easy to grow. This snowdrop prefers a sunnier spot than the spring snowdrops (see p. 97) and a position where the bulbs can dry out more during summer, but some shade is also necessary. As with other snowdrops, the bulbs can be successfully moved while in growth or in late summer to early fall, while still dormant. Propagation is best by division. Hardiness zone: 7.

G. reginae-olgae

The flowers appear before the foliage and are very similar to those of the common spring species, *G. nivalis*. The leaves are different, however, having a silvery gray stripe along the center. It requires more sun than its spring-flowering relatives.

GLADIOLUS

Most of the gladioli cultivated in gardens are the spectacular summer-flowering hybrids developed from several South African species (see p. 162). However, a much hardier species from the eastern Cape in South Africa flowers in fall. *G. papilio* can be grown in sun or partial shade, where it will not dry out too much during its summer growing season. It does well in shrub borders. While not very showy, it provides interest when the summer bulb display is nearing an end. It increases by stolons and forms extensive patches 3½ ft (1 m) or more across; propagation is by division in spring. Hardiness zones: 5-6.

G. papilio

G. papilio (syn. *G. purpureo-auratus*) (*above*)

This gladiolus grows about 3½ ft (1 m) high and carries up to 10 smoky dull purple, yellow, and green cowl-like flowers with hooded upper petals.

LEUCOJUM
Snowflake

The stronger-growing early and late spring-flowering snowflakes are much better known than the tiny autumnal ones (see p. 103), but the latter have a delicate charm and are ideal for growing in an outdoor terrarium. The potting is carried out in late summer because flowering occurs in early autumn; the medium should be fast-draining with plenty of sand. Watering should continue through until late spring, when it can be withheld until the following autumn. For propagation, remove offsets when repotting or, alternatively, collect seed; if sown in the autumn, seed may produce flowering-size bulbs in just 2-3 years. Hardiness zones: 6-7.

L. autumnale (*below*)

Threadlike flower stems 4-6 in (10-15 cm) high carry up to 4 tiny, white, pendent, bell-shaped flowers that are followed by equally slender leaves. Grow outside in a warm, sunny spot in a rock garden.

L. autumnale

L. roseum

This species has soft pink flowers and is best grown in an outside terrarium as it is tender.

MERENDERA

A relative of the colchicum, the merendera is an attractive plant, although smaller and less showy. Grow it in an outside terrarium or in a sunny, well-drained spot on a raised bed or in a rock garden where the corms can dry out during the summer rest period. Propagation is by seed in fall, or by division in early fall. Hardiness zone: 6.

M. montana

M. montana (syn. *M. pyrenaica* or *M. bulbocodium*) (*above*)

This plant has wide, funnel-shaped pink-purple flowers, each with a large white eye in the center. The flowers are about 1½-2¼ in (4-6 cm) in diameter. The narrow leaves appear after the blooms, forming a rosette.

NERINE

The South African nerines are delightful autumn-flowering members of the amaryllis family. They have long-lasting pink to bright red flowers with narrow, crinkled petals, giving them a sparkling crystaline appearance. The bulbs range from the frost-hardy to the tender, but even the hardy ones are best grown against a warm wall, where they receive some protection in severe winters. Plant the large bulbs with the neck just protruding from the soil, either in early spring, as in the case of the hardy *N. bowdenii*, or in late summer or early fall for the more tender greenhouse varieties.

Nerines will tolerate acid or alkaline conditions, but the soil or potting medium must be well drained and not too rich in fertilizers, which encourage strong leaves at the expense of flowers; additions of sand are ideal for quick drainage. Greenhouse pot bulbs should be dried off in summer after the leaves have died down; they flower best if left undisturbed, but if they become too crowded they should be repotted in late summer with as little disturbance as possible. Propagate by offsets or by seed, which may take at least 3 years to produce flowering-size bulbs. Hardiness zones: 7-8 for *N. bowdenii* and its forms; 9 for other species and hybrids.

N. bowdenii

N. bowdenii (above)

This is the hardiest species, flowering in mid-autumn with stout 1½-2 ft (45-60 cm) tall stems, each carrying an umbel with up to 12 glistening, bright pink flowers; these have elegant undulating petals. The variety 'Mark Fenwick' is a more rigorous taller version, growing up to 3 ft (90 cm) high, with larger heads and deeper pink flowers than other varieties of the bulb.

N. filifolia

N. filifolia (above)

N. filifolia is only 10-12 in (25-30 cm) high and has umbels of small, wavy-petaled pink flowers. Keep it frost-free in cold areas.

N. flexuosa

N. flexuosa (above)

This pink nerine is usually about 1 ft (30 cm) tall, with reflexed and crinkled petals.

N. masonorum

N. masonorum (above)

One of the smallest nerines, this is only 6-8 in (15-20 cm) tall with threadlike leaves and slender stems bearing up to 10 small pink flowers held in an umbel.

N. sarniensis

Although called the Guernsey lily, *N. sarniensis* is South African in origin. It has 1½-2 ft (45-60 cm) high stems, straplike leaves, and scarlet flowers. Because of its color, it has been much used in hybridization.

Hybrid cultivars

Many exciting hybrid cultivars are available for greenhouse cultivation. They require frost protection because they are in leaf in winter, but it is not necessary and is actually harmful to keep them in conditions that are too warm. In summer, bulbs require a rest period but avoid baking the bulbs under glass in full sun or they may roast. 'Corusca Major' is an old favorite, with bright scarlet flowers held on 1½-2 ft (45-60 cm) tall stems; it is grown for the cut-flower trade. 'Baghdad' sends up umbels of soft carmine red flowers later in autumn than most. 'Blanchfleur' is an excellent pure white variety.

SCHIZOSTYLIS

This valuable autumn-flowering member of the iris family can be grown in sun or partial shade in a soil that does not dry out excessively in summer. Because the small rhizomes produce stolons, the plants can eventually spread into relatively large patches, perhaps 3 ft (90 cm) across in ideal conditions, and they never really become dormant. For propagation purposes, clumps can be lifted and divided in spring when the worst of the frost is past. The rhizomes should be replanted with a shallow covering of soil not more than 1 in (2.5 cm) deep. Hardiness zone: 6.

S. coccinea 'Major'

S. coccinea (above and page 211)

The 1-2 ft (30-60 cm) high stems of *S. coccinea* carry racemes of funnel-shaped red flowers, each about 2 in (5 cm) in diameter.

They are produced amid narrow, erect leaves. 'Major' has even larger red flowers, 'Mrs. Hegarty' is an attractive pale pink and 'Alba' is a good clear white one.

S. coccinea 'Mrs. Hegarty'

STERNBERGIA

Although these showy fall bulbs are similar to large yellow crocuses, sternbergias are, in fact, members of the amaryllis family. Occasionally referred to as fall daffodils, their only similarity is the color and daffodil-like bulb. Being mainly Mediterranean plants, they require hot, sunny spots in well-drained neutral or alkaline soil. In colder climates, they are best placed at the foot of a sunny wall where the bulbs will ripen to form flower buds during their summer dormancy. They should be planted in autumn at a depth of about 2 in (5 cm) but may take a year or two before flowering. Once established, they are best left undisturbed to form clumps. Propagation is by division of clumps in early fall. Hardiness zones: 6-7.

S. clusiana

S. clusiana (*above*)
This is one of the largest-flowering species, producing green-yellow goblet-shaped

flowers in midautumn before the strap-shaped gray-green leaves appear. It is best planted in a cold frame for winter protection and soil warmth in summer.

S. lutea

S. lutea (*above*)
S. lutea has large, bright yellow funnel-shaped flowers amid glossy green straplike leaves in early autumn.

S. sicula

S. sicula (*above*)
This looks like a smaller version of *S. lutea*. The flower stems are only 2-3 in (5-7.5 cm) high, and the narrow, dark green leaves have a pale stripe running along the center.

ZEPHYRANTHES
Rain lily or windflower

Another autumn member of the amaryllis family, the rain lily has funnel- or wineglass-shaped flowers. They require a hot, sunny spot where the bulbs will dry out in summer and form flower buds for the coming season. They are best planted in spring and left undisturbed for as long as possible; they thrive in light, sandy soils. Propagation is by divisions of clumps in early fall. Hardiness zones: 9-10.

Z. candida

Z. candida (*above*)
This plant is the hardiest species, with rushlike leaves and 6 in (15 cm) tall stems. The flowers are white with green centers.

Z. grandiflora

Z. grandiflora (*above*)
Z. grandiflora is less hardy than other species and requires a frost-free greenhouse in cold areas. It has large, rosy pink flowers about 3 in (7.5 cm) long.

Z. rosea (*below*)
This zephyranthes is only hardy in mild areas and may be grown in a sunny border. Its 2 in (5 cm) long, funnel-like flowers are pale pink.

Z. rosea

WINTER

Garden highlights

In cold regions winter offers little of garden interest, apart from a few winter-flowering shrubs and one or two ornamental trees with colored bark. Although lots of bulbs will grow outside at this time of the year, only a small selection will flower, provided the weather is not too harsh. In areas with mild winters, however, some spring-flowering bulbs like crocuses may flower in late winter. These cheerful highlights add color to an otherwise drab or monochromatic setting. To make the most of these bulbs, plant them close to the house so they can be appreciated from the comfort of indoors as well as outside.

One of the best winter-flowering bulbs for North America and Canada is *Crocus laevigatus* 'Fontenayi' (zone 6). A colorful plant with purple flowers striped a dark purple on the outside, it benefits from a sunny but sheltered spot to protect it against inclement weather. The best companion plants are shrubby Mediterranean natives like lavender and rosemary, which require similar gritty, free-draining soil conditions and have attractive gray-green leaves that complement the slender chalices of the crocuses. Other herbs, such as winter savory, hyssop, sage, and wild thyme, can also be used; push a few of the crocus corms through a fine, leafy carpet of creeping *Thymus serpyllum* and wait for the spearlike buds to pierce the foliage and erupt into splashes of lilac-mauve.

A good winter display can be achieved using *Cyclamen coum* (zone 6), a hardy bulb that starts to flower in mid- to late winter. There are many colors to choose from, including bright magenta-purple, carmine-pink, and white, each accompanied by either plain dark green or silver-zoned foliage. These bulbs grow well among winter heathers but look equally good massed on their own, allowing the beauty of the individual flowers to be appreciated.

(previous page) *This combination of* Cyclamen coum, *winter aconites, and snowdrops naturalized under bare trees, forms a bold swathe of glowing color.*

(below) Narcissus cyclamineus, *with its dainty backswept petals, invites close inspection and is striking massed around the base of this shrub.*

(right) *Woodland is ideal for growing extensive drifts of naturalized snowdrops, which thrive in the winter sunlight.*

For handsome winter foliage, nothing beats *Arum italicum* 'Pictum' (zone 6). This tuber has rich green leaves marbled with white veins and mixes well with crocuses or cyclamens. It is also decorative when grown with hellebores (Christmas or Lenten roses); the pale green-flowered *Helleborus argutifolius* looks particularly attractive pushing up through a group of arums. A shady corner is the perfect place for a planting of *H. niger* and *A. i.* 'Pictum,' with the white flowers of the Christmas rose silhouetted against the marbled foliage of the bulbs.

An equally exciting combination involves *Cyclamen coum*, the arum, and the shrubby *Rubus cockburnianus* (white-washed bramble), an odd-looking relative of the blackberry, with pure white thorny stems in winter. While it creates a dramatic effect against the dark soil, it makes an impressive appearance rising out of a clump of fresh green arum foliage. You can create a similar effect by using the contorted golden stems of *Salix matsudana* 'Tortuosa' (corkscrew willow). Both shrubs, however, must be regularly trimmed to promote a new crop of bright stems each year.

(left) *Snowdrops and winter aconites combine to good effect here to provide a colorful display that is especially welcome in dull weather.*

(below) *The delicate-looking* Crocus tommasinianus *is one of the hardiest late-winter bulbs and at its most rewarding when used boldly, as here.*

(above) *Borders near a house need year-round appeal, as provided here by* Arum italicum *'Pictum' and* Helleborus orientalis.

(main picture) *This alluring tapestry of color is made all the more intriguing by the natural variation in the shades of* **Cyclamen coum,** *from magenta to soft pink. Long after flowering has ended, the attractive leaves of the cyclamen will continue to provide interest around the base of the trees. The colorful introduction of the contrasting golden* **Crocus flavus** *'Dutch Yellow' (inset) and dazzling white snowdrops (below) makes the planting even more vibrant.*

Naturalizing

The same selection of bulbs can also be used for naturalizing in winter to provide a welcome show of color. However, none are suitable for naturalizing in grass; instead, they must be colonized in bare soil and left undisturbed to reproduce freely into clumps over the years.

In North America and Europe, the very fine purple-flowered *Crocus laevigatus* 'Fontenayi' multiplies, forming a sparkling sheet of color in the depths of winter. It does best when allowed to spread alone, but it will tolerate shrubs that do not have shallow root systems, such as *Prunus triloba, Cornus mas* (Cornelian cherry), or *Hamamelis mollis* (Chinese witch hazel).

Cyclamen coum, with its magenta-purple blossoms, will often naturalize if left alone in a humus-rich, well-drained soil. The plants stand out best against a background of stone or earth, or silhouetted against some of the more interesting trees. Birch provides a suitable backdrop; *Betula pendula* (silver birch), with its somewhat rugged silvery bark, and the pendulous *B. pendula* 'Youngii,' with its weeping twiggy branches, provide perfect settings for clusters of cyclamen.

The snowy white form of *Cyclamen coum*, known as 'Album,' will also naturalize freely. For the most dramatic effect, plant a group in front of the glossy, mahoganylike trunk of *Prunus serrula*; few winter scenes can surpass the skeletal beauty of the prunus etched against a bright blue sky, surrounded by a colony of *C. c.* 'Album.'

In difficult shady areas with richly organic soil, *Arum italicum* 'Pictum' can be colonized. This easygoing, hardy member of the arum family has attractive green- and silver-marbled foliage, and in late spring, it produces creamy white spathes, followed in fall by striking orange-red fruit held just above the leaves on neat, tight spikes. The leaves appear in fall and intensify in color during the increasingly short winter days, persisting until the end of the season.

These showy arums are best planted around deciduous shrubs, particularly those that flower in winter. One of the best combinations involves the arum and the pink-flowered *Viburnum × bodnantense* 'Dawn,' a scented shrub that starts flowering in late fall and continues into spring, when the leaf buds break into growth. The eye-catching trailing stems of *Jasminum nudiflorum*, wreathed in waxy primrose-yellow blossoms, also provide a fine contrast to the foliage of the arum. The arum is also useful as ground cover beneath *Euonymus fortunei* 'Silver Queen.'

Rock gardens

Again, it is the winter-flowering crocuses and cyclamens that provide interest in the rock garden at this time of the year. These bulbs are good for adding color and form. After flowering, they die down to make way for spring and summer alpines.

In Northern America and Europe, a well-drained, sunny spot provides a natural home for *Crocus laevigatus* 'Fontenayi.' For the greatest impact, plant a small patch (about 10 or 12 bulbs) on its own, so that the purple flowers stand out against a stark background of rock. Their beauty is further brought out by a top dressing of wood chips. When selecting companion plants, choose ones with noncompeting root systems as well as attractive foliage.

For a good visual mix, grow *Crocus laevigatus* 'Fontenayi' with *Arenaria caespitosa* 'Aurea' (sandwort). This golden-leaved plant, with a shallow root system, contrasts pleasingly with the crocuses, as does *A. balearica*, with its bright green leaves. *A. balearica* is more delicate than its relative: distribute the bulbs thinly among the foliage, otherwise the crocuses will smother their neighbors with decomposing flowers when they die back.

(below) *There is nothing more cheering in the winter frost and snow than the sight of tiny winter aconites and snowdrops breaking through a crust of ice to open their petals wide in the winter sun.*

The rock garden is an ideal setting for the tiny *Cyclamen coum*. It can be planted on its own against a rocky backdrop, or it can be mixed with other plants for a more varied display. Since it will tolerate light shade, it is particularly useful for planting beneath a yew or dwarf pine, which offers in turn protection from bad weather.

Although barely hardy and in some areas normally cultivated in an outside terrarium, *Narcissus bulbocodium romieuxii* (zones 7-8) can be grown in a well-drained sheltered spot of the rock garden. This relative of the hoop-petticoat daffodil has flared, pale sulfur-yellow blossoms and grassy foliage.

(above left) Cyclamen persicum, *with its exotic-looking flowers and heart-shaped, silver-marbled leaves, is perfect for lighting up a dark corner.*

(above right) Arum italicum *'Pictum' is an invaluable asset in borders during winter, both as a foil for shrubs and as a ground cover.*

(below) Narcissus bulbocodium *is unlike any other member of the narcissus family and should be planted where the flowers can be admired.*

Containers and window boxes

Plants grown in window boxes and containers do not survive cold winters, but in more temperate regions it is possible to enjoy container plants throughout the year. If uncommonly cold weather does threaten, small containers can be moved into the warmth inside until the danger of frost has past.

A visit to a local garden center can yield some brightly colored bulbs suitable for containers and window boxes, such as narcissi, cyclamens and hyacinths. Hyacinths are particularly popular and few winter displays are worth considering without the bright colors and sweet fragrance of these bulbs, although they are extremely vulnerable to cold weather. However, a foundation planting of evergreens such as ivies like *Hedera helix* 'Anne Marie' and 'Parsley Crested' will provide some protection. The same ivies are suitable for mixing with crocuses and cyclamens, and a few clumps of the paper-white narcissi will add some color. On the borderline of hardiness (zones 7-8), these narcissi make a delightful scented display. For a large container, they can be used to underplant dwarf conifers and, in window boxes, can be mixed with variegated ivies and a few primulas for a colorful mixed planting.

Forcing

Winter is the time for forcing into early bloom bulbs that would otherwise flower outside later in the season (see p. 49). The bulbs must have as much light as possible and, while they are in flower, they will need frequent watering to ensure that the soil is always damp. After flowering, once the danger of frost has passed, they can be planted outdoors, where they will eventually multiply into patches.

Hyacinths are commonly forced and are often available as "prepared" bulbs for early flowering (see p. 39). Among the more obtainable are 'Delft Blue' and 'Ostara,' which both have blue flowers; the crimson 'Jan Bos'; 'L'Innocence,' a pure white hyacinth; and the primrose-yellow 'City of Haarlem.' Grow them as single plantings, with several of each bulb combined if you wish, but do not mix the cultivars because they will flower at different times. The best companion plants for these are ferns like *Pteris* and similar plants like *Selaginella*. The glossy, rich green *Selaginella martensii* is one of the easiest to grow, tucked in among a few forced hyacinths. Provided it receives a

(below) *Nothing matches the fragrant perfection of hyacinths when they are forced in containers for an indoor display as early as midwinter.*

(above) *This delightful, fresh-looking window-box planting, combining white cyclamen and small-leaved ivies, is ideal for a shady location.*

(right) *For a cheerful window-box composition, mix together* Narcissus *'Tête-à-Tête,' dwarf conifers, primroses, and variegated ivy.*

daily misting of water, it should thrive, even in dry rooms. Once the hyacinths have faded, the ferns can be repotted and will make good house plants.

The fragrant multiflowering hyacinths, known as Roman hyacinths, resemble refined, elegant bluebells. They are usually sold by color and have the advantage of naturally flowering early in the season. They do not mix readily with other plants, but will grow among fresh green sphagnum moss, provided both are misted every other day.

Amaryllises (hippeastrums), with their large, colorful trumpets, flower naturally during the winter months. For the full benefit of the wonderful sculptured flower, a single specimen should be placed on its own in a prominent place, such as a windowsill or table. For more of a display, a few different-colored

(above) *The glowing, mixed colors of hyacinths and winter-flowering pansies make a fine feature in this window box.*

amaryllises can be planted together in a large container, with a few green-leaved ivies like *Hedera helix* 'Parsley Crested' and 'Sagittifolia,' or some *Ficus pumila* (creeping fig).

The delicate *Narcissus papyraceus* 'Paperwhite' is another popular choice. With their succulent, upright clusters of bright green leaves and tight heads of small white blossoms, these daffodils look most attractive when surrounded by fresh, damp green moss or trailing green or silver-variegated ivies, such as *Hedera helix* 'Anne Marie' and 'Variegata.' Because they are not hardy, they should be discarded after flowering.

Many small-flowered hardy bulbs can also be forced into early blossom; plant them in their individual pots rather than crowding different kinds into the same large container. Some of the most successful are the pale blue *Scilla mischtschenkoana* (syn. *S. tubergeniana*) and the dark blue *S. siberica* 'Spring Beauty,' the striped squill *Puschkinia scilloides* (syn. *P. libanotica*), the dwarf *Iris histrioides* 'Major,' and the colorful cultivars of *I. reticulata* in shades of blue, including 'Harmony,' 'Joyce,' and 'J.S. Dijt.' The bright yellow *I. danfordiae danfordiae* is also very striking.

Outdoor bulbous plants indoors

Unprepared bulbs can be encouraged into early flowering if they are brought inside, where the heat will advance the flowering process.

Crocuses respond well to this kind of treatment. They look good planted in imaginative, colorful containers, including terra-cotta crocus bowls, which have small planting holes to accommodate each corm. The best crocuses include the pure white *Crocus vernus* 'Joan of Arc,' the violet-purple *C. v.* 'Remembrance,' and *C. v.* 'Dutch Yellow,' along with the bunch-flowering *C. chrysanthus* hybrids. Some of the best dwarf beauties include 'Blue Bird,' 'Cream Beauty,' 'Snow Bunting,' and the orange-bronze 'Zwanenburg Bronze.'

(above) *All the dwarf irises lend themselves to container growing because their dainty flowers may otherwise be overlooked.*

Indoors

Even if relatively little happens outside in the garden during the winter months, indoor cultivation can provide the ideal opportunity to grow some of the tender bulbs that will not survive outdoor winter conditions.

The scented *Cyclamen persicum* (zone 9) is a popular indoor tuber. An elegant plant with slender, upright stems, it has beautiful backswept blossoms in blush-pink or white, held above boldly marked ivy-shaped or rounded leaves. It will last much longer if placed in a cool porch or greenhouse rather than a warm living room or kitchen. The bulbs can be kept from one year to the next planted in fresh soil, either indoors or, during the summer months, outside.

Lachenalias (Cape cowslips)—winter-flowering in zone 10 only—are some of the easiest plants to grow indoors and are ideally suited for the windowsill. Although each variety is enjoyable for its interesting foliage and unusual flowers, the free-flowering *Lachenalia aloides* is the most colorful. It boasts pendulous yellow, red-tipped blooms and handsome purple-mottled leaves. It is a clump-forming plant, and a potful quickly blossoms with flowers that, if kept cool, will last for most of the winter. *L. bulbifera* is also very striking, with dark-spotted foliage and spikes of pendent, deep orange or red flowers. The lavender-blue-flowered *L. mutabilis*

is much less colorful but equally attractive. To reap the full benefit of its majestic appearance, it is best displayed on its own as a specimen plant—although you can create a truly vibrant display by teaming it with one or two containers of bright blue forced squills.

Veltheimia bracteata (zone 10) is another reliable indoor bulb. An unusual-looking plant, it has tall stems crowned with a cluster of drooping tubular pinkish-red flowers. For the best effect, combine it with a few pots of bright red poinsettias or *Solanum capsicastrum* (winter cherry).

(above) *These neat clusters of small white* Narcissus papyraceus *flowerheads are bound tightly together in a witty, fragrant arrangement.*

A limited number of freesias (zone 9) can also be grown indoors in winter if they are placed in a cool, bright room. With their sweetly scented, brightly colored flowers, they are a welcome sight. Ivies are particularly good companions, especially *Hedera helix* 'Green Ruffles.'

(above) *The glowing crimson of these cyclamens is set off perfectly by the color of the marbled, basket-style container.*

Cut flowers

Apart from *Arum italicum*, which is used a great deal in flower arrangements, there are very few winter-flowering bulbs suitable for cutting. A handful of cyclamens can be plucked from a clump and placed in a small glass or teacup, but crocuses dislike being picked and will not last for more than a day or two in water.

For this reason, most indoor displays are supplemented with store-bought flowers. Narcissi, tulips, and gladioli are among the most popular, although lilies are also frequently available year-round, together with various forms of anemones and ranunculus.

For a seasonal flavor, however, the flowers can be mixed with the foliage of *Arum italicum* 'Pictum' and winter berries like cotoneaster. *Cotoneaster* 'Cornubia' produces carmine berries held in big bunches on naked branches. *Hippophae rhamnoides* is also good for indoor decorations. Although thorny, its vibrant orange fruit looks well beside the simplicity of white tulips. Eucalyptus is another good foliage plant for winter arrangements.

(left) *A traditional-looking winter arrangement, the warm reds of amaryllis, cyclamens, gladioli, and tulips are set off by evergreen foliage.*

(right) *A few stems of waxy white amaryllis blooms with willow branches and simple foliage to make a sparse yet dramatic arrangement.*

ARUM
Lords and ladies or cuckoo pint

Although not winter flowering, some of the hardy arums are worth growing for their ornamental foliage, which lasts through the dullest months of the year, continuing well into spring (see p. 88), before dying down for summer. The cut leaves also last well in water and are very useful for winter flower arrangements. The tubers should be planted in fall unless bought in pots, in which case they can be planted at any time. Plant them at a depth of about 6 in (15 cm) in a semishaded position in any fertile acid or alkaline soil. When settled, the tubers will produce offsets and form clumps 8-12 in (20-30 cm) wide in 3 years; after that they can be lifted and divided in the fall. Hardiness zone: 6.

A. italicum 'Pictum'

A. italicum (*above*)

This is an extremely valuable winter plant producing very decorative rich green arrow-shaped leaves with a striking marbled pattern of cream-colored veins. *A. italicum* 'Pictum' (syn. 'Marmoratum') is a particularly attractive form.

CROCUS

Autumn- and spring-flowering crocuses are well known for providing a fine display during those seasons, but there are few to bridge the winter gap. For this reason, *C. laevigatus* is especially welcome; it flowers at any time from early to late winter, pushing up a few blooms whenever there is a mild spell. The corms are planted in fall in an open, sunny, preferably sheltered position, in well-drained soil; if the ground is heavy and damp, mix in sand. In time they increase into clumps, and they can be lifted and divided in late summer. Hardiness zone: 6.

C. laevigatus (*below*)

This Greek species is variable in color and flowering time. 'Fontenayi' is one of the best variants, with lilac-blue flowers that are strongly striped and veined dark purple on the outside and have yellow throats. It is pleasantly scented. Although quite hardy, it makes an excellent terrarium plant.

C. laevigatus

CYCLAMEN

While most cyclamens flower in spring or fall (see pp. 93 and 206), *C. coum* and *C. persicum* bloom during winter.

C. coum is very hardy and starts to flower by the new year in mild areas. It can be planted in fall in partial shade, sheltered from cold winds, in a light, open soil enriched with organic matter; use leaf mold rather than acid peat. Alternatively, purchase cyclamens as pot plants at any time and cover them with ³/₄ in (2 cm) of soil. Since each plant may cover about 4-6 in (10-15 cm) when in leaf, plant them about that far apart.

C. persicum, a tender species, comes in a great range of colors and sizes and is a popular pot plant, usually sold by florists in full flower in winter. This cyclamen does not last long indoors since it dislikes the heat; it does much better if given a light, cool position at a maximum temperature of 50°F (10°C) in a frost-free porch or greenhouse. From seed to flowering takes just over one year. The seedlings should be potted individually, the larger types requiring a final pot size of 5 in (13 cm) in diameter and the small ones 4 in (10 cm). In winter the young plants should be grown in a greenhouse at approximately 55-60°F (13-16°C), and in summer they need to be kept in growth by watering and a dose of weak fertilizer until they flower. Even spring-sown plants may flower the following winter or spring if grown continuously. Older tubers that have finished flowering can be kept for the next year, but they are best given a rest period; dry them out and repot them in early fall and renew watering. Propagation is by seeds sown in autumn or winter; *C. coum* takes about 2-3 years to produce flowering-size tubers. Hardiness zones: 6 for *C. coum*; 9 for *C. persicum*.

C. coum

C. coum (*above*)

This cyclamen reaches only 1¹/₂ in (4 cm) in height and has rounded leaves about 1 in (2.5 cm) in diameter, either plain dark green or patterned silver. The flowers are small, at ¹/₂ in (1.3 cm) long, but are carmine pink with a dark stain around the mouth. 'Album' has white flowers and 'Pewter' has silvery leaves.

C. persicum

C. persicum (*above*)

This is the wild species with attractive silver-patterned, heart-shaped leaves topped by fragrant white or pale pink flowers, which display long, reflexed petals. Formerly, large-flowered forms were selected, but these were unscented, so they were crossed with the wild species again to produce smaller-flowered plants in more colors than the wild ones.

C. persicum cultivar

C. persicum cultivars (*above* and *below*)
The 'Kaori' types of cyclamen have compact rosettes of foliage and many small red, pink, or white flowers standing well above the leaves. 'Firmament' is a hybrid with medium-size flowers in a wide range of colors. The compact, stronger-scented forms are called 'Dwarf Fragrant,' 'Dwarf Scented,' or 'Sweet Scented.' 'Pink Ruffles' has salmon-pink petals that are frilled at the edges, and 'Decora' has silver-patterned foliage and a wide range of flower colors.

C. persicum cultivar

FREESIA
The numerous wild species of freesia are South African plants. These species are rarely cultivated, but some have been hybridized to produce a range of large-flowered cultivars in many colors. The hybrids are naturally winter-growing plants that flower in early spring and, with slight forcing, can be brought into flower in midwinter. Their colorful, fragrant funnel-shaped blossoms also make popular cut flowers that last well in water.

The corms can be bought in early fall and are best planted with 6 per 5 in (13 cm) diameter pot, filled with a sandy potting medium. It is useful to insert support

sticks. After potting, sink the pots up to their rims in sand and water the bulbs well. By late fall, when the shoots appear, the pots can be moved into a cool greenhouse and kept in a bright, airy place at not more than 50°F (10°C). When the buds show color, bring them indoors, although the flowers will not last as long in the heat. After flowering, keep them in growth until the leaves die back, then keep them on the dry side over summer.

Freesias can be propagated by offsets detached at repotting time in fall, or by seeds sown in early spring at about 65°F (18.5°C). If they are kept growing through the summer with watering and liquid fertilizer, they will often flower the following winter. They all have narrow, erect leaves and are mostly 1³/₄-2¹/₂ ft (53-76 cm) high at flowering time, with the flower stem bent near the apex. Hardiness zone: 9.

F. alba
This freesia has spikes of fragrant white funnel-shaped flowers, sometimes flushed purple on the outside, and marked with yellow on the lower petals.

F. armstrongii (sometimes included with F. corymbosa)
This is one of the parents of the hybrid cultivars. Although an attractive shade of rose-pink with yellow markings near the base, the flowers are unscented.

F. refracta

F. refracta (*above*)
The variable flower color of this freesia ranges from pale yellow to a green or purple color, with deeper yellow-orange marks on the lower petals. Although not showy the flowers have a good scent. *F. refracta* has been hybridized with the above two species to produce large, fragrant freesias.

F. 'Elegance'

F. 'Elegance' (*above*)
F. 'Elegance' displays white flowers suffused with chartreuse on the outside.

F. 'Romany'
One of the many double freesias, this variety flaunts large, fragrant pale purple flowers.

F. 'Yellow River' (*below*)
This freesia has spikes of large, sweetly scented bright yellow flowers.

F. 'Yellow River'

HIPPEASTRUM
These tender bulbous plants from South America are incorrectly sold as amaryllises (the true amaryllis, the Cape Belladonna lily, is a much hardier South African species—see Fall Directory, p. 203). There are many wild species of *Hippeastrum*, but most are unobtainable. The most common are the larger-flowered hybrids. Propagation is by division of offsets in fall. Hardiness zone: 9.

H. reginae
This large-flowered species has stout stems 1¹/₂ ft-2 ft (45-60 cm) high; it carries 2-4 slightly drooping red flowers marked with a green star in the center.

H. reticulatum

H. reticulatum (*above*)
This is a daintier species, about 1 ft (30 cm) high, with up to 6, red-purple flowers that display a darker net-veined pattern.

H. rutilum
Approximately 1 ft (30 cm) high, this species has 2-4 flowers, ranging from crimson to red or orange, often with a green stripe

Hybrids
The hybrids are about 2 ft (60 cm) high when in flower, with 2-4 flowers per stem.

H. 'Appleblossom'

H. 'Appleblossom' (*above*)
This bulb has soft pink flowers with a pale stripe on each petal and a pale throat.

H. 'Belinda'
The rich, deep red velvety flowers of *H.* 'Belinda' shade to darker red at the throat.

H. 'Star of Holland'
The large, bright red flowers of this hybrid have a white band along the center of each petal, producing a white starlike effect.

H. 'White Dazzler'
This is a vigorous pure-white variety.

HYACINTHUS
Hyacinth

Hyacinths are fully described in the Spring Directory (see p. 100) because that is their natural flowering time. However, they are perhaps best appreciated as forced bulbs for midwinter indoor flowering, where their fragrance can be enjoyed to the full. For early winter flowering, it is necessary to buy prepared bulbs that have been stored under special conditions the previous summer; these must be planted in early fall. If the flowering time is not so important, ordinary bulbs are suitable and less expensive, and they can be planted a little later.

Plant the bulbs in any loose potting mixture or fiber, with the bulbs almost touching and the tops just peeping above soil level. Then place the pots in a cool room, shed, or garage and keep them damp while the roots develop. After about 8 weeks, the young leaves and flower buds should be pushing up, and you can bring the pots into a light place indoors; this must be cool, or they will elongate rapidly and topple over. Unprepared bulbs are grown in exactly the same way, but they flower later in the new year.

A great range of large-flowered varieties are now available in shades of blue, pink, red, white, peach, yellow, and purple, in single and double forms, as well as the smaller 'Roman,' 'Cynthella' and 'Multiflora' types, which are often even more fragrant, like the original wild type. Propagation is by division in early fall. Hardiness zone: 5; for winter flowering, grow under glass or indoors.

LACHENALIA
Cape cowslip

These small, neat bulbous plants from South Africa produce dense spikes of tubular or bell-shaped flowers over strap-shaped leaves. The foliage is often ornamental. The bulbs are dormant during summer, growing in fall and winter. Athough not hardy, they require minimal heat in cold regions to keep them frost-free. A cool, bright greenhouse or windowsill is ideal.

Plant the small bulbs in autumn in a sandy, well-drained medium and immediately water them. At least 3 bulbs—spaced about 1 in (2.5 cm) apart—are needed for a good display. Azalea pots or pans give an adequate soil depth, since

the bulbs do not need to be planted any deeper than ¹/₂ in (1.5 cm). After flowering, when the leaves die back in spring, they can be dried off but not sunbaked, until fall, when they can be repotted. Propagation is by offsets, which are usually produced freely. Hardiness zone: 10 or frost-free under glass.

L. aloides

L. aloides (syn. *L. tricolor*) (*above*)
This has glaucous leaves marked with green or purple blotches and 4-6 in (10-15 cm) spikes of pendent tubular flowers. These may be yellow with red tips, plain golden yellow or multicolored.

L. bulbifera

L. bulbifera (*above*)
This striking plant usually has dark-spotted leaves that are topped by 4-6 in (10-15 cm) tall spikes of pendent tubular flowers in shades of deep orange to red. It produces bulblets at the base of the leaves.

L. contaminata
This plant has dense, 2-6 in (5-15 cm) tall spikes of much shorter bell-shaped flowers that stand out horizontally and are white with maroon tips on the outer petals.

L. glaucina

L. glaucina (syn. L. orchioides var. glaucina) (*above*)

The dense, 4–8 in (10–20 cm) tall spikes of *L. glaucina* have many small blue to purple flowers tipped dark purple, all facing obliquely upward.

L. mutabilis

This colorful species exhibits 4–8 in (10–20 cm) tall spikes of small bell-shaped flowers with dark-tipped pale blue outer petals and brown-tipped bright yellow inner ones. The entire upper part of the spike consists of bright blue sterile flowers.

L. rubida

This very attractive plant has spotted leaves topped by 4–7 in (10–18 cm) tall spikes of long, pendent tubular flowers. These range from coral-red to deeper ruby-red in color, sometimes tipped with a darker color.

NARCISSUS

Narcissi (daffodils) are the mainstay of the spring bulb garden display and are described under that section (see p. 105), but a few flower so early, especially in mild areas, that they can be classed as winter flowering. There are 2 to recommend; all differ widely in their cultural requirements. Propagation is by division of clumps in fall. Hardiness zones: 6-8.

N. papyraceus
Paperwhite narcissus

This narcissus has clustered heads of small, fragrant white flowers, usually about 1 ft (30 cm) high. Although it can be grown outdoors in sheltered spots or mild areas, it is more often treated as a subject for forcing into an early flower display in a greenhouse or on a windowsill. The bulbs will produce flowers about 6 weeks after planting without needing the cool, damp preparation period

required by hyacinths. However, it is best not to keep them in a warm living room because their stems will become weak and the flowers will start to droop.

Almost any loose potting medium or bulb fiber is adequate since the buds are already formed inside the bulb when purchased in fall; they only need water to make them develop. After flowering, if you want to save them for the following year, keep them in a cool, bright frost-free place and use a potash-rich liquid fertilizer to strengthen the bulbs. After the leaves die down in late spring, dry out the bulbs and keep them in a warm, but not sunbaked, place until fall, when they can be repotted or planted in a sheltered spot in the garden. However, the results are not always reliable; for forcing purposes, it is better to buy new bulbs each autumn.

N. bulbocodium romieuxii

N. bulbocodium romieuxii (syn. N. romieuxii) (*above*)

One of the hoop petticoat types, this is a small species, only 4–6 in (10–15 cm) high. The sulfur-yellow flowers have narrow petals surrounding a wide funnel-shaped trumpet and are produced in midwinter, sometimes by mid-December. Grow them in pots in an outside terrarium or frost-free greenhouse where the delicate blooms can receive some protection. A well-drained sandy soil mix is best. Bulbs should be dried in summer during the dormant period, but not sunbaked, and repotted in fall.

VELTHEIMIA

Unfortunately, these delightful winter-flowering bulbs from South Africa are not frost-hardy, but they make excellent pot plants for a heated glasshouse, greenhouse, or cool windowsill. The large bulbs should be potted with the tips just showing; plant them in well-drained potting soil in early

fall and start them growing by slight watering, increasing as growth commences. Give them as much light as possible. After flowering, keep them in growth until late spring, when watering can be reduced. *V. capensis* will die down completely and must be kept warm and dry for the summer, but *V. bracteata* remains in leaf and requires a little water from time to time. The bulbs occasionally produce offsets that can be detached at repotting time. Seeds are also produced, but they take several years to produce flowering-size bulbs. Hardiness zone: 10.

V. bracteata

V. bracteata (*above*)

This plant has shiny, bright green broad leaves and 1–1¼ ft (30–38 cm) tall, dense spikes of pink-red tubular flowers.

V. capensis

V. capensis (*above*)

The tubular pink flowers of *V. capensis* are carried in dense spikes about 1 ft (30 cm) high; it has narrow gray leaves that are very wavy at the edges.

V. 'Rosalba'

This attractive cultivar has tubular creamy flowers suffused with pink in the lower part.

GLOSSARY

Acid soil Soil that tests below 7.0 on a pH scale. To sweeten acid soil use lime.

Alkaline soil Soil that tests above 7.0 on a pH scale. To neutralize soil use sulfur, peat moss, or finely shredded bark.

Alpines Diminutive plants that in nature usually grow above the tree line in mountainous regions. In cultivation, these plants are usually grown in a rock garden or outside terrarium.

Alternate Used to describe a plant's growth habit. It means that the leaves grow in a staggered manner along the stems.

Annual A plant that flowers, fruits, and produces new seed before dying in the course of one season or year.

Apex The pointed end or tip of a leaf or petal.

Axil The junction at which a leaf and stem join.

Baking Some bulbs require a dry sunny location after flowering. This condition allows the bulbs to "bake" or ripen in order to produce next year's flowers.

Basal Leaves that grow directly from a bulb or rootstock without an intervening stem are called basal leaves.

Basal plate A hard central disc at the base of a bulbous plant. It holds the scales together and produces roots.

Bedding plant Annuals or biennials that are used in large groups to create a mass of color or a formal display.

Bent Any perennial grass that has spreading panicles of tiny flowers; ideal for lawns.

Biennial A plant that lives for two years. Grown from seed, it makes leaves the first year. It flowers and produces seed the second year.

Bone meal An organic fertilizer made from ground animal bones

Bract A leaf that grows just below the flowerhead and is often mistaken for a true petal.

Bulb A swollen underground stem covered with scales that are attached at the bottom. In the center is a flower bud. The surrounding scales store nutrients and protect the bud. Tulips and daffodils grow from true bulbs.

Bulb fiber A soilless planting medium used to grow bulbs in pots. It usually contains shredded peat, oyster shells, and charcoal.

Bulbil A baby bulb that grows from a mature plant. A natural form of plant propagation.

Bulblet A young bulb that has been separated from the parent plant and is in the process of growing into a full-sized bulb.

Channeled A leaf that has a "V"-shaped cross-section.

Coir A soilless planting medium used for growing bulbs in pots. It is made from tropical fibers.

Cold frame A bottomless box with a hinged or removable glass top. Used in the garden for protecting young plants from adverse weather conditions.

Compost Used to condition and fertilize existing soil structure, compost is the remains of decomposed leaves, lawn clippings, garden debris, and vegetable waste that has been broken down by bacteria to form a humus-rich material.

Compound A leaf or flower divided into two or more parts.

Corm An underground storage unit that resembles a bulb, but does not have scales. Crocuses and gladioli grow from corms.

Cormel A young corm that forms around the base of a mature parent corm.

Corolla A collective term for petals; most commonly used to describe the six petals surrounding the corona of a daffodil.

Corona The cup or trumpet of a flower; most commonly used to describe the central projection of a daffodil.

Cultivar A plant derived from a species, created through the intervention of people and not by a natural mutation or cross-pollination in the wild; for example, *Iris sibirica* 'Silver Queen.' 'Silver Queen' is the cultivar.

Cutting A piece of a plant that is separated from the original one for the purpose of propagating identical plants.

Damping off A "disease" that causes young plants to wilt and die. It is sometimes caused by environmental factors.

Deadhead To remove spent flowers or unripe seed pods from a plant.

Deciduous A plant that loses all its leaves annually at the end of the growing season.

Dibber The name of a tool used to poke holes in the ground prior to planting. Also sometimes used to denote the planting process.

Die back Some plants die back, or die down, meaning they wither and die above ground,

leaving only the root alive below ground. Also, a disease of plants characterized by the death of the young shoots.

Division A method of propagating plants by dividing them into small clumps, each with shoots and roots attached.

Dormancy The period when a plant rests. This state can be affected by length of daylight, temperature, or supply of water.

Dot or highlight plant A plant used among other plants to add contrasting color, height, or form to the display.

Double A flower with a double row or multiple rows of petals.

Drifts Certain plants, such as daffodils and crocuses, look good planted in large informal clumps known as drifts.

Dry off The process of withholding water to induce dormancy in a plant.

Elliptic Used to describe the shape of a leaf that is broad in the center and narrow at each of the ends.

Evergreen A plant that retains its leaves throughout the year.

Eye The term given to a bud that grows on a tuber.

Falls The three, usually larger, outer reflexed petals; most commonly used to describe the outer petals of an iris.

Family Plants are divided into different families for the purpose of botanical classification. For example, the *Iridaceae* family includes the genus of *Iris*, *Crocus*, and *Crocosmia*.

Fescue Any grass of the genus *Festuca*; ideal for garden lawns and naturalized bulbs.

Flowers of sulfur A powdered form of sulfur used as a fungicide. Often sold in pharmacies as well as garden centers.

Force To stimulate natural conditions to induce a plant to flower out of the usual season.

Frond The leaf of a fern.

Frost-hardy A hardy plant that is able to survive periods of freezing weather.

Fungicide A substance that inhibits or kills fungus growth.

Genus Plant families are divided into genus for the purpose of botanical classification. For example, the genus *Iris* includes the following species: *Iris sibirica*, *Iris reticulata*, and *Iris cristata*.

Germination The period of time it takes for a seed to sprout leaves. Some quick-growing seeds germinate in less than a week, others take months.

Glaucous A term used to describe leaves or flowers that have a waxy texture and a blue-colored tint.

Ground cover A low-growing plant that covers the surface of the soil.

Growing medium Soil-based or soilless substances in which plants are grown.

Growing season The period during which a plant is actively producing leaves and flowers.

Half-hardy Plants that will survive a few degrees of frost but will not survive prolonged or severe cold weather.

Harden off The process of gradually getting an indoor or greenhouse-raised plant used to outdoor conditions.

Hardy A plant that can survive winter conditions. The ability to withstand degrees of frost varies from plant to plant.

Heavy soil Soil that is composed mainly of clay. Usually needs additions of sand and organic matter to improve drainage.

Heel To temporarily cover the roots of a plant with soil until it can be planted in the garden.

Herbaceous A plant with non-woody, soft stems. The top growth usually dies down to the ground in winter, but the roots remain alive underground.

Humus Well-rotted organic matter in soil.

Hybrid A plant that is produced by the cross-fertilization of two different plants.

Incurved Term used to describe a petal that curves inward toward the center of a flower.

Inflorescence The part of a plant that bears the flower or flowers.

Internode The section of stem between two nodes.

Interplant To plant two or more plants together in a flower bed to create a mixed display of different colors and textures.

Leaf mold Partially decomposed leaves that can be used to improve soil.

Light soil Soil that is composed mainly of sand. Usually needs additions of top soil and organic matter to improve fertility and water retention.

Lime A substance used to reduce the acidity of soil. Available in both quick- and slow-release formulations.

Liquid fertilizer Nutrients suspended in a liquid solution. Can be used to water the soil or spray on the foliage.

Loam The best type of soil for a wide range of plants. It contains an ideal mix of clay and sand.

Microclimate A smaller environment within a much larger one. For example, a damp border sheltered by walls on two sides may be suitable for plants that would not grow in other parts of the garden.

Mulch A material applied in a layer around the base of a plant to enrich the ground, conserve moisture, or protect the plant.

Native A plant may be native to one or more regions or countries. A "native" plant is one that is cultivated in the region in which it grows naturally.

Naturalize To establish and grow a plant as if in the wild; to colonize a plant.

Node The point on a stem from which a leaf, shoot, or flower bud grows.

Offset A young plant produced at the base of the parent; a natural form of propagation.

Opposite Used to describe a plant's growth habit. It means that the leaves grow from the same spot on opposite sides of the stem.

Peat Decaying, humus-rich material that is often added to light, sandy soils to increase moisture retention.

Peat moss Gathered from natural bogs, this moisture-retentive soil additive is composed of decayed organic matter. Sphagnum peat moss is the most readily available.

Pendent A flower or leaf that hangs down.

Perennial A plant that lives for more than two years.

Perlite Small granules of a volcanic mineral; often added to growing mediums to increase moisture retention.

Pesticide A substance used to inhibit or kill insects that attack plants. Organic pesticides are derived from natural ingredients.

pH A measure of the acidity or alkalinity of soil. Soil test readings range from 0 (the most acidic) to 14.0 (the most alkaline). A neutral reading of 7.0 is acceptable to the widest range of plants.

Photosynthesis The process by which plants manufacture their own food; a synthesis of organic compounds from carbon dioxide and water using light in the presence of chlorophyl.

Plunge To sink a pot up to its rim in soil, peat, or sand.

Prepared bulbs Some bulbs are specially treated so they can be forced into early flowering indoors. These bulbs are known as prepared bulbs.

Propagation The production of a new plant from an existing one.

Raceme The part of a plant that bears flowers along a main stem.

Reflexed Term used to describe a petal that curves backward with the point facing the ground.

Rhizome Sometimes called rootstocks, these swollen stems grow horizontally below the soil surface. Roots grow from the bottom and shoots emerge from the upper surface or sides. Cannas and certain types of iris are grown from rhizomes.

Rooting hormone A chemical powder or liquid used to encourage root development when propagating cuttings.

Rootstock See **Rhizomes**.

Rose The spray attachment of a watering can used to disperse and regulate a fine spray of water, especially used for seed.

Rosette A circular cluster of leaves growing from the base of a shoot.

Scales Fleshy leaflike structures that store the nutrients needed by a bulb to survive dormancy and early growth.

Scaling A technique used to propagate lilies.

Scooping and scouring Techniques used to propagate hyacinth bulbs.

Seed head A faded flowerhead containing seed.

Seedling A very young plant that has grown from seed.

Selections A plant possessing a desirable new trait, color, or growth habit created by natural cross-pollination, mutations, or hybridizing efforts.

Sepal The outermost, leaflike part of a flower.

Shoot Emerging growth from a seed, bulb, root cutting, rhizome, or tuber.

Shrub A woody plant that is smaller than a tree. Most have more than one stem.

Single A flower with a single layer of petals.

Slow-release fertilizer A fertilizer that gradually releases nutrients into the soil over a period of time.

Spadix An unusual flower form in which the true flowers are clustered around a fleshy base and semi-enclosed by a capelike sheath, called a spathe. Calla lilies produce this type of flower.

Spathe The sheath that surrounds a spadix — this is an unusual flower form.

Spawn A group of baby corms that grow at the base of a mature corm. A natural form of plant propagation.

Species Plant genus are divided into species for the purpose of botanical classification; for example, *Iris sibirica. Iris* is the genus; *sibirica* is the species.

Specimen A special tree, shrub, or plant grown for its striking or unusual appearance.

Spike The term used to describe a group of flowers clustered along an erect stem.

Spur A hollow projection of a flower; for example, *Corydalis.*

Stake To support a tall-growing vigorous plant with sticks or canes and string.

Stamen The male reproductive organ of a flower.

Standard A term applied to the three inner, often erect, petals of a flower; most commonly used to describe an iris.

Stem propagation A way of increasing a variety of tubers by rooting detached stems.

Stolon Underground stems that produce new plants. A natural method of propagation.

Straplike A tongue-shaped leaf.

Sun-bake See **Baking**.

Tender A plant that is vulnerable to frost damage.

Tilth A layer of soil with a perfect texture for successful gardening.

Top-dress To apply a layer of fertilizer or compost to the soil without digging or mixing it in.

Transplant To transfer small seedlings into trays or pots so that they have more room to grow into full-sized plants.

Trumpet The cuplike structure of a flower. Most commonly used when describing daffodils.

Tube A flower in which the petals join together at the base to form a hollow stalk.

Tuber Usually underground, these swollen stems produce roots and shoots. Gloxinias, cyclamens, and tuberous begonias are grown from tubers.

Tunic The dry, papery outer-covering of a bulb or corm.

Tunicated A term used to describe bulbs that have a papery outer layer, called a tunic. Tulips, hyacinths, and narcissi are all examples. Bulbs that lack this outer layer are called imbricated.

Umbel A flat-topped or domed flowerhead in which the flowers are borne on stalks rising from the top of the main stem.

Underplant To plant low-growing plants around larger plants.

Variegated A leaf that is marked with an irregular pattern, usually cream, white, or yellow on green.

Variety A subdivision of a species in which the plant was created by a natural mutation or cross-pollination in the wild. For example, *Iris sibirica alba.* The variety is *alba*, which means white.

Vegetative propagation Any method of propagating a plant that does not include seed.

Vermiculite A soil additive that is used to improve the texture of planting mediums. It is made from natural mica deposits.

Water in To water gently around a newly planted bulb to settle the soil around the roots.

Whorl A pinwheel-like formation created by three or more flowers or leaves that grow out of the same place.

DIRECTORY OF SUPPLIERS

U.S.A.

B. & D. Lilies
330 P Street
Port Townsend, WA 98368
Tel: 206-385-1738

Blue Dahlia Gardens
Box 316
San Jose, IL 62682
Tel: 309-247-3210

Breck's Bulbs
6523 North Galena Road
Peoria, IL 61601
Tel: 309-691-4601

W. Atlee Burpee
300 Park Avenue
Warminster, PA 18974
Tel: 800-888-1447

The Daffodil Mart
Route 3, Box 794
Gloucester, VA 23061
Tel: 804-693-3966

DeJager Bulb Co.
Box 2010
South Hamilton, MA 01982
Tel: 617-468-1622

Dutch Gardens
P. O. Box 200
Adelphia, NJ 07710
Tel: 908-780-2713

Fairyland Begonia & Lily Garden
1100 Griffith Road
McKinleyville, CA 95521
Tel: 707-839-3034

The Lily Garden
36752 SE Bluff Road
Boring, OR 97009
Tel: 503-631-8153

McClure and Zimmerman
P. O. Box 368
Friesland, WI 53935
Tel: 414-326-4220

Park Seed Co. Inc.
Cokesbury Road
Greenwood, SC 29647-0001
Tel: 803-223-7333

John Scheepers, Inc.
P. O. Box 700
Bantam, CT 06750
Tel: 203-567-0838

Swan Island Dahlias
P. O. Box 700
Canby, OR 97013
Tel: 503-266-7711

Van Bourgondien Bros.
P. O. Box A
Babylon, NY 11702
Tel: 516-669-3500

Van Engelen Inc.
Stillbrook Farm
313 Maple Street
Litchfield, CT 06759
Tel: 203-567-8734

Wayside Gardens
1 Garden Lane
Hodges, SC 29695
Tel: 800-845-1124

White Flower Farm
Route 63
Litchfield, CT 06759
Tel: 203-496-9600

CANADA

Aimers Seeds and Bulbs
81 Temperance Street
Aurora, Ontario, L4G 1R1
Tel: 416-841-6226
Fax: 416-727-7333

Leonard W. Butt
Huttonville
Ontario, L0J 1B0
Tel: 416-455-8344

Cruickshank's Inc.
1015 Mount Pleasant Road
Toronto, Ontario, M4P 2M1
Tel: 800-665-5605/416-488-8292
Fax: 416-488-8802

Dominion Seed House
Box 2500
Georgetown
Ontario, L7G 5L6
Tel: 416-873-3037
Fax: 800-567-4594

Ferncliff Gardens
8394 McTaggart Street
S. S. 1 Mission
British Columbia
V2V 6S6
Tel: 604-826-2447
Fax: 604-826-4316

Gardenimport Inc.
P. O. Box 760
Thornhill
Ontario, L3T 4A5
Tel: 800-565-0957/416-731-1950
Fax: 416-831-3499

Lee Valley Tools Ltd.
1080 Morrison Drive
Ottawa
Ontario, K2H 8K7
Tel: 800-267-8767/613 596-0350
Fax: 613-596-6030

McFayden Seeds
30-9th Street
P. O. Box 1800, Brandon
Manitoba, R7A 6N4
Tel: 204-725-7300
Fax: 204-725-1888

McMath's Daffodils
6340 Francis Road
Richmond
British Columbia, V7C 1K5
Tel: 604-277-8096

W. H. Perron & Cie Ltée
2914 Curé-Labelle
Chomedey, Laval
Québec, H7P 5R9
Tel: 514-332-3617

Suttell's Dahlias
5543 Blezard Drive
Beamsville, Ontario
L0R 1B3
Tel: 416-945-5765

AUSTRALIA

Blue Dandenongs Bulb Farm
P. O. Box 8
Old Emerald Road
Monbulk, VIC. 3793
Tel: (03) 756-6766

Broersen Seeds & Bulbs Pty Ltd.
365-367 Monbulk Road
Silvan, VIC. 3795
Tel: (03) 737-9202

Doyne & Staff Pty Ltd.
Lot 1, Ure Road
P. O. Box 174
Gembrook, VIC. 3783
Tel: (059) 68-1758

Drewitt & Sons
P. O. Box 212
Woori Yallock, VIC. 3139
Tel: (059) 67-4307

Fell's Nursery
P. O. Box 419
Virginia, SA 5120
Tel: (08) 380-9074

Flowerbulbs Tasmania
C/-Post Office
Collinsvale, TAS. 7012
Tel: (002) 39-0104

Golden Ray Gardens
1 Monash Avenue
Olinda, VIC. 3788
Tel: (03) 751-1395

J. N. Hancock & Co.
Jacksons Hill Road
Menzies Creek,VIC. 3159
Tel: (03) 754-3328

Jackson's Daffodils
P. O. Box 77
Geeveston, TAS. 7116
Tel: (002) 97-6203

Jersey Farm Pty Ltd.
Lot 3
Old Cape Shanck Road
Rosebud, VIC. 3929
Tel: (059) 86-4694

Lake Nurseries
P. O. Box 149
439 Silvan Road
Monbulk, VIC. 3793
Tel: (03) 756-6157

Patchwork Nursery
P. O. Box 50
The Patch, VIC. 3792
Tel: (03) 756-7277

Pine Heights Nursery
Pepper Street
Everton Hills, QLD 4053
Tel (07) 353-2761

Pronk's Bulb Farm
Yankee Road
Newbury
Trentham, VIC. 3458
Tel: (054) 24-1330

Tedworth Bulb Farm
P. O. Box 72
Kempton, TAS. 7030
Tel: (002) 59-1143

Tempo Two
P. O. Box 60A, 57 East Road
Pearcedale, VIC. 3912
Tel: (059) 78-6980

Tesselaar Bulbs & Flowers
Padua Bulb Nurseries
357 Monbulk Road
Silvan, VIC. 3795
Tel: (03) 737-9811

Bryan H. Tonkin
'Sylvan Vale'
Kalorama, VIC. 3766

Van Diemen Quality Bulbs
R. S. D. 20
Table Cape
Wynyard, TAS. 7325
Tel: (004) 42-2012

Wyndyhill Flowers Pty Ltd.
P. O. Box 189
Macclesfield Road
Monbulk, VIC. 3793
Tel: (03) 756-6669

INDEX

Page numbers in *italic* refer to the illustrations

ACKNOWLEDGMENTS

The publisher would like to thank the many individuals and organizations who allowed them to reproduce their photographs in this book. The publisher and Clive Nichols would also like to thank the many individuals and organizations who allowed them to photograph their gardens. Page numbers are followed by codes denoting left (l), right (r), center (c), top (t) and bottom (b); location and garden owners are given in brackets where relevant.

Jacques Amand/John Amand 95 bl, 165 br; **A-Z Botanical Collection** 115 tr, 153 tc, 156 bc, 165 tr, 166 l & c, 169 bl, 209 bc, 228 tr, 231 c; **Gillian Beckett** 159 r, 177 c, 211 bl; **Eric Crichton** 31 t, 128-9 b, 131 r, 178 r, 190-1, 195 r, 207 c & br, 215, 229 tr, 231 tr; **John Fielding** 87 r, 88 tl, tr & c, 89 l & r, 90 tr & b, 91 tr & br, 92 tc, tr & b, 95 tr & br, 97 tl & tr, 99 bl, 100 bc, 101 tl, r & bc, 102 tl, tr, c & bl, 103 tc, 106 tl, tc, tr, bl, bc & br, 107 tr & c, 108 tl & tr, 110 bc, 113 tr, 114 t, cl, c & bl, 115 cl & br, 117 cr, bc & br, 118 cl & bl, 137, 150 tl, 152 tr, l, cr, 153 tl, tr & br, 158 tl, c, bl & bc, 160 tc & br, 161 tr & bl, 162 c, 165 tc & bl, 166 bc, 167 l, 169 bc, 171 bl, 174 t, 175 l & c, 176 tl, 178 c, 180 l, 182 c, 195 l & c, 206 cl, bl & br, 207 tl, 209 br, 228 bc; **Fleurmerc bv,** 154 b, 182 br; **Garden Picture Library/Linda Burgess** 21, /Menk Dijkman 120-1, /John Glover 30 b, 76, /Jerry Pavia 180 c; **John Glover** 6 t, 107 bl, 130 l, 133; **Derek Gould** 126 b, 191 r; **Jerry Harpur** 35 br, 60, 61, 70 b, 123, 132 bc, 139 tr, 186, 188, 189, /Beth Chatto 29, 187; **Marijke Heuff** 20, 30 c, 31 b, 68 bl, 122, 124-5, 127, 128-9 t, 194, 214, 220; **International Flower Bulb Centre** 91 tl, 96 tl, 100 cr, 104 bl, 115 tc, 118 c & br, 119 t, c & cr, 150 l, 155 r & b, 161 tc, 162 tc, tr, l, cr & br, 163 tl, tc & bl, 211 br; **Andrew Lawson** 87 tc, 88 br, 89 t, 90 tr & c, 92 tl, 94 tl, tr, c & br, 95 tl, 96 tr, bc & br, 97 bl, 99 tc & c, 100 tr & bl, 103 cl & br, 104 tl, c & br, 107 tl, 108 bl, bc & br, 109 tr, cl, c & bl, 110 tl, tc, r & bl, 112 l, tr & br, 113 l, c & br, 114 cl & br, 115 tl & c, 117 c, 118 tr, 119 l & br, 124 tc, 132 bl, 135, 150 br, 152 c, 153 c, 154 c, 155 l, 158 tr & br, 159 l & c, 160 l & bc, 161 br, 163 tr, 166 tr, 167 r, 168 l, tc, tr, bc & br, 169 tc, tr, cl, cr & br, 170 tl, tc, c, c r, bl & br, 171 tl, tc, cl, 171 tr & cr, 173 tl, tr, c & bl, 174 cl, r, bl & bc, 177 tl & r, 178 l, 180 r, 181 l & tr, 182 tr, cr & bl, 203 c & r, 204 t, cl, c & r, 205 tc & br, 206 c, 207 cr, 208 tr & br, 209 t, 211 tl & tr, 226 tr & br, 229 tl, bl & br, 231 tl; **Brian Mathew** 94 cr, 107 bc, 161 tl, 173 br, 205 tr, 208 l, 211 tc, 226 l; **Ian McKinnell** 1, 2, 8, 26-7, 36-7, 38, 80-6, 93, 99, 105, 111, 116, 138 bc, 140-9, 151, 157, 164, 172, 179, 183, 196 tr, 196-7, 198-201, 202, 207, 210, 222 tr, 222-3, 223 br, 224-5, 226, 230; **Clive Nichols** 30 t (Abbotswood Garden, Gloucestershire), 68 tl (Mr and Mrs Baker, Old Rectory Cottage, Berkshire), 184-5, 192 tr, 73 br (John Bond, The Saville Garden, Surrey), 58-9, 62 t, 70 tl, 71, 217 t (Sarah Butt, Bennington Lordship, Hertfordshire), 135 (Capel Manor Horticultural and Environmental C, Middlesex), 66 tl, 66-7, 72, 73 b (Darlington Hall, Devon), 96 t (Eggleston Hall Gardens, Co. Durham), 23 t, 22, 126 t (Wendy Lauderdale, Ashtree Cottage, Wiltshire), 130 (Wendy Francis, The Anchorage, Kent), 192 tl (The Sir Harold Hillier Gardens and Arboretum, Hampshire), 64, 65 l, 78 t, 78-9 b, 76 bl, 79 tr (The Keukenhoff Gardens, Holland), 126 c (Pam Lewis, Sticky Wicket, Dorset), 138 l, 223 tr (The Lygon Arms Hotel, Broadway, Worcestershire), 23 t, 34 t, 103 l (Elizabeth Macleod Matthews, Chenies Manor, Bucks), 73 r (Mrs Merton, The Old Rectory, Burghfield, Berkshire), 68-9, 70 tr (Mr and Mrs Norton, East Lambrook Manor Garden, Somerset), 33, 63 t, 75 c (Ripley Castle, North Yorkshire), 62 b (Mrs H. H. Robinson and Mrs J. Brookes, Denmans, West Sussex), 16, 23 b, 65 r, 75 t, 125 bc (Royal Horticultural Society's Garden, Wisley, Surrey), 34 br (Mr and Mrs Terry, 28 Hillgrove Crescent, Hereford and Worcestershire), 193 (Mrs Thorp, Coates Manor, West Sussex), 138 tr (Caroline Todhunter, The Old Rectory, Farnborough, Oxfordshire), 212-3 216, 218 bl, tl, 218-9 (Colonel Watson, The Door House, Gloucestershire), 67 b (Wolfson College, Oxford), 6, 23 b, 65 r, 75 t (Rosemary Verey, Barnsley House, Gloucestershire), 77 (Mrs Voges, Holland); **Hugh Palmer** 132 br; **Jerry Pavia** 32, 74, 251, /Joanna Pavia 25 r, 217 b; **Photos Horticultural/Michael Warren** 91 ac, 97 tc & bc, 99 r, 104 bc, 107 br, 107 br, 108 tc, 112 c, 117 l, 173 cr, 176 cl, 180 bc, 181 br, 203 l, 208 c, 211 cr, 228 tl & bl, 231; **Reed International Books Limited** 89 c, /Jerry Harpur 87 bl, 100 cl, /George Wright 32; **Christine Skelmesdale** 152 tc, 153 cl, 154 r, 156 r, 167 c, 176 r, 177 bl, 204 bl, 205 bc, 206 tl, 211 c; **Harry Smith Collection** 87 bc, 88 bl, 90 cl & bl, 91 cl & c, 94 bl, 95 tc & bc, 96 bl, 99 tl, 101 c, 102 br, 109 bc, 112 bc, 150 bc, 156 tc & l, 160 cr, 166 br, 175 tr & br, 176 c, 182 tr, 206 bc, 209 c, 226 c, 228 br; **Curtice Taylor** 24, 69 r; **Elizabeth Whiting Associates** 6 b, 134; **Timothy Woodcock** 222.

List of plates in Plant Directories

Page 86 *Anemone* (De Caen)
Page 93 *Narcissus* 'Tête à Tête'
Page 98 *Iris* 'Purple Sensation' (Dutch)
Page 105 *Muscari armeniacum*
Page 111 *Narcissus* 'Cheerfulness' (Tazetta)
Page 116 *Tulipa* 'Ballade' (Lily-flowered)
Page 151 *Begonia* x *tuberhybrida*
Page 157 *Gloxinia* cultivar
Page 164 *Gloriosa superba*
Page 172 *Lilium* 'Bellona'
Page 179 *Ranunculus asiaticus* (double-flowered)
Page 183 *Zantedeschia aethiopica*
Page 202 *Cyclamen persicum* cultivar
Page 210 *Galanthus nivalis*
Page 227 *Hippeastrum* 'White Lady'
Page 230 *Iris danfordiae*